Phonographic Memories

Critical Caribbean Studies

Series Editors: Yolanda Martínez-San Miguel, Carter Mathes, and Kathleen López

Focused particularly in the twentieth and twenty-first centuries, although attentive to the context of earlier eras, this series encourages interdisciplinary approaches and methods and is open to scholarship in a variety of areas, including anthropology, cultural studies, diaspora and transnational studies, environmental studies, gender and sexuality studies, history, and sociology. The series pays particular attention to the four main research clusters of Critical Caribbean Studies at Rutgers University, where the coeditors serve as members of the executive board: Caribbean Critical Studies Theory and the Disciplines; Archipelagic Studies and Creolization; Caribbean Aesthetics, Poetics, and Politics; and Caribbean Colonialities.

Giselle Anatol, *The Things That Fly in the Night: Female Vampires in Literature of the Circum-Caribbean and African Diaspora*

Frances R. Botkin, *Thieving Three-Fingered Jack: Transatlantic Tales of a Jamaican Outlaw, 1780–2015*

Carlos Garrido Castellano, *Beyond Representation in Contemporary Caribbean Art: Space, Politics, and the Public Sphere*

Njelle W. Hamilton, *Phonographic Memories: Popular Music and the Contemporary Caribbean Novel*

Melissa A. Johnson, *Becoming Creole: Nature and Race in Belize*

Alaí Reyes-Santos, *Our Caribbean Kin: Race and Nation in the Neoliberal Antilles*

Milagros Ricourt, *The Dominican Racial Imaginary: Surveying the Landscape of Race and Nation in Hispaniola*

Katherine A. Zien, *Sovereign Acts: Performing Race, Space, and Belonging in Panama and the Canal Zone*

Phonographic Memories

Popular Music and the Contemporary Caribbean Novel

Njelle W. Hamilton

Rutgers University Press
New Brunswick, Camden, and Newark,
New Jersey, and London

Library of Congress Cataloging-in-Publication Data

Names: Hamilton, Njelle W., 1977– author.
Title: Phonographic memories : popular music and the contemporary Caribbean novel / Njelle W. Hamilton.
Description: New Brunswick, New Jersey : Rutgers University Press, [2019] |
Series: Critical Caribbean studies | Revision of author's thesis (doctoral)—Brandeis University, 2012, titled Sound writing : popular music in the contemporary Caribbean novel. | Includes bibliographical references, discography, and index.
Identifiers: LCCN 2018049829 | ISBN 9780813596600 (hardcover) | ISBN 9780813596594 (paperback)
Subjects: LCSH: Caribbean fiction (English)—20th century—History and criticism. | Music and literature—Caribbean Area—History—20th century. | Popular music in literature.
Classification: LCC PR9205.05 .H36 2019 | DDC 813/.509357809729—dc23
LC record available at https://lccn.loc.gov/2018049829

A British Cataloging-in-Publication record for this book is available from the British Library.

∞ The paper used in this publication meets the requirements of the American National Standard for Information Sciences—Permanence of Paper for Printed Library Materials, ANSI Z39.48-1992.

www.rutgersuniversitypress.org

Manufactured in the United States of America

In loving rememory of those I lost en route:

My father, Joseph Benjamin Hamilton
(1939–2015),
who engendered my love for music,

and

Monique Vidal Dalle
(1962–2016, EgyptAir 840),
who prophesied about all I'd achieve "by faith."

Contents

Preface

I grew up in an era of physical music media—8-track tapes, LPs, cassettes, and CDs—and the technologies on which to play them. Most of my memories either have a soundtrack or relate to listening to music, manipulating music players, collecting music, writing music, or writing about music in some way. The subject of this book, how music encodes memories and helps us to remember, became all the more personal when my father passed away as I was writing it. (An avid music collector, he and my mother ran *Hamilton's Christian Books and Records Store* in Port Antonio, Jamaica, as I was growing up.) Writing about musical remembering suddenly became infused with personal nostalgic energies. My own reflective and creative practice as I grieved him made me realize how much this book constellates the several selves I have cultivated throughout my life: music listener and collector, music fan, songwriter and singer, musical novelist, and now sound studies scholar.

Looking back now, I also realize that I trained my memory on music. The Jamaica of my childhood had one television station that went off the air from midnight to 6 a.m., and since my family was rarely at home, most of our news and entertainment came from the radio. The many hours spent listening to the radio meant I developed a highly auditory memory and imagination: a gift for mimicking voices and accents and for imagining entire visual worlds from the soundtrack offered by the radio. The repetitive music roster meant learning songs the wrong way—misheard lyrics, songs cut off by advertisements—or hours calling into to Richie B on a weekday afternoon so he could play Tiffany's "It's the Lover Not the Love" so I could (a) record it and (b) learn it for a school talent competition. Since my father had a turntable system at home and at our books-and-records store, I had the fortune of learning songs by heart because he played his 8-tracks and 45s and LPs—Skeeter Davis, Andraé Crouch, Royal Routes—so often I learned all the words, melodies, harmonies, and even the instrumentation. Once I started going to high school and had pocket money, I spent it all buying cassettes and, with my new Walkman as my constant companion, spent many hours playing my own favorite songs and albums on repeat.

Three things came back to me as I started writing down my memories of my father (Hamilton, "Mourning Mixtape") after he passed away: First, owning cassettes and a Walkman—the ability to rewind a song so I could transcribe the lyrics and learn the song—coincided with my songwriting. Second, it also coincided with my tendency to spatialize music; because I listened to music while commuting to school, certain songs from my youth will always trigger the memory of riding in the bus or car. Replaying certain albums will bring back entire episodic memory sequences because I had them on repeat at a particular place in a particular moment of my youth. Tevin Campbell's *T.E.V.I.N.* (1991) never fails to trigger the memory of a weekend in the mid-1990s when we were marooned at home due to heavy rains and flooding. There is teenage me looking out my bedroom window at the floodwaters creeping up the backyard as I listened to "Strawberry Letter 23" or a young adult me walking through the city of Avignon in southern France listening to Mariah Carey's *Charmbracelet* (2002) on repeat as I tried to find the city hall. (How long does it take to walk around the ramparts of Avignon? Three *Charmbracelet*s.) Third, I realized that my brain would replay entire albums as if it were its own Walkman or iPod, and it would do so with remarkable high fidelity—the pitch, tempo, the grain of the singer's voice, even lyrics I hadn't learned yet would play in my head as if I were hearing them on the stereo. Sometimes this would manifest as anticipation when actually listening to an album: in the pause between tracks, my brain would already start playing the opening strains of the next. What this reflection on my own life made clear was that lifelong habits of music listening endowed me with what I call in this book *phonographic memory*. My exposure to technologies of repetitive music listening means that my own brain functions like a music player. But this is also true of my songwriting self, which developed in tandem with owning my own recorded music. Although I kept a songbook, I remember the lyrics and melodies to most of my early songs because I sang them over and over in those days. Not so today—I struggle to remember my newer songs, and it is unclear whether that is due to age, writing fewer songs, performance anxiety, listening to music less, or listening to a wider range of (mostly digital) music on shuffle rather than the same few favorite albums.

Writing this book allowed me to reflect on my own remembering and music listening practices. It also gave me the opportunity to listen to many old favorites and discover new ones. A key part of chapter 3, for instance, required me to replay Ella Fitzgerald's version of "Body and Soul" so I could learn its lyrics, melody, tonal center shifts, and when and how much to inhale in order to hold those high, long notes. Most importantly, writing this book gave me the critical language and historical context to understand the genres and idioms that were formative in my own upbringing. Finally, writing about music literally brought me back to Jamaica—the book's final words were written following a trip home in December 2017 to attend the homecoming show of reggae sensation Chronixx (Jamar McNaughton). Already *Dread and Terrible* (2014) had created a memory palace of listening to it for the first time, on repeat, as I sat on a bus from Boston, Massachusetts, to New York City that summer, en route to his free concert in Brooklyn. Now the songs on *Chronology* (2017) will forever be encoded with the memory of jamming with my sister, nephew, and brother-in-law—who chose that moment to tell his son that he played bass guitar on the song "Ghetto Paradise." Good times.

Phonographic Memories is about how music helps us remember anterior selves, places we've been, and experiences that have marked us. Even as it focuses in particular on Caribbean music and its representation in contemporary fiction as a trigger for cultural memory, it remains attentive to the process and experience of encoding and retrieving autobiographical or episodic memory through music listening. I read these musical novels as long-playing records of Caribbean music and situate myself as a listener to the memories they record and replay. I invite you to listen along with me.

A playlist of music can be found on the publisher's website: https://www.rutgersuniversitypress.org/phonographic-memories/9780813596594.

Phonographic Memories

Introduction

Near the beginning of Erna Brodber's 1994 novel *Louisiana*, a young Caribbean American anthropologist, Ella Townsend, is sent to the U.S. South armed with newfangled recording technology to gather and archive the living memories of a community of African Americans. In fact, Ella bears much resemblance to writer and anthropologist Zora Neale Hurston, who in the 1930s traveled throughout the U.S. South and the Caribbean documenting black folk culture on twelve-inch gramophone discs, on seven-inch reel-to-reel tapes, and in field notes. Part of *Louisiana*'s project is to render in fiction the opportunities and limitations of new technologies in recording sound and memory. Prior to the invention of the phonograph and the development of tapes and discs for recording at the turn of the twentieth century, ethnographers like Hurston had to take extensive field notes describing the sound, tempo, lyrics, and other extralinguistic features of the music. Of course, the challenge of such transcriptions is that they were *written* translations of sound, which had to be supplemented by the memory of the ethnographer. With the advent of sound recording technology, researchers could now capture and replay voices and songs with some measure of fidelity.

Louisiana expands and disrupts our conceptions of both recording technology and remembering. Although the text of the novel is framed as the transcription of Ella's tape recording of a single interview, the first version of the tape transcript runs for fewer than twenty pages. The remainder of the novel attempts to reconstruct what Ella hears when she replays the recording. Even as the tape's content exceeds the normative capacity of the technology—it yields up more data upon rewinding and relistening—the tech itself has finite storage. Consequently, the role of recording and replay jumps to Ella herself; she becomes a recording and playback "device" for voices, sounds, and memories—even those that are not ordinarily audible. Brodber depicts Ella as a blank slate, devoid of biographical and cultural memory: she was abandoned by her parents when they migrated from Jamaica to the United States shortly after her birth, and while they eventually returned for her, “They don’t say very much about the place that they came from” (18). Despite Ella’s early uprooting from her birthplace, place memory has been encoded in deep recesses of her subconscious and is reawakened by listening to the voices and songs of the women she interviews. For instance, hearing the Jamaican folk song “Sammy Dead” in the present triggers the memory of hearing that song as a baby in her grandmother’s arms (88). Without her own memories, she has the mental capacity to remember on behalf of her Afro-Caribbean and African American interlocutors who have repressed or forgotten personal and collective traumas. As a sound and memory medium, she amplifies subconscious memories that she then transmits to amnesiacs so they can remember in turn. Beyond illustrating how musical technology enables remembering, Brodber imbues Ella with what I call *phonographic memory*—the auditory counterpart to photographic memory. Her capacity for high fidelity encoding and replay depicts her memory as a surrogate for recording technology, even as her virtuosic hearing and remembering transcend the capabilities of any known format.

Ella’s depiction as an embodied recording device raises pertinent questions about the relationship between recording and remembering that this book will take up. How does listening to music reawaken autobiographical memory—even memories that were never encoded and the memories of others? What does it mean that Caribbean music triggers Ella’s memory even though she left Jamaica as a young child? Can human memory and geographical sites function as alternate recording devices? And if music encodes place memory, can listening to music associated with a specific place bring us back not only psychologically but physically?

Phonographic Memories: Popular Music and the Contemporary Caribbean Novel argues that even as recording technology enhances the fidelity of memory, the unique features of Caribbean music cultures endow listeners with a capacity for high-fidelity recall that is both occasioned by and rivals technology. As this introduction will elaborate, the structure of our brains and the structure of music work together to make music an unusual mnemonic device; its inherent characteristics of repetition, rhythm, and perhaps its appeal to our pleasure and emotional centers mean that even nonmusical people tend to remember music and its associated contexts with a high degree of fidelity (Sacks xii). Listening to recorded music adds habit memories—practices of handling technology that reinforce the purely mental aspect of listening with embodied repetitions that give new dimensions to memory as a sensual and deeply felt experience. Because of the anatomy of the human brain and the structural characteristics of music, listening to recorded music that has become personally or culturally meaningful to the auditor often serves as a potent cue to call up neural links to memories, even those that have become buried or fragmented due to time, travel, or trauma. Aside from the deep connections between memory and music in general and between memory and recorded music in particular, Caribbean music idioms such as Trinidadian calypso, Cuban bolero, Guadeloupean gwoka, Jamaican reggae, and Indo-Trinidadian chutney have long been connected to both precolonial memory and to cultural memory practices from which postcolonial national identities have been forged since the 1960s.

Bridging literary studies, ethnomusicology, and neuroscience, *Phonographic Memories* is the first monograph to perform a sustained analysis of the influence of Caribbean popular music on both memory and the contemporary Caribbean novel. The book moves from radio- to phonograph- to cassette- to digital-era remembering in order to trace how shifting formats, technologies, and global trends in music and culture impact how Caribbean peoples restructure memories and construct themselves in the world, at home, and in fiction. With particular focus on literary "phonotopes" (musical references) in five contemporary novels from the anglophone, francophone, and hispanophone Caribbean, I consider the broader music cultures that sustain collective memory and situate Caribbean subjects in specific localities. These "musical fictions"—Lawrence Scott's *Night Calypso* (2004), Oscar Hijuelos's *The Mambo Kings Play Songs of Love* (1989), Daniel Maximin's *Lone Sun* (1981), Colin Channer's *Waiting in Vain* (1998), and Ramabai Espinet's *The Swinging Bridge* (2003)—depict characters turning to national popular music to encode and retrieve memories. They illustrate the social function of Caribbean popular music and musicians to fill in the gaps of memory. *Lone Sun* and *Night Calypso* feature characters who write or perform music to create memories or to negotiate forgetting on behalf of themselves and others. *The Swinging Bridge* and *The Mambo Kings Play Songs of Love* focus on listeners who engage in intentional habit memory, privately playing or remembering music to voluntarily remember personally meaningful pasts. *Waiting in Vain* shows diasporic auditors listening to music together in intimate settings or at large public events that create both personal associations and collective identities. While private mobile or domestic listening creates and rehearses individual memory records—in other words, autobiographical memory—collective musical cultures and practices create broader cultural memory that allows social groups to consolidate identity, define belonging, and narrate and transmit historical memory through song and performance.

Inspired by Channer's assertion that Caribbean music can provide regional writers with a "vital and valid . . . literary model" ("Preface" 13), *Phonographic Memories* proposes a critical practice that is attentive to the literary narration of Caribbean music and the discourses and representations inherent in each idiom. Each chapter situates a novel in the musical contexts from which it draws thematic and structural inspiration while considering how those music idioms—calypso, bolero, gwoka, reggae, and dub—enable radical new theorizations of Caribbean memory. Because of its connection to the West African griot tradition as well as its consolidation in the 1930s through early phonograph recording, calypso (chapter 1) developed a reputation as the song form that records Trinidadian history and enables amnesiac or traumatized listeners to remember the past down through time. The bolero's imbrication of romantic and national lyrics (chapter 2) makes it a fruitful form to explore the nostalgic memory of postrevolution Cuban exiles. Both gwoka (chapter 3) and reggae (chapter 4) soundtrack emergent nationalist movements in the 1960s and 1970s, as defined by narratives around a romantic return to roots—practices and sites of black memory and liberation. But the construction of national politics is itself a form of memory work, including which constituents belong and are included in collective memory. As a recording technique that allows for the creation of space in and removal of voices from existing records, dub (chapter 5) models revisionist and ethical remembering useful for subaltern communities. In addition to tapping into the themes and narrative conventions of Caribbean popular music, therefore, the five authors use music to signal cultural belonging and to sound citizenship—what it means to be Trinidadian, Cuban, Guadeloupean, Jamaican, or cosmopolitan—at the turn of the twentieth century. These novels conceptualize memory as both a psychological and a physical process, including the rehabilitation of damaged psyches and bodies and returns to the native land. In so doing, they privilege the Caribbean soil as the location of culture and the site of memory where amnesiac subjects might reconstitute fragmented memories and identities.

Phonography: Recording Memory

By bringing sound studies and the neuroscience of memory into dialogue with trauma theory, this book intervenes in the burgeoning field of memory studies more broadly and Caribbean memory studies more specifically. *Phonographic Memories* is the first book to consider the impact of Caribbean music and sound recording technology on autobiographical recall, not just cultural memory. The examples herein depict the recall of episodic memory (when characters consciously pull from long-term storage details of a specific moment from their distant past) as well as semantic memory (knowledge, skills, ideas about music and identity gleaned both consciously and unconsciously from immersion in a culture). In the former, listening to music aids in both the encoding and recall of associated personal episodes, while in the latter, communities and societies associate certain musical idioms with group identity. The book illustrates how the formats, content, and cultural significance of music inform how individual auditors remember.[1] These five musical fictions explicitly depict the techniques, technologies, and trajectories of Caribbean music idioms and their role in memory work even as they also show how both analog and recorded music cultures impact memory and subjectivity.

Despite the relative lack of high-fidelity recording and playback technology throughout much of the twentieth century, format aficionados often associate the long-playing phonograph record with fidelity, authenticity, and return (inspired by its circular form).[2] Memory has been conceptualized in several modes that cohere with the temporal, spatial, embodied, and physical characteristics of the recorded object. With its playback setup of a turntable and horn, the record privileges focused, public, and stationary listening and has become a metaphor for collective listening and the fidelity of cultural memory. Although many musical fictions privilege the record, my conceptual frame includes musical technologies more broadly, including sound system speakers, cassette tapes, dub plates and digital media. Beyond using music as a shorthand cultural signifier, the deployment of particular formats in Caribbean musical fictions indexes different attitudes to memory. For instance, radio-era musical memory work (chapter 1) focuses on virtuosic listening and embodied performance as modes of creating and curating memory, while cassette-era fictions (chapter 5) often foreground the recording-erasure dichotomy, interrogating systems of inclusion and exclusion in both cultural master records and memory documents. In contrast, musical fictions informed by the digital era (see coda) often imagine culture and memories as memes—extractable and highly mobile, with the ability to form new associations in what might be called memory playlists.

The term *phonographic memories* underscores that recorded music is both a writing technology and a mnemonic device. Although we often think of recorded music as purely sonic rather than as a writing technology, the word *phonograph* means "sound writing." The terms *gramophone*, *graphophone*, *phonograph*, and *phonautograph* all point to their inventors' beliefs that they were indeed graphing sound, and original figurations of recording stressed writing or inscribing, meanings lost as recording gained its twentieth-century sonic valence.[3] Although Leon Scott (1857) and Thomas Edison (1877), inventors of the phonograph and related technologies, were variously interested in mechanically reproducing and expanding the function of the human ear, the implications for preserving memories immediately became apparent. Sound recording technology disrupts temporality by arresting a time-bound sound event—a spoken word, a musical performance—and inscribing it onto a physical object that, when played or "read," brings the past viscerally into the present. The process of consolidating long-term memory has three stages: encoding, storage, and retrieval (Slotnick 13), and throughout this book, I connect these stages to the processes of encoding, storing, and retrieving music using media such as the vinyl record.[4]

As a technological appendage to human memory, recorded music outsources aspects of memory production, enabling listeners to retrieve and replay memories that have been fragmented by time, travel, or trauma—the three sources of memory loss this book discusses. Even while memories can become degraded by temporal or spatial distance from their source, remembered music is replayed with remarkable fidelity. This is partly because our hippocampus, "a structure deep in the center of the brain that is known to be crucial to memory encoding and retrieval," functions much in the same way as a recording device, encoding our every experience for later retrieval (Levitin 165). Thus, when combined with music, memory has a powerful prosthetic aid to record experiences and retrieve them across space and time. Music listening both deepens the encoding, grafting memories more faithfully for high fidelity reproduction, and cues retrieval. This means that it can produce both episodic and semantic memory simultaneously and, in some cases—as I show in chapter 2—can replace, overwrite, or distort the initial episode, or create "false memories" (Loftus and Laney). Intense emotional experiences processed by the amygdala have a ready-made circuit to the neighboring hippocampus, our memory storage center. The more unique the cues, the more potent and effective they are at memory playback: "As soon as we hear a song that we haven't heard since a particular time in our lives, the floodgates of memory open and we're immersed in memories. The song has acted as a unique cue, a key unlocking all the experiences associated with the memory for the song, its time and place" (Levitin 166).

I define as *phonographic* those memories that are encoded and cued by the repetitive replay of music. *Phonographic memory* thus describes the memory work that inheres and is enabled by the repeated audition of music. The term builds on but is distinct from Raymond Murray Schafer's "sound souvenirs" and Michael Bull's "auditory nostalgia." For Schafer, rehearing familiar sounds unwittingly triggers associated memories in those who were the original "earwitnesses," the auditory counterpart to the eyewitness. For his part, Bull traces how contemporary auditors use portable music players to consciously create personal and mobile aural environments through which they can transport themselves elsewhere in place and time, away from the encroachment of collective sonorities. These terms all foreground the use of music technologies to remember the past and to negotiate present-tense identities and subjectivities. By locating musical memory work in the specificity of the Caribbean context, however, I further argue that the region's music-dominant soundscapes and the centrality of repetition in its idioms endow auditors in general and musicians in particular with a memory capacity that often approximates and rivals sound recording technologies. Caribbean music cultures create audiles, not just people "in whom auditory knowing is privileged over knowing through sight" (Sterne, *Audible Past* 96) but specifically subjects with virtuosic listening skills that enable them to hear and remember sounds and music with remarkably high fidelity. The engraving of music on the mind results from frequent and repeated listening, each repetition deepening the grooves of the memory record and moving the sound event from short-term to long-term memory. Repetition and rehearsal further associate songs and the features thereof with culture, periods of time, and shared references. This ability of music to increase the fidelity of recollection and to encode and later replay social and psychological contexts is a significant factor in its popularity for both Caribbean peoples and diasporic novelists alike.

While contemporary musical fictions always feature recorded music, they expand musical recording and archiving to other sources. These five musical novels privilege memory, the voice, and the body as alternate records, even as they incorporate modern recording technology and music formats. They register the interplay between analog and modern technology, between live and recorded music, and between Caribbean and Western epistemologies of memory and historiography. As such, the term *phonographic memories* highlights the ways that Caribbean musical memory approaches, supplements, and sometimes surrogates for phonographic technologies, especially given the unequal access Caribbean peoples have to music commodities and since official records often instantiate forgetting and silencing. In their dramatizing of the effects of various traumas—loss, sexual violence, cultural marginalization, exile—these novels subvert notions of the infidelity of pure memory and illuminate how the repetitive nature of Caribbean music culture enables a pseudotechnological memory capacity that is even further enhanced, rather than degraded, by trauma. *Phonographic Memories* thus complicates the consensus in memory studies that memory work is a post hoc reconstruction, invention, or performance.[5] These novels suggest that performance and narration both create memory where there is none and enhance and trigger the recall of memories that are repressed.

My deployment of recording analogies for memory might seem to go against at least a century of rethinking the early archaeological, imprint, and storage cabinet models of memory espoused by Plato, Socrates, and Freud (King 13; Ricoeur 9–14; Trouillot 14–15). In Caribbean memory theory, the focus is often on collective memory and the quarrel with history, even when illustrated through individual subjects,[6] and both autobiographical and cultural memory are framed in terms of forgetting and loss. For Édouard Glissant, the Middle Passage experience produced a rupture akin to traumatic shock between the Caribbean subject and the precolonial past and homeland. According to this view, historical memory did not encode, therefore, the Caribbean subject is "stripped" of his past, his memory "wiped clean" (*Caribbean Discourse* 105). Where Glissant uses language like erasure, absence, and rupture, Kamau Brathwaite argues that much of African culture survived until emancipation, when the civilizing mission of postplantation society forced these retentions into repression and transformation (creolization), but that they can later be salvaged from the collective unconscious (*Roots* 194–195). For both Glissant and Derek Walcott, however, sites of memory are really sites of cultural production. In this way, what is "remembered" of the precolonial past is not the "real" thing but a remade version or "branch" (Walcott, *Twilight* 68).[7] Hence creolization's impact is not only on how Caribbean migrants have to make do with unfamiliar implements in order to recreate memories but on how remembering in the new space already remakes the memory.

Prevailing Caribbean metaphors therefore suggest that memory is not retrieved but recreated, if not invented (Roach 4). Such "remembering" is really an attestation of forgetting: if remembering is a subjective, thus human, process, then the oft-referenced archives of the sea and landscape are illegible and inaccessible to us. Submarine memory is in fact a metaphor for the work of the poetic imagination, where the artist creates memory archives in place of absented memory. In other words, memory work means (re)constructing the present and future from fragments. In contrast to the "afterwardness" and "anamnesis" (unforgetting) models in Western memory studies, Caribbean remembering therefore often entails an *initial* encoding, creating memory where none was before. Beginning with the calypsonian's memory work in chapter 1, I show how a key social function of the Caribbean musician is to rectify a prior or partial forgetting. Caribbean memory work often presumes that we have already forgotten. Those who might have had episodic memory of precolonial culture are long gone; therefore the past may be "remembered" today as inherited, embodied memory (habits and mannerisms learned consciously or unconsciously from ancestors), semantic memory (knowledge about the past), or reconstructed memory artifacts and commodities (representations of how those in the present imagine episodes from the past).

Caribbean performance scholars therefore often use language that suggests that retrieval and invention are indistinguishable. While Walcott imagines a kind of Adamic invention and an affiliation to Crusoe's creation of new realities from found objects (*Twilight* 70), choreographer L'Antoinette Stines and performance theorist Joseph Roach see "expressive movements as mnemonic reserves, including patterned movements made and remembered by bodies" (Roach 26). This notion that the body retains memory and data unavailable to consciousness and thus to Western modes of knowing shifts the retrieval and curation of memory to people of color and reframes the black body as a memory technology in its own right. The prevalence of tropes such as body memory and place memory (chapters 3 and 4) in the Caribbean speak to divergent ideas about memory work in cultures forged from systemic and violent forgetting. The turn to performance in recent Caribbean criticism therefore belies a belief not in the persistence of episodic memory but in how implicit and semantic memory can be transmitted and performed in and as cultural norms. Performance scholars thus suggest that the body might be the privileged site where memory traces are archived; this reframes earlier notions of the body as a legible record of colonial trauma (chapter 1). In this way, proponents of performative and embodied memory echo Pierre Nora's distinction between two different sites of memory: *milieux de mémoire*, or "real environments" with collective practices where "real" memory is constructed, and *lieux de mémoire*, "sites" or reconstructed versions of lost memory practices

(284–285). This disdain for the recreated memory object or site recalls Walter Benjamin's anxieties over the evacuation of aura—the evidence of the manual labor of the "real" author or live performer—once technological reproduction in photography and film emerged at the turn of the twentieth century (220–223). In the Caribbean, Nick Nesbitt summarizes this take on "Antillean historical experience" as "the erasure of communal memory and its replacement by the mnemonic commodity" (xiv). Following Glissant's and Nora's notion of "real" memory as collective, lived, and embodied, Nesbitt views the mnemonic commodity as an emptied out object that serves to commoditize and monetize memory.

Phonographic Memories, however, reclaims the mnemonic commodity; the musical fictions I discuss throughout this book valorize the popular song and musical media for enabling amnesiac Caribbean peoples to "remember" both personal and collective experience. This is the tenor of M. NourbeSe Philip's many writings on memory. In her essay, "In the Matter of Memory," she agrees with the body as a container metaphor that undergirds performance studies but elaborates that the work of the artist as griot is to "compensat[e] for the earlier erasure of memories" by surrogating words, a voice, and a body (4). "Memory is always imaginary," she writes, but "we search for the tangible substance of those memories—the physical matter so to speak that could underpin our memories—of initial belonging, then loss" (12). Here, as throughout her work, she connects her project as a writer with that of the musician—specifically, the calypsonian. Philip has suggested that calypsonians create and perform memory for amnesiac listeners, reconnecting them to the ancestral memories from which they have been disconnected, whether by colonization, socialization, or migration ("Fugues, Fragments" 83). Both writer and musician aim to (re)create memory after a forgetting. In this way, she anticipates the alignment of the griot functions of novelist and musician alike in the examples in this book.

I build on the work of ethnomusicologists, cultural theorists, and authors like Philip who have shown how Caribbean music idioms function as repositories of cultural memories. In her introduction to *Music, Memory, Resistance*, a collection of essays on calypso's influence on literature, Patricia Saunders notes that "when [. . .] memory becomes susceptible to time, distance and the imagination, music is one of the 'sign-posts' that allows us to reconstruct our past out of the splintered recollections in the recesses of our minds and bodies" (xx). These remarks on the mnemonist function of Caribbean musicians cohere with the broader social roles of the region's oral storytellers, or *conteurs*—among them, to preserve memory and to act as spokespersons for the community (Aching 132–133). Music enables local communities, ethnic groups, societies, and nations to remember. As Michael Turino has explained, to create national culture, stakeholders determine which emblems and practices are promoted to "develop or maintain national sentiment"; such national symbols often emanate from folk "lifeways" and are considered to have broad cultural resonance so as to enable the newly formed or emerging nations to "maintain their unique identity" and to not "disappear as distinct . . . operative units on the international scene" (14–15). For his part, Nadi Edwards connects Caribbean popular culture with "the nationalist projects of political and cultural autonomy; its presence conferred authenticity on emergent national literatures, visual arts, dance and theatre. Given the émigré status of much of the region's literati, popular culture also signified the nostalgia of homeland, the expressive umbilical cord that linked writers in metropolitan exile to the distant sources of their art" ("Talking about Culture" vi). It thus stands to reason that, despite the ongoing critiques of nation-based essentialism, musical nationalism and essentialist memory work remain so prevalent in discourses around Caribbean popular music and the novels inspired by them.[8]

My argument in this book connects these strands of Caribbean memory theory. First, the materiality of music listening and Caribbean music's connection to dance allow listeners to tap into both their own conscious recall and unconscious corporeal memories. Second, even as autobiographical memory may become faulty, the accuracy of recall can be strengthened by the griot function of Caribbean music and the ability of music in general to heighten memory encoding. Third, where memory does not exist at all, the musician creates surrogate memory for the listener, thereby forging imagined communities of auditors joined by shared listening and shared remembering.

Present Tense, Past Perfect: The "Ex-Isle" Condition

Given the centrality of music in Caribbean culture, music has long been part of a broad vernacular thrust in crafting an autochthonous postcolonial literary aesthetic rooted in pre-scribal folk traditions. But unlike earlier folk-oriented musical literature, set in the (often rural) Caribbean and aimed to construct a literary aesthetic from African diaspora folkways,[9] the five musical fictions I discuss here, published between 1981 and 2004, focus less on the Caribbean-folk/Western-modern binary than on crafting a literary tradition from already modernized Caribbean cultural forms. With the migratory push from and within the Caribbean in the last decades of the twentieth century, many of the most visible Caribbean-born writers live at least part of the year in diaspora, and their fiction belies a preoccupation with the migrant condition. Contemporary musical fictions seem to fit these trends on the surface. Although written from diasporic locations—London, Spanish Harlem, Paris, Brooklyn, and Toronto—and dealing with hyphenated identities and questions of belonging, they nevertheless evince a decidedly essentialist conception of identity, fixating on return to pre-exilic homelands (whether physically or psychologically). With a few exceptions, their characters display anxiety over assimilating to North American and European identities and (re)turn to Caribbean culture—nation languages, foodstuffs, and especially music—to stave off the loss or degradation of cultural memory.

Music serves to mark Caribbean peoples as other, to transport them to the past or across the ocean, or to create a sonic bubble that insulates them from hostile spaces and sounds.

These five musical fictions emerged out of a post-1970s period of intense anxiety in the region about national and cultural identity. On the political front, the euphoria over variously successful resistance efforts to colonial and neocolonial powers settled into civil unrest or disquiet from within and pressures from without. Internally, the region confronted the rise of dictatorships and terror regimes in the northern Caribbean, near civil war and mass demographic flights of brown elites and Indo- and Chinese Caribbean peoples in Trinidad and Jamaica, and renewed separatist agitations in the French Antilles. Even as these states negotiated questions of sovereignty, they were also negotiating late Cold War geopolitics that saw continued U.S. interference in self-governance in Cuba, Jamaica, Grenada, Haiti, and elsewhere. On the cultural front, major shifts in global music markets saw the rise of musical nationalisms as efficient and potent markers of identity and difference, particularly in the face of U.S. cultural hegemony and the homogenization of culture. Although postcolonial and cultural studies romanticized the postmodern destabilization of the nation-state and its attendant ideologies (purity, universality, authenticity), as famously advanced by Gilroy's *The Black Atlantic*, such ideas emanating from powerful first world cultures ignored how underprivileged nation-states and what Yarimar Bonilla calls "non-sovereign" countries broadcasted and constructed their national identities on the global stage. I contend that Caribbean sonic nationalism serves as a form of resistance to globalization and neocolonial encroachments into Caribbean sovereignty. *Nation music*—my term for the sonic analog to Brathwaite's "nation language" (*Roots* 270)—has been marshaled by states, intellectuals, or ordinary folk to sound alternative subjectivities and continues to enable a new generation of mobile Caribbean peoples to maintain affective ties to Caribbean homelands.

Although often featuring contemporary frame narratives, contemporary musical fictions look back to older idioms coded as nation music. *Phonographic Memories* thus tells the story of how these music idioms have been narrativized as *the* sound of the nation through a combination of politics and recording and subsequently how Caribbean peoples turn to these records of cultural identity and memory in order to negotiate memory loss. By the 1970s, many Caribbean nations had developed strong nationalist musical traditions that enjoyed significant global success, but soon new technologies also began to transform musical practice. As Curwen Best details, the computerization of music production and the proliferation of music studios consolidated the transformation of many Caribbean folk forms from participatory to studio music. These technologies also enabled music producers to repatriate many aspects of production from the United States and Europe to Caribbean-based facilities like Dynamic Sounds in Jamaica. While the first half of the century saw mambo and calypso crazes driven by American interest in exotic music, in the 1970s, as local studios fed robust local music industries, genres such as reggae, soca, and zouk impacted the international market. Local acts could now produce music to break into foreign markets and speak to Caribbean citizens living both at home and abroad. This musical "colonization in reverse" (Bennett 106) broadly aimed to assert Caribbean specificity on the global stage. By the 1980s, the rise of music video culture as well as changes in Caribbean demographics in the United States drove changes in the world music market and charts, ushering in a torrent of Caribbean acts—Robin Imamshah, Miami Sound Machine, Maxi Priest, Black Uhuru, and others—which topped the Billboard and U.K. charts and garnered Grammy awards.

The international success of Caribbean music and musicians created a new kind of citizenship and identity at the turn of the century, even as new music technologies and performance routes opened up alongside newer migratory patterns. While international superstars like Stevie Wonder and Mick Jagger converged on Kingston, Jamaica—a tiny dot on the world map—to jam with rising superstar Bob Marley, the Fania All-Stars, with its assortment of Cuban, Puerto Rican, and other Latinx acts, filled the fifty-thousand-seat Yankee Stadium in New York in 1973, making visible and audible the scope and diversity of the Latin music catalog and audience. Meanwhile, the migratory patterns of Antilleans in France and the establishment of Creole cultural centers in the 1980s largely contributed to the success of Guadeloupean zouk group Kassav', who would play a sold-out show at the Zenith in Paris in 1985 and to an estimated audience of 250,000 at the first Caribbean Carnival in Paris in 1986. If globalization is particularly marked by the commoditization of culture and memory, Caribbean countries could now export and market music to the world as it had with banana and bauxite. Caribbean cosmopolitanism and migration increased the market for cultural consumables—not just global goods but those that mark consumers as simultaneously Caribbean and cosmopolitan.

As this book will demonstrate, these late-twentieth-century musical, migratory, and technological changes affected what being Caribbean sounded like at different historical moments. Contemporary musical fictions betray the influence of a shift in perception of national popular music idioms both in the Caribbean and on the global music stage. Because of the global recognition of Caribbean musicians and music forms, Caribbean popular music often functions as a portable but potent signifier of identity for Caribbean nationals and auditors at home and abroad. In tandem with the spatial diasporization evoked by terms such as "Troisième Île," "Kingston 21," and "Little Havana" that designate Paris, New York, and Miami, respectively, as off-shore territories of Caribbean islands, popular music simultaneously reinforces national identity and creates musical transnations, connecting auditors who share its hearing or values.[10] As a result, the mobility of music in the global age expands the capacity of once local, national, or regional music idioms to interpellate displaced Caribbean peoples and to create new communities of sound. Musical remembering consequently reconnects Caribbean listeners to anterior selves and to collective national and regional identities, with memory figured as not only a psychological but also a physical return.

Canonical Caribbean memory theory has focused on the trauma of exile *to* the Caribbean as the region's foundational condition[11] and how, with vast "black water" between the old home and new, the vital process of immersion and renewal that sustains culture and keeps one abreast of new developments is disrupted. For a new generation of Caribbean writers who have crossed the water in a different direction, from island to island and from the Caribbean to New York, Toronto, London, and Marseille, the routes of memory and the nostalgia for home look at once different from and familiar to the traditional Caribbean exile narrative. Largely sublimating primary exiles and their impact on collective memory, these five authors turn their attention to newer displacements and traumas, the depredations of postcolonial and contemporary issues, and they often engage primarily with autobiographical memory. My focus on these newer musical fictions thus moves Caribbean memory studies from its conventional focus on exile to the Caribbean to contemporary exiles from and in the Caribbean.[12]

I privilege the term *exile* rather than *migration* and *diaspora*, even though my conception of exile includes both migrants and diasporic citizens. I use *diaspora* as a geographic term to designate locales outside the Caribbean where significant communities of Caribbean peoples have settled and formed identifiably Caribbean subcultures. In contrast, I use *exile* to describe the condition of living elsewhere from where one considers "home." This might be in diaspora, elsewhere in the Caribbean, or even in one's home country in the case of internal exiles and subaltern communities. Exile thus includes both physical and psychological displacement; as the last two chapters will show, ethnic minorities can be in exile even while remaining in the Caribbean and before physical migration. Exile in this book carries the notions of loss, mourning, and nostalgia as evoked in "Rivers of Babylon." In this Rastafarian chant repurposed from a psalm on Jewish exile, The Melodians mourn that, sitting "by the rivers of Babylon / there we wept / when we remember Zion." Exile in this figuration telegraphs an identity always or predominantly oriented to and defined by distance from home, however conceived. Here I co-opt the added nuances of Maximin's original French in *L'Isolé soleil*, where he slips between "exiled" (*exilé*) and what I would translate as "ex-isled," "off-shored," or in Jamaican Patwa, "off the island" (*ex-îlé*; *Lone Sun* 102; *L'Isolé soleil* 115).

The term *ex-isle* foregrounds the gap between self and island. The hyphen between *ex* and *isle* becomes a discursive space and a site of loss and terror, much like the tangled Atlantic waters with dangerous currents that displace or disorient. The *ex-* prefix indexes both temporal and spatial absence; exile introduces a spatial gap between the subject and "home" and a simultaneous temporal gap between an idealized remembered self and the present. Exile is thus a form of *décalage* (displacement in space or time). Both a time difference and a delay, its "jetlag" denotation belies the incompatible temporalities produced by remembering: the recollector is simultaneously in the present and in the past (*elsewhen*), in the new location and in the original homeland (*elsewhere*). This coheres with Michel-Rolph Trouillot's suggestion that "the past—or, more accurately, pastness—is a position," a perception of a gap between "here" and "over there" (15). Recorded music and music technologies make audible the temporal dimension of exilic experience: recording facilitates repeating, rewinding, or relistening to the exact same song each time—as opposed to the always-changing live performance—which creates a temporal and audible glitch between present and past. As Brent Hayes Edwards theorized, the term *décalage* also images the exile moving about the world with a limp (an uneven gait from being unpropped up, or *décalé*) and occupying a limbo in space and time, unable to move forward due to being caught in the past. It foregrounds that some things "refuse to pass over when one crosses the water" (14). In other words, exiles might presume that the anchoring memories that let them know *who* they are regardless of *where* they are have come under threat of loss; otherwise, they would consider themselves wanderers or cosmopolitans.

In his 2003 single "Asignatura Pendiente" ("Assignment Pending"), Puerto Rican Latin pop superstar Ricky Martin expresses the desire to "*comprarme un boleto y regreso al ayer*" (to buy myself a ticket so I can return to yesterday), with a suggestion that the island home represents a return in both space and time as well as a psychological regression back to "*el niño que fui*" (the boy I was). "Isla Bella" (2015) further depicts a crucial motive for nostalgic returns to the Caribbean past and soil: "*Mi alma necesita transfusión, sangre de mi tierra*" (my soul needs a transfusion [of the] blood of my [native] land). Much like in Martin's music, contemporary musical fictions construct Caribbean homelands as sites of memory—not in Nora's sense of a poor physical replica of "real" memory (288) but in an earlier Platonic sense of "memory palaces" or Yates's "memory places" (Ricoeur 59). Memory sites in this book refer to physical sites that have recorded and remembered autobiographical and cultural memory, especially sites where the auditor experienced and encoded significant memories or emotionally meaningful music. Part of the reason these musical fictions imbricate memory and place is due to the way the brain's anatomy enables us to spatialize memory. Indeed, one key strategy to enable extraordinary recall is called *method of loci*, mentally mapping information onto a familiar space (Slotnick 66). Several chapters throughout this book depict this association between memory and place through the planting of the umbilical cord, which is believed to root one in that specific soil. When the exile has been physically separated from the site of memory, the movement away (ex) leads the exile to turn to musical remembering to reproduce the home (isle) in the unhomely (*unheimlich*) space. The dual physical and temporal displacement echoed in the term *fugue* creates what Walcott calls an "amnesiac blow" (*Collected Poems* 88). Fugue has a temporal, spatial, and musical dimension; it involves unconscious wandering from a geographic location, the place where one ought to be but is not (Rudnicki xiv). While fugal time ordinarily cannot be captured, the person can return to the place from which she has wandered so long as her memory returns. This book therefore examines how even as music transports the auditor back in time and space in her imagination, such remembering often also inspires a physical return to spaces of origin or belonging.

With their nostalgic focus, contemporary musical fictions might seem out of place amid recent discussions of a "celebratory diasporic consciousness" in Caribbean literature.[13] Although written by diasporic authors, these musical fictions remain Caribbean-oriented and situate music listening in the service of remembering and returning to the homeland, even if only in the imagination. They seem to reify Caribbean specificity and a decidedly retrograde nostalgic attachment to home and roots, with hyphenated characters who code-switch into and out of Caribbeanness as circumstances warrant and who at crucial moments turn from cosmopolitanism. These musical fictions often depict postnationalism and dislocation as traumatizing, producing a crisis that sends the wanderer in search of a refuge in an alternative and prior identity. Rather than "the pleasures of exile,"[14] contemporary musical fictions portray a range of experiences. Exile might be precipitated by a politics of exclusion or by quests for betterment through employment, studies, or creative work. In some cases, exile follows personal loss and trauma, including physical and sexual violence; in other cases, exile begins as temporary migration and itinerant employment but turns into de facto exile following instability in the Caribbean. The varied reasons for displacement from home mean that exiles' sense of belonging in their places of sojourn differs, at least initially. As Kezia Page argues, the "foreign" space might provide new modes of sociality and belonging unavailable in the homeland ("Diasporic Sensibility" 226). These texts suggest that a celebratory diasporic consciousness might not become consolidated without a period or process of deep memory work, as Caribbean peoples on the move grapple with the past to formulate a (more) secure sense of the present and future.

In contrast to early models of Caribbean exilic memory, which focused on the impossibility of return to the site of memory, these contemporary musical fictions show how the contemporary circulation of Caribbean peoples and music complicates traditional notions of memory. I argue that the proximity of diasporas to the sites of origin, coupled with the globalization of Caribbean music, creates a sense that return is possible. Unlike the forced deportations of enslaved Africans to the Caribbean as "stripped migrants" (Glissant, *Caribbean Discourse*

50), Caribbean people moving in and beyond the region can often carry memory commodities with them or access them via new technologies.[15] Music travels as records, cassettes, or CDs; on phones or computers; as digital downloads or streaming files; on radio airwaves or in the cloud; from computer to computer; and also in the memories of listeners.

Musical fictions move "the pleasures of exile" to the pleasures of repeated music listening and remembering. Repetition not only enhances memory transmission in oral-dominant societies like the Caribbean; it also provides pleasure through *re*cognition, the return of a meaningful and forgotten sound, memory, or image of the self. The Caribbean auditors throughout this book replay nation music and the past because doing so gives them pleasure in relation to the perceived pain of the present or a pressing future. *Phonographic Memories* therefore ultimately demonstrates how sound recording technology's capacity for repetition and replay with exactitude enhances the ludic function of musical remembering even when in the service of negotiating trauma.[16]

With their focus on the performative memory work of Caribbean music and musicians, contemporary musical fictions suggest that Caribbean memory can be retrieved and reconstituted through the performative and mnemonic work of the musician. Hand in hand with the antiphonal features of Caribbean musical idioms, Caribbean memory is not only an individual psychological process but a collective and collaborative activity. This book thus theorizes a mode of memory work that is ultimately mediated through the musician, the music, or the technology. In this way, I extend recent studies on memory in the era of mass media that have called into question whether contemporary remembering sees a retrieval of our own memories or a rehearsal of data circulated by audiovisual media. Alison Landsberg has argued that the prevalence of media technologies has created "prosthetic memories" in contemporary viewers who "remember" events and experiences that are not their own (i.e., 9/11) and that these secondhand memories create new affinities among communities instead of remaining in racial, ethnic, or national silos. Shalini Puri advances the term "adoptive memory" to describe "a memory that seeps into one from the outside . . . [and that] enables the first-person narrative to transcend an eyewitness account, and to fuse with a wider collective. . . . The first-person narrator thus becomes a vehicle or repository for a memory that exceeds her own direct experience" ("Memory-Work" 495). *Phonographic Memories* likewise considers how music and music media can surrogate for absented cultural memory; curators of memory use their extraordinary facility to remember on behalf of others and share and broadcast their retrievals with others. The recorded object becomes a surrogate for our own memories; as the musician voices our experiences at a distance, whether in first person or third, we hear our experiences narrated from someone else's perspective and in another's voice. As a result, the musical novel also becomes a playback device for music and memory and therefore requires new reading and listening strategies.

Literary Phonotopes: Reading for Music

Although incorporating music into literature is a long-standing and region-wide tradition, *Phonographic Memories* is the first book-length study of Caribbean musical fictions across a variety of music idioms. Impeded by disciplinary differences, the specificity of national cultures and musics, and the relative paucity of (ethno)musicological studies on individual idioms and the region as a whole,[17] studies of popular music in Caribbean literature tend toward article-length analyses of single texts or chapters on single music genres in regional cultural studies collections.[18] In contrast, my comparative analysis of musical fictions from Trinidad, Cuba, Guadeloupe, and Jamaica reassesses the synchronicities in music, memory, and literary form across the region. Departing from the cartographies of linguistic and colonial histories, I conceptualize a Caribbean musical and literary region that (re)connects, for instance, Cuba with a close neighbor like Jamaica and Guadeloupe with the rest of the Caribbean. Further, while the prevalence of African diaspora forms leads to a focus on black musicality in literary criticism, this book explores how auditors from a range of ethnicities engage in musical remembering, including how they negotiate the impact of Afro-Caribbean musical hegemony on their subjectivity. By putting into conversation texts, authors, music, and theorists from different traditions and considering writers from disparate ethnic backgrounds together, I unearth a region-wide Caribbean poetics of musical remembering.

Phonographic Memories bridges what are still separate cultural, literary, and theoretical practices to consider the technologies and formats of musicking and their impact on both Caribbean memory and the novel form. It therefore distinguishes itself from the focus on predominantly analog and embodied music and performance in recent monographs by Carol Bailey, Jason Frydman, Martin Munro, and Jeannine Murray-Román, which have filled in critical gaps by considering literary representations of sound, noise, drumming, and oral performance writ large in transnational (albeit monolingual) archives. By focusing on popular music—idioms that emerged or were consolidated as the sound of the nation in the post-1960s era—this book asserts that contemporary musical fictions are informed by conceptions of memory and identity circulated by modern, technologically advanced Caribbean music. I underscore how, while Afro-Caribbean musical idioms have often been thought of as premodern, their emergence through the specific modernizing context of the plantation system and then their later transformation through encounter, technology, and urbanization created alternate modalities of modernity rooted in sound and musicality, or what Alexander G. Weheliye terms "sonic Afro-modernity."[19] Caribbean popular music idioms are urbanized and technologized studio versions of earlier participatory and presentational forms, and both forms sometimes still coexist (Bilby 24–25).[20] This book therefore argues that Caribbean memory work in the era of music recording figures remembering not necessarily as a return to analog and precolonial folk traditions—even as this kind of memory work is still in view—but as a (re)turn to modern, technologized, and mediated cultural forms and the remembering techniques they model.

Phonographic Memories joins a rich tradition of musico-literary criticism within both African American and Caribbean studies. Building on the work of Kamau Brathwaite, Carolyn Cooper, Kwame Dawes, and Gordon Rohlehr, who have pioneered critical practices rooted in the jazz, reggae, and calypso aesthetics, I also chart new terrain in theorizing Caribbean literary aesthetics based on underexplored music idioms such as bolero, gwoka, dancehall, and dub. My focus on explicit musical references and the listening cultures evoked in each novel is grounded in an awareness of the tendency to privilege hegemonic music as a reading strategy or to "mishear" literary devices as musical aesthetics. The "aesthetic" model belongs to a critical tradition where sonorous and musical features are read into textual effects. The texts read as examples of such aesthetics need not reference that music form at all or even belong to the same national tradition as the music applied to it.[21] *Phonographic Memories* instead deploys an ethnomusicological model, which aims to situate musical texts in the cultural and historical contexts of the music forms they explicitly reference. For Dawes, musical aesthetics have as much to do with the musical influences that inform a writer's work—and by extension, the cultural milieu at the heart of the novel—as to overt musical references; as such, his "reggae aesthetic" seeks out in Jamaican fiction characteristic reggae elements such as the self-assured use of Jamaican Patwa and a grounding in black consciousness (*Natural Mysticism* 103–118).

The prevalence in the Hispanic Caribbean of consciously musical fiction such as Edgardo Rodríguez Julia's *El entierro del Cortijo* (*Cortijo's Wake*; 1983), and Guillermo Cabrera Infante's *Tres tigres tristes* (*Three Trapped Tigers*; 1965), which feature ekphrastic descriptions of musical interludes as well as encomiums to famous or fictional musicians, has given rise to a strain of criticism that focuses on explicit musicality. Critics like Juan Flores and Christopher Winks first give extensive attention to the musicological features of forms like Puerto Rican *bomba* and *plena* before performing what I call a *critical listening* to the transposition of those features in explicitly musical passages. While the aesthetic mode pays attention to how the aesthetics of music are transformed from sonorous to textual, the sonic turn focuses on the representation of sound and sonority in literature more broadly. In *Sounding Off*, a reading of sonorous fictions from francophone West Africa and the Caribbean, Julie Huntington calls this "texted sound" and coins the term *instrumentaliture* to describe the hybrid aesthetic in which writers transform the novel into a "transcultural transpoetic space" (18); Carter Mathes refers to this as "literary sound" (10), while Weheliye refers to such novels as "literary sound recordings" (83).[22]

Inspired by Weheliye's theorization of phonography as a reading, writing, and hearing practice that "neither . . . abandons the *graph* for the *phono* or vice versa" (38), I deploy the term *phonographic* not to limit my discussion to the vinyl record but to invoke its etymological valence as a hybrid musical and textual document, combining recorded music (*phonê*) and writing (*graph*). I am therefore as interested in the formal impact of musical aesthetics on the Caribbean novel as in the memory making qualities of recorded music. A phonographic aesthetic incorporates silenced and unspeakable histories and voices into the "mix" inasmuch as it brings into the inherently scribal mode of the novel the sounds and associated memories of Caribbean popular music. Rather than focusing on sound qua sound, however, my neologism *phonotope*—a riff on Bakhtin's conception of the chronotope, the narration of time-space in the novel (*Dialogic Imagination* 84)—proposes a critical attention to the narration of music and music making in the Caribbean novel. Literary phonotopes include textual representations of musical interludes as well as lyric fragments, song titles, and musical allusions that interrupt or supplement the prose narrative. I approach novelistic phonotopes as constructed sonority akin to the soundscape of a film or television show: consciously chosen and embedded within the narrative to evoke a mood or imply setting (as both background and foreground), to characterize, and to provide all sorts of anticipatory and mnemonic effects. In this way, I listen to not just texted sound but texted music. In other words, since each novel has an underlying soundtrack that is variously foregrounded as text, subtext, or context, I situate each novel in the musical contexts from which it draws thematic and structural inspiration while considering how that novel's phonographic aesthetic expands extant conceptions of Caribbean memory. If recorded music both captures and replays memories and associated contexts, my critical posture is to perform the "playback." What might readers and characters hear when playing and listening to such records, and what does a combined reading and hearing of Caribbean musical fictions uncover?

Contemporary musical fictions depict not just listening to music but also broader cultures where music listening is integral to collective memory and where aurality is a mode of being. Like Brodber's Ella, listening subjects in musical fictions are often perceptive and virtuosic and listen both to hear and to remember. Readers listen alongside them, eavesdropping on how listening to music (re)constructs subjectivity and enables recollection and, later, narrative composition. To listen means to position oneself in space and time in relation to sound, to orient oneself in aurality. A musical novel becomes an auditorium, a contained "listening device" where music is bound up in printed words

(Baucom 47). Centering on music-mediated memory work, which often appears in response to a trauma or crisis, the musical fictions in this book invite us to lend a critical "listening ear" (Stoever 13) to textual and cultural silences and the hegemonic structures that render some sounds, genres, texts, and subjectivities inaudible. Alexandra Vazquez has advocated attentiveness to "those bits of history that get skipped over or left unattended. Details are, for many of us, wonderfully disruptive fissures that crack many a foundational premise behind all sorts of narratives" (20). I extend Vazquez's conception of "details" to those moments when phonotopes—often in the form of italicized lyric fragments or the narration of musical interludes—disrupt and fissure the prose narrative and cause the reader to pause, pay attention, and "imagine the sound" (Mathes). Vazquez insists that listening in detail is a critical imperative: "To not listen to what the performers are doing . . . would be to enact another kind of violence upon them" (12). Likewise, I argue, to *not* listen to the music in the text is to resilence it in a replay of the colonial silencing of subaltern voices.

Ethical listening as a critical method thus situates the reader and critic in relation to the "material details" that writers use to evoke music and to re-sound and amplify it for others (Vazquez 26). It is not without significance that Vazquez's text demonstrates how to *listen* but not "what the [music or musicians] *sounds* like" (12). In the end, these sounds are all produced and transduced in the mind's ear. Here I am borrowing Jonathan Sterne's term *transducers*—"devices . . . which turn sound into something else and that something else back into sound" (*Audible Past* 22)—to think about the translation of music into novelistic prose and how such a process raises questions about what we *do not* hear in various types of records, written or musical. Since they are comprised solely of text and static visual data, musical novels are a "lossy" format for sound data; music has to be transduced or converted into printed words. Like analog to digital or vinyl to CD or MP3 conversions, much is lost of the sound event when music is transduced into words. Readers only partially participate in the listening project since they cannot "hear" texted lyrics and descriptions of sound without their own sonic memories of those sounds. For instance, not all readers will have the requisite cultural knowledge to replay phonotopes as they are heard by authors or fictional characters. As a Jamaican reader, when I see the italicized words "*Sammy dead-oh*" in *Louisiana*, my memory can playback the melody of the song, and if so desired, I might even be able to remember a specific instance of singing or hearing and any associations I have with it. Even as musical fictions record sounds and music, they rely on the reader's own cultural memory to complete the literary document in the antiphonal mode central to Caribbean musicality. *Phonographic Memories* thus expands our understanding of what constitutes a recording technology—beyond obvious examples like the LP, record players, and sound systems—to include bodies, psyches, and literary texts. Indeed, as diasporic authors tap into music as an archive of memory that adds layers of signification to the literary text, the Caribbean novel itself mimics and extends the function of Caribbean musical recordings.

Book Overview

The role of the musician in helping others negotiate amnesia or trauma recurs throughout the chapters of this book. Chapter 1 explores how, whereas lay citizens can afford to forget, the calypsonian—with his virtuosic listening skills, phonographic memory, and techniques of masking—creates and curates memory on behalf of the community, enabling others to remember in their turn. Scott's *Night Calypso* (2004) is set in the context of the recording of Trinidadian calypso and the development of early listening technologies that, alongside the emergent phonograph industry, made the early twentieth century audible and mass-reproducible. Exile to a leper colony and recourse to the calypsonian's techniques offer the traumatized focal character, Theo, the physical and narrative distance to performatively salvage recessed memories from the collective unconscious and to retrieve and replay traumatic memories on behalf of himself and others.

Chapter 2 explores the role of recorded music as a memory aid that both enables and disables the successful negotiation of memory. The formal reliance on the repeating LP and what I call a bolero aesthetic—the simultaneous romantic and nationalist nostalgia of Cuban "songs of love"—in *The Mambo Kings* (1989) sets up the Cuban exile condition as a tension between nostalgia and acculturation. The Castillo brothers, who migrate to New York from Cuba in the 1950s to pursue success as mambo musicians, become trapped in a constant quest to return to their homeland, which often can only be realized through repetitive replay of recorded music and its associated memories. Hijuelos frames nostalgic memory as not merely the replay but the distortion of the originary event, making retrieval even more impossible and replay even more addictive. Indeed, in the same way that excessive play warps wax records, excessive reminiscences warp memory, and the warped performance paradoxically becomes fixed *in* and *as* memory.

Chapter 3 centers on three female characters in *Lone Sun* (1981) who experience various forms of psychic and bodily trauma and the way that their provisional *re-membering* is enabled by listening to both African American jazz and the improvisational drum-based gwoka music of Guadeloupe. Tracing the characters' turn from jazz to gwoka, from Paris to Guadeloupe, and from assimilated Frenchness to liberated national consciousness during the 1940s and 1960s, I investigate the novel's depiction of a range of creative work: from the scribal practices of Marie-Gabriel, who narrates herself into being by textually re-membering her parents' bodies and stories, to the musical strategies of her father, a jazz musician who discovers in gwoka a liberatory practice that enables women to restore bodies and psyches shattered by French colonization.

By crafting a novel that reassembles fragments of herstory, music, and memory, Maximin highlights the gendered implications of remembrance (the repeated *psychological* reassembling of memories) and re-membering (the *physical* reassembling of the disarticulated members of the female body).

The focus of sites of memory—the body and the homeland—is also a key aspect of Colin Channer's *Waiting in Vain* (1998). Chapter 4 tunes in to the spatial and embodied dimensions of cultural memory in Channer's novel. Channer's characters pursue physical, psychological, or performative repatriation as a balm to the trauma of exile and the loss of the fidelity of cultural memory. I attend to the technologies that enable the circulation of Jamaicanness throughout and beyond the island's shores in the 1980s and 1990s—the sound system, the commuter bus, sound clash mixtapes, and the radio—as well as characters who function as a "sound system" to amplify Jamaicanness in diaspora and to facilitate the re-memorization and repatriation of diasporic yardies. Referencing recent advances in DNA and genome studies to interrogate the novel's framing of cultural memory as a root-seeking repatriation project, I argue that the deployment of numerous agricultural metaphors figures Jamaicanness as an indelible trait that can be recovered by roots music and marshaled in the service of nation-building. The novel therefore conceptualizes memory work not merely as a psychological process, a desire to return to a past time or an anterior self, but as a necessarily physical one, a quest to physically return to and become rooted in one's native soil. But this romance of the nation marginalizes Jamaicans of other ethnicities, who might have to turn to performative fugue instead.

Chapter 5 returns the focus more explicitly to listening to recorded music and the use of recording technologies in remembering. In the final chapter, I consider how gender and ethnicity enable the interrogation of the hegemonies inherent in Afro-Caribbean popular music. I examine the practices of music listening in *The Swinging Bridge* (2003) that enable Indo-Caribbean women to negotiate their marginalization within collective music forms. Rather than a single nation music, as in previous chapters, the narrator re-members her Trinidadian identity through what I call a memory mixtape—a collection of remembered songs from a variety of genres that soundtrack both the novel and her memories. The novel's primary phonotope of the cassette tape also calls attention to salient features of Caribbean sonority and memory as well as compositional practices most valuable for subaltern subjects. Even as I focus on the tension between sound and unsound practices, I theorize paradigms of memory work that mimic cassette-era technologies and practices—from mobile and isolated listening to creative editing of original recordings. Inserting their own voices and stories into unsound religious, patriarchal, or national "master" records, subaltern women deploy feminist performative and authorship practices drawn from Indo-Trinidadian chutney music and Jamaican dub music. Whereas in previous chapters characters imagine an idyllic Caribbean homeland filled with sounds of belonging, the final chapters show how Afro-Caribbean music might exacerbate and record the marginalization of other ethnic groups and the recording techniques that will be vital in negotiation that marginalization. I close with a coda that looks forward to recent examples of digital-era music fictions to assess how new music technologies like dub and new formats like MP3s reshape modalities of being and sounding Caribbean as well as upend the format of the Caribbean musical novel.

By bringing together these disparate texts from across the Caribbean and putting these different musical genres into conversation, I hope to demonstrate the fruitfulness of sustained sound readings and hearings of phonographic novels beyond those that I study here. In its theorization of a region-wide investment in musical aesthetics, *Phonographic Memories* affirms the continued importance of Caribbean music in providing contemporary novelists ethical narrative models for recording and sounding marginalized memories and voices. Like their characters, whose music-mediated memory work enables them to return home and subsequently to move through the world with their memories and Caribbeanness intact, these authors chart an exciting future for Caribbean novels that circulate throughout the literary world with an ingrained self-assurance in their musicality and vitality. As music technology advances and Caribbean peoples continue to circulate and return, music remains not only a "vital and valid . . . literary model" (Channer, "Preface" 13) but also a vital and valid critical model as well.

CHAPTER 1

Phonographic Memory

TRACING THE CALYPSONIAN'S WORK IN LAWRENCE SCOTT'S *NIGHT CALYPSO*

Calypso does remember.

—M. NourbeSe Philip, "Fugues, Fragments and Fissures"

Do you remember the days of slavery?
History can recall, history can recall [. . .]
While I remember, please remember.

—Burning Spear, "Slavery Days"

One could hear Burning Spear's "Slavery Days" as a stirring attempt to trigger the memory of key aspects of the Afro-Caribbean experience. Indeed, it is the second track on the Jamaican reggae act's 1975 *Marcus Garvey* album that is filled with historical events and figures. One such figure is the titular Garvey for whom knowledge of black history was a core component of rehumanizing African diaspora peoples in the first three decades of the twentieth century. But the lyrics of "Slavery Days" are curious: its refrain asks reggae listeners in and since 1975 if they "remember the days of slavery." If "remembering" is figured as the retrieval of an experience personally experienced and stored in the annals of memory, then Winston Rodney's question seems nonsensical on the surface. Since slavery was abolished in the anglophone Caribbean in 1834, his listeners did not personally experience and therefore neither have forgotten nor can remember the whipping, beating, and enchainment that the song recounts. As the song goes on, Rodney makes two claims that illuminate both his conception of remembering and his understanding of the role of the Caribbean musician: "history can recall" and "I [the musician] remember." Here, the "history" that "can recall" is not official history but the song itself; in other words, the song narrates historical events neither recorded in canonical archives nor transmitted in remembered stories. The creation and curation of a historical record in song aims to plant "memories" in the mind of listeners far beyond the temporal and spatial locations of the initial horrific events narrated and beyond the personal experiences of those for whom the song's events constitute first-person testimony.

I begin this chapter on Trinidad calypso with this anachronistic story from 1970s Jamaica to draw attention to the region-wide mnemonic function of Caribbean popular music and musicians that undergirds this book. If *Phonographic Memories* examines how Caribbean music enables remembering, this opening chapter establishes the role of the Caribbean musician as creator and curator of collective memory. Since the Middle Passage and plantation slavery ruptured memory and subjectivity, dealing what Derek Walcott calls a "deep, amnesiac blow" to the region's inhabitants (*Collected Poems* 88), where are the records of the Caribbean past and what techniques and technologies might allow for their retrieval and replay? As I argue in this chapter, that is the work of musicians like the calypsonian. In "Fugues, Fragments and Fissures," M. NourbeSe Philip proposes that "calypso does remember" (80). As direct descendants of the West African griot tradition of recording and transmitting collective memory, calypsonians "serve to wake us from our dissociative states" by "improvis[ing and] filling the gaps in our memory" (84, 80). She describes the calypsonian's primary function as "the performance of memory. . . . But that memory is a two-edged sword on the one side of which is amnesia and on the other forgetting" (80). Starting from this premise, I trace the techniques that calypsonians use to remember and record traumatic memories unavailable to consciousness or in other archives, even as such recuperation remains partial and provisional.

To this end, this chapter performs a critical listening of the calypso phonotopes in *Night Calypso* (2004) by Trinidadian novelist Lawrence Scott. If his earlier fiction locates calypso and Carnival as performative modes for recuperating and narrating Caribbean memory, in his third novel, Scott depicts a Caribbean rife with alternate memory archives, including bodily wounds and sound recordings of popular music. Whereas lay citizens can afford to forget, the novel shows how individuals gifted with phonographic memory remember on behalf of the community, carry collective memory in their minds and bodies, and transmit it down through time through performance. In *Witchbroom* (1992), Scott's white Creole protagonist listens to the stories of others in order to assemble them in a narrative Scott calls "Carnival tales," but in *Night Calypso*, Dr. Vincent Metevier, the white Creole narrator, must listen to the "night calypso" crafted by Theo, a twelve-year-old orphan who bears mysterious bodily scars and whose composite racial heritage marks him as the product of a creolization rooted in sexual violence. In both novels, Scott interrogates the place of white Trinidadians in postcolonial nation-building while privileging Afro-Trinidadian memory practices.

Framed by two brief sections set in 1983, *Night Calypso* spans World War II and the immediate postwar period (1938–1948) when Trinidad's location at the southernmost tip of the Caribbean archipelago placed it at the frontline of the war. German U-boats often found their way into Trinidadian waters, and the United States set up naval bases on the island to monitor and launch attacks against German incursions into the region. The novel reimagines this watershed period in Western history and the turning point for trauma and memory studies from an alternative perspective. It chronicles the psychological and political struggles of a group of lepers and other outcasts exiled to a leprosarium run by French nuns on El Caracol, a fictional island off the coast of mainland Trinidad. Populating the novel with historical doubles and characters who begin as stock types of the key players in Trinidad and Tobago's wartime history, Scott depicts the war as part of the Caribbean's historical memory: that of white Creole Trinidadians like Vincent, who belongs to a class of landed elites grappling with challenges to their economic power; of Jews like Vincent's assistant Madeleine Weil, who flees the pogroms for the Caribbean and refashions herself as the nun, Sister Thérèse; of the fishermen who discover dead German sailors in their nets; of the mothers and daughters who discover the power of the Yankee dollar and the "social invasion" that the naval bases cause in their sexual and economic lives; of Indian and African laborers and labor leaders struggling for bread and justice; of the lepers cast off the mainland to live or die in leper colonies; and of the calypsonians who had constant fodder for their sung commentary even as their practice was censored during this period.

Believed mute when he is first sent to the island to seek psychological help from the doctor, it takes many overtures by Vincent and others before Theo responds, selectively and unevenly, not only to touch but also to conversation. With the emotional and physical safety afforded by Vincent's care for and informal adoption of the boy, it soon becomes clear that Theo's aphasia is a psychological rather than physical disability due to his having repressed a story of sexual trauma. Despite "choking on [his] own words" (*NC* 37), Theo must find a mode of telling that will allow him to narrate the story of his visible and invisible injuries. As this chapter will show, despite the efficacy of Vincent's training in psychoanalysis and mediate auscultation, and even with the coterminous emergence of early-twentieth-century modern technologies like the phonograph record and the gramophone, *Night Calypso* privileges corporeal memory rather than recording technology and calypso rather than the talking cure to negotiate the amnesia and aphasia that attend Caribbean trauma.

Although it refers to a song form, calypso (alternately *kaiso*) is best understood as a discursive practice and narrative form set to music. Rich with rhetorical masking features that allow the calypsonian to effect social and political commentary, it is readily transducible to other narrative forms and has long inspired the region's writers. Kamau Brathwaite regards the calypsonian as the "musical counterpart of the novelist" ("Caribbean Literature" 46), while Funso Aiyejina coined the term *novelypso* to describe novels that mimic the form, content, and techniques of calypso music and the masking and memory work of the calypsonian or chantwell ("Novelypso").[1] Two Trinidadian authors in particular have established the novelypso tradition: Samuel Selvon transposes the style of the chantwell into novelistic narrative voice (*The Lonely Londoners*, 1956), while Earl Lovelace (*The Dragon Can't Dance*, 1979) explicitly incorporates calypso lyrics, calypsonian figures, Carnival tropes, and the broader rhetorical strategies of the chantwell. Scott combines both in *Night Calypso*: lyrics of actual calypsos of the World War II period appear as chapter titles, are sung by characters, and serve to comment on the story in a similar way to Lovelace, Scott's unofficial literary mentor.[2] These real calypsos complement the titular "night calypso," Theo's term for the remembered tale he narrates in "sleeptalking" mode. Even though Theo's tale includes moments of calypso singing, his neologism frames his tale as the narrative equivalent to sung calypsos. Like Selvon's chantwell narrator, Theo employs the narrative and rhetorical masking strategies that the music form derives from its association with Carnival, the annual pre-Lenten masquerades of Trinidad and Tobago. However, Scott's chantwell is not the novel's overarching narrator but a character who crafts an extended "calypso" within the novel.

Through this metafictional mode, Scott illustrates how the calypsonian performatively salvages and surfaces repressed memory fragments, then composes them into a public record of collective memory that enables amnesiac listeners to remember in their own turn. In this way, Scott reframes calypso's "I" narrator—a marker of personal witnessing—into collective memory and depicts memory work as a shared project constructed through the call-and-response between musician and audience. The emphasis on performative retrieval and replay establishes two key aspects of Caribbean memory that will recur throughout this book. First, without intact memories, postcolonial Caribbean recollection is only partial and fraught with fragmentation and degradation. As a result, Caribbean memory work is not a process of reencountering the past as it was but reconstructing and curating it through performance and storytelling. Second, as the music played in Carnival tents and during road marches, calypso is closely related to forms of dramatization associated with "playing mas"—Carnival masquerade—and thus highlights the corporeality of Caribbean memory.

As I will show, calypso offers the traumatized storyteller innovative narrative techniques to salvage recessed memories from both the collective unconscious and the wounded body. Focusing on Theo's deployment of chantwell techniques of linguistic, narrative, theatrical, and sartorial masquerade, I investigate how he bypasses the unnarratability of trauma and circumvents some of the limits of modern calypso to make women's voices and memories audible. Significantly, whereas calypsonians, like other musicians, are skilled at memorizing their compositions, in transducing the musician's memory work into novel form, Scott constellates in Theo three exceptional modes of high-fidelity recording and remembering: the musician's memory, the vinyl record, and trauma. Theo's phonographic memory surrogates for recording technologies as high-fidelity media and enables an inclusive genealogy of musicking that does not sideline people without access to modern or Western technologies. By localizing phonographic memory in Theo's chantwell skills, Scott displaces the listening and recording technologies extant during the time of the novel, even those that prove efficacious in Vincent's treatment of his other patients.

Sound(ing) History: Calypso as Record

Night Calypso depicts several early-twentieth-century listening technologies and modes of listening even as it often sidelines modern technologies to center calypso itself as an audible record of Trinidadian history.[3] Four major circumstances of the "turbulent thirties" contributed to calypso's emergence in its present form. The presence of American marines in calypso tents helped to professionalize the song form, and the money they freely spent in the towns created a bustling economy in the demimonde centered on calypso and prostitution. But as a result of the Theatre and Dancehalls Ordinance (1937–1951), calypsonians had to present their songs for censorship before recording or performing them as white and brown elites tried to snuff out the rising working-class political voice and black merriment. Ironically, while censorship meant the dumping of many records into the sea, it also led to a variety of alternate recordings in newspapers, pamphlets, and booklets, as well as to innovative censorship-evading linguistic techniques. But the emergent recording industry in the thirties also enabled calypsonians to ink lucrative recording contracts with American companies such as RCA Victor, Okeh, and Columbia Records, and several calypsonians including Rafael "Roaring Lion" de Leon and Raymond "Atilla" Quevedo embarked on recording sessions in New York City. During the thirties, Decca Records even sent delegates to Port of Spain to record the annual calypso competitions, and they often left with enough recordings to last until the next year's competition. The censorship, the recording missions, and the vigorous debates around calypso in the newspapers of the day gift present-day auditors with a rich archive of sonic and written records of the song form.

As the people's spokesman, calypsonians recorded, critiqued, and broadcasted news of the events that would become key plot points in *Night Calypso*: the 1937 labor riots, the arrival of Jews in the southern Caribbean, a German U-boat attack in Trinidadian waters on Ash Wednesday 1942, the resentment against American marines and the socially disruptive influence of the Yankee dollar in the towns and tents, the birth of steel pan on VE and V-J Day, and even the censorship of calypso and the ban on Carnival. Much of the plot not only has a soundtrack indexed by chapter titles and calypso couplets but also dramatizes historical events recorded in calypso songs of the day. As Theo himself demonstrates, these songs were often hot off the press, composed and circulated in the mouths of tent audiences within hours or days of the events described therein.[4] An alternative archive for calypso and subaltern histories, the novel incorporates fragments of calypso lyrics of and about the period, which are in turn sonic records of key moments in history.[5] Scott in fact imaginatively reconstructed a narrative of those times from Gordon Rohlehr's documentation of wartime calypso records in *Calypso and Society* (1990). In other words, the novel documents calypso's (trans)formative period, particularly given that calypso remains one of the few indigenous records of life on the island during the war.

In a novel about listening techniques and technologies as much as narrative practices, the chantwell combines both in order to discern and compose untold stories into audible history to be recorded for posterity. Considered the historical antecedent to the Caribbean chantwell, West African griots chronicled collective history by composing and memorizing sung genealogies. In the griot tradition, history is a collective story that is sung and heard, and "once composed, [the griot's] song is not forgotten" (Hale 38). As history in song, calypso likewise enables historians to reconstitute a chronicle of the island's history and attitudes to world history beyond those recorded in the elite newspapers of the day. Notwithstanding, the extant calypso archive is an incomplete historical record of that time, with untold stories lost to the unfathomable archive of the sea. Even further, although the presence of recording technologies often assuages our sense that we can record experience for posterity, no technology can as yet capture with perfect fidelity the entirety of lived experience. Sound technology's capabilities of the day were often mono, low-fidelity, static-ridden, and selectively recorded with the inbuilt censorship of having to make decisions about what to record based on economic, political, or technical exigencies.

By focusing on a period in which history was made acutely audible via sound reproduction technologies, even as European states strove to violently erase the living memories of subaltern constituents, Scott emphasizes the tension between recording and forgetting and the simultaneous absence and presence of historical records. Although this was a time of increased recording, historians would need to turn to alternate archives and historiographic techniques—not just musical records but also *remembered* records. Despite censorship, irrepressible calypsonians found other modes of transmission. Vincent notices that "the calypsonians kept their commentary going on the time. . . . The Doctor's House was a buzz of humming and singing, replacing the ban on Carnival by the governor. . . . The fishermen were the calypsonians" (*NC* 171). The novel shows the fishermen, and later Theo, listening to and memorizing censored calypsos and then broadcasting them to others by singing and, even further, by reliving and reenacting the historical events that the calypso narrates. Recording makes historical events replayable and repeatable, but even before the advent of recording technology, the repeated performance of calypso songs in the tents and road marches enabled their transmission with a kind of fidelity that anticipates recorded music but was entirely ingrained in oral transmission. Scott establishes calypso's credentials as both audible and embodied history; here, history is condensed into a three-minute song that is replayable in conscious or subconscious retrievals. In so doing, he suggests that under the right circumstances, memory might substitute for sound recording technology.

Phonographic Memory

Trauma functions in the novel much like the phonograph recording process. Leon Scott's 1856 phonautograph, for instance, "used a cone-shaped horn to capture sound and 'focus' it on a flexible membrane stretched across the small end. Sounds captured by the horn made the membrane vibrate rapidly. Linked to the membrane through a delicate mechanism was a pointed stylus to which the vibrations were transmitted. . . . If the cylinder was turned rapidly during this, the stylus would scribe a thin line in the soot, rendering a visible record of the sound" (Morton 2). This silent but "visible record" is nevertheless pregnant with sounds that must be coaxed out by a playback mechanism. Scott likewise depicts Theo's body as a visible record of colonial violence, but this recording requires the appropriate playback mechanism to make its data audible.

Trauma is, of course, Greek for "wound," originating in bodily injury then expanded into psychoanalysis to denote psychic injury. The wounds of Vincent's patients are both physical and psychological, the physical often serving as a legible yet silent testimony to profound psychological trauma. Trauma marks and imprints the body with what Roberta Culbertson calls "the memory of the event" (174), making the wounded body a silent archive and a site of memory. Narratives that foreground bodily inscription therefore suggest that we might have to look to the wounded body to recover memory records lost to other historical archives.[6] The physical wound is distinct from the scar—the one fresh and present, the other signaling that the injury has healed. In-between is the scab, where the wound is still recent, but healing is in process. Physical wounds might heal into faint scars, while psychic wounds often recess but remain potentially painful and damaging. Scars—indices of past injury—invite remembering and the recounting of what Vincent calls "the story of the scar" (*NC* 27) and therefore serve as a visible record of physical or psychological injury that disables and disorders narration. Theo's silence and scars are in fact indices of recording and an invitation to play back the sounds encoded in the grooves. I consider the interplay in the novel between healed physical scars and their corresponding psychic wounds as registering the crucial work of music, memory, and storytelling in working through the lingering traumas of colonization.

The experiences of Vincent's wounded patients reveal three related effects of trauma: bodily wounds, amnesia, and the compulsion to explain the illness even when it is often impossible to coherently narrate. The lepers' atrophied limbs numb them to pain, which leads to unwitting self-harm and, in one case, death. For Sister Thérèse, the mental trouble over her repressed Jewish identity and the incursion of German sailors into Caribbean waters creates a shock so profound that it triggers the resurgence of her repressed identity in a psychic war that uncannily testifies to the political war looming on the horizon. In fact, her night of broken glass occurs on the eponymous Kristallnacht (November 9–10, 1938); her psyche produces a version of the events occurring in Europe, which becomes externalized in her unconscious self-harm. Vincent calls her dramatized regurgitation of her father's censored letters and their account of the war and the extermination of the Jews a "bloodletting of words," as if the letters have caused a surplus of words that she must expunge in order to heal (*NC* 160–163). Although vocal possession allows her to retrieve and testify to the experiences of others that haunt her, this is an oblique retrieval; vocal possession makes her trauma available for interpretation by the doctor, even as she herself cannot tell it plainly.

In Theo's case, he bears numerous bodily scars, including "a suture, a stitched wound, running from the base of his neck to the coccyx" (*NC* 26). Although his scar is potentially legible, a type of "braille" (28), it has a certain opacity. As Theo tells his interlocutor in the frame narrative, set in 1983 long after the recounted events, "I've got a scar right down my back, and yet another scar you cannot see" (459). The legible physical scar thus maps to a psychic wound that "simultaneously defies and demands . . . witness" (Caruth 5). Whereas it often renders him mute by day, at night, Theo's numbing and dumbing wound reanimates when he awakens in a terrible state of fright, manifest in his wide-eyed perch on the edge of Vincent's bed, and his night calypso is his only means of release. Reflecting the paradoxical imperative of speaking the unspeakable, Theo is often rendered silent by a surfeit of words and memories backed up inside his throat. His partial aphasia indexes a larger cultural silence due to the colonialist repression of Caribbean orality, the seat of collective memory where the Caribbean subaltern speaks. Theo's initial silence also registers not a forgetting as much as a repression in order to survive. Philip suggests that not-telling, what might resemble aphasia, is not necessarily a sign of the absence of memory or the presence of traumatic amnesia but often an inability to narrate despite the overwhelming desire to narrate. To not-tell or to not-remember is an act of survival and will; it protects the survivor from being overwhelmed by a traumatic memory. Amnesia and aphasia within a postcolonial text are thus discursive choices, "mutilating the text" to register the violence that produced the injury (*Zong!* 193). As his memories emerge as *Pawòl*, or utterance,[7] Theo's listeners realize that he chokes and tells in stutters and fragments because his memories are too horrible to even contemplate much less to utter.

Over a span of six years, in approximately ten discontinuous nocturnal tales, Theo draws on calypso techniques to remember and narrate the "ancestry of . . . interference" that runs from the time of slavery to the present (*NC* 151). There are a few common triggers—usually Theo's empathetic response to witnessing the trauma of others in the present: encountering for the first time soon after his arrival on the island a leper's severely disfigured face or witnessing the premature sexualization of Christiana, a teenaged schoolmate. Something in the postures and context of the sexual act—a helpless young girl in an animal posture, bearing the desire of an older man—triggers a belated shock that throws him back into the past. That night he replays the repressed memory of that very scenario, this time with his great-grandmother Christina Dellacourt, his grandmother Alice, and his mother, Emelda, as hapless prepubescent victims of the sexual appetites of successive white French Creole masters named Pierre de Marineaux, or Mister, and often their fathers or brothers as well.

A chance encounter with the Mister of his tale near the end of the novel leads to his dreadful revelation that, although the Dellacourt women chose to abort their pregnancies (or commit suicide) rather than bring more daughters into the world to "get take" (150), Theo does not escape the same violation. The Mister of his generation encountered Theo in the de Marineaux cocoa fields, flogged him severely, and forced him to perform fellatio. Hearing his mother using the nickname Coco, which reminds him of his abjection, Theo set fire to the plantation house. However, while his mother perished in the flames, Mister and his white family survived. Later, when Theo was subsequently sequestered in a monastery for his safety, the Father Superior would leave a key inside Theo's room for him to let in his own violator. Theo tried to flee his unending torment by attempting to fly from his room window—either to Africa like the Guinea slaves or to his death—at which point Father Dominic sent him off the mainland to Vincent for healing. In addition to the narrative replay and sometimes confusing carnivalesque intertwining of unfit fathers—priests who rape novices and fathers who rape daughters and sons—the night calypso also reveals that Theo has inherited not only the victimization of Ma Dellacourt, Alice, and Emelda but also their memories.

This is the story of the scar: the systemic rape of black women, girls, and boys even while preserving the fantasy of white purity and with the complicity of the Church. The Dellacourt women would "get take on a quiet afternoon, to the tune of the catechism class downstairs, under the house, teach by the mistress of the house" (*NC* 150). In contrast to Freud's theorization of a screen memory as a comforting recollection that blocks an anterior and even more disturbing traumatic experience (see Rothberg 12–16), Theo's and his foremothers' experiences interlock in a web of interrelated traumatic memories, each more disturbing than the last. Theo's own violation can be read as the original trauma, but its memory is hidden under layers of similar assaults in his own timeline.

Chronologically, however, Theo's own experience is a more recent screen to the historical trauma he uncovers in his remembering of the Caribbean's original sin. *Night Calypso* reveals that at the heart of traumatic Caribbean histories is the truth of disturbing paternity, where the father is at once one's brother and also the father of one's child. As such, beyond the experience itself, the consequence of intergenerational sexual violence is both a confused incestuous ancestry and a confused linearity.

In order to diagnose his patients and decide on a mode of treatment, Vincent needs to understand their symptoms; therefore, establishing what happened, to whom, and by whom are vital projects. But since the "reality or truth" of trauma "is not otherwise available" to consciousness (Caruth 4), this poses a challenge for the talking cure method. A traumatic experience is a limit case, one that is far outside the bounds of normalcy and comprehension. As a mode of protection and survival, the mind might disassociate from the present or fixate on an object or sound. Theo, for example, fixated on the softness of the cocoa pods to distract from sexual violence, while his great-grandmother focused on the sound of "the catechism class downstairs" as she was apprehended by the Mister of the house (*NC* 150). The existential horror of traumatic events often affects the survivor's perception of time, whether it dramatically slows or the entire period collapses into a vacuum of forgetting. Such protective maneuvers can result in a "faulty" recording of the experience. Given that long-term memory retention requires attention (Snyder 10), significant chunks of traumatic experience might be lost or overwritten. Beyond its multiple occurrences, Theo's experience is all the more devastating because he would have been too young to have the requisite understanding of his experience or the requisite language to explain it to others. The resulting "crisis of witnessing" frustrates the quest for empirical accounts of what really happened (Felman and Laub xvii). Psychoanalysts posit that traumatic memory is not forgotten but repressed beyond conscious knowing; while the patient might not be able to consciously reproduce—remember, recollect, or perhaps even recognize—the event as narrative, which implies consciousness and control, it remains in the memory system and can make itself known through repetition compulsion where passive memory becomes action and embodied memory (Freud, "Remembering" 150).

How can one tell a story of one's beginnings to account for the collective experience of ruptured families—torn apart at the slave port and the auction block—and the fundamental incestuousness of Caribbean genealogies? And how might one retrieve traumatic memories when their retrieval is painful and dangerous to the patient and when the experience of trauma itself shatters the ontological and cognitive conditions required for the coherent encoding and retrieval of memory? While the talking cure mostly proves successful for Thérèse-Madeleine, Theo's turn to calypso suggests that he requires narrative techniques beyond Vincent's Western training, specific to the Caribbean, and capable of handling the aporia of childhood sexual trauma. True, in *Caribbean Discourse*, Édouard Glissant tells the story of Caribbean history using the language of psychoanalysis: neurosis, shock, repression, latency, and return (65–66). But whereas the talking cure focuses on the individual psyche, Glissant reframes Freudian psychoanalysis to theorize a social phenomenon. As *Night Calypso* elaborates, those working through individual trauma must first grapple with the recuperation not just of repressed autobiographical memories but of collective memory as well.

Scott bypasses Western psychoanalysis and listening technologies to instead center Caribbean music as the primary modality for retrieving and narrating traumatic memory. Even further, Scott shows how even as the body remembers (Saunders xx), traditional technologies of sounding the body are ineffectual in Theo's case. The novel's setting marks a time of listening as "mediated, skilled, and technologized" (Sterne, *Audible Past* 100), modeled by the stethoscope used by doctors like Vincent to listen to and diagnose the sounds of the inner body and sonar (Sound Navigation and Ranging) used in missions against German U-boats to listen to submarine sounds and seek out submerged threats.[8] In the same way that psychoanalysis rendered the subconscious accessible and knowable, so too did sonar and the stethoscope, both of which were coterminous with and incorporated elements of the emergent recording industry. Although Theo's body bears multiple scars, the data that will allow Vincent to diagnose and treat him lies beneath the surface. In his capacity as listener-healer, Vincent's uses the stethoscope to retrieve nonvisual information and to listen to the body's hidden language in concert with reading its surface inscription. Vincent's medical training prepares him to consider Theo's body as a container of sounds that might explain his illness. He discovers, however, that while the information surmised by auscultation can reveal a narrative of physical illness, Theo's testimony refuses empirical examination; in other words, what ails him is not available to Vincent's listening apparatus. Subverting the privileged mode of diagnosis, Theo makes the voice the instrument of diagnosis and reverts diagnostic power back to the patient rather than the physician, whose use of the technology requires and asserts his skill and power.

In contrast to the Hegelian deployment of the myth of the Dark Continent as a metaphor for African opacity and to dismiss those considered "behind" or incompatible with modern, rational techniques and technologies, Theo asserts that the black unknown is scrutable, meaningful, and modern, but access requires the right technology and training. Instead of the modern gaze, reading and hearing the black unknown requires heightened audile skills, precise attunement of the ear, and a facility with local technologies and cultural practices so as to transduce salvaged data into a form comprehensible to the audience. Here I extend Jonathan Sterne's definition of an *audile* from one who privileges audition as a way of knowing to a person with extraordinary *listening* techniques—learned, repeatable skills—on the level of modern technology (*Audible Past* 96, 92). The oral-dominant music culture of early-twentieth-century Trinidad required repetitive and participatory song structures. Before the advent and widespread adoption of recording technologies on the island, calypso also depended on and honed finely tuned listening and memorization in musicians and listeners alike. This structural and culture repetition enables a pseudotechnological memory capacity, what I call *phonographic memory* throughout this book. Whereas short-term memory only holds information for a few seconds before it decays, in addition to repetition, intense or unexpected experiences like traumatic shock can allow data to persist and ultimately move into long-term memory storage (Snyder 53).

Theo's ears rise to the level of modern technology, enough to displace both Vincent's stethoscope as a diagnostic tool for traumatic memory and the 33rpm LP as the format for recording calypso and its sociopolitical commentary. He is often "all ears," an avid listener to live voices as to radio-transmitted sounds. He has gleaned his mother's tale from overhearing her "speaking like she in confession" (*NC* 285), and in regurgitating the overheard tale, he allows her voice and suffering to emerge. He records overheard stories and replays them across space and time for new listeners with fidelity to plot and voice—as if his own voice were a high-fidelity record. He mimics but reorders stories he has imbibed in order to narrate "living history" (94)—historical memory that, like calypso, is timely and relevant, links past and present, and gives voice to untold and unspeakable experiences. Theo does the same with the stories of Jesse, the African American GI with whom he explores the pre-Columbian middens. Mimicking Jesse's voice, during his night calypso, Theo replays verbatim his conversation with Jesse for Vincent and Thérèse (as Madeleine). In so doing, Theo reveals his chantwell-like process in real time as his listeners witness his filing away in his archival system a story he has recently heard, recording both sound and content with remarkable fidelity.

Highly sensitive so as to become profoundly marked even by physical and emotional trauma suffered by others, he is also exceptionally perceptive and empathetic; in order to add his commentary and to know what to select, he hears and intuits even the unspoken. His gift is thus prophetic: he is able to narrate in a night calypso the fate of the German soldier who is killed in a U-boat attack near the doctor's house before he and others witness the actual event (*NC* 346). According to Rohlehr, "The job of the calypsonian was . . . to create fictions out of the stuff of experience. In these fictions, the calypsonian often presented himself as a witness of the action being described" (122). By depicting Theo's phonographic memory as able to access—or imagine—memory before witnessing it, Scott extends the calypsonian's position as perceptive witness and witty observer. He is not remembering, if remembering is figured as retrieval of episodes from the recollector's psyche. Instead, his ability to tap into the collective unconscious figures memory as psychic salvage.[9] Even further, Theo's attunement to the fate of the submarine operator both mimics and displaces the sonar technology of the German marine.

Theo's turn to the chantwell's memory work enables him to create an audible record that serves as both a tool against amnesia and a tool for anamnesis—to recreate memory after a forgetting (Ricoeur 27). Often beginning with or including couplets and refrains from sung calypsos, each memory fragment in Theo's night calypso is topical, speaking to the social reality of his listeners and connecting distant history and current events (journalist function) in order to make the audience aware of the atrocities of the past (historian function). Throughout his story, Theo decodes the novel's historical allusions and illuminates recent events. Even as characters enact the historical labor riots of what is for them recent Trinidadian history, Theo reveals a second level of historical and narrative doubling: "Mama Say that Mister know about history, that this kind of thing happen before. She say, we go be safe, even if them coolie in the sugar and nigger in the oilfield make trouble" (*NC* 35). For the reader, "this kind of thing happen before" both in the temporal past and in the pages of the novel. Theo's history lesson comprises both the World War II present and the colonial past, illuminating that Trinidadian history features compulsively repeated traumas. Theo also uncovers how both the names and the power relations repeat: "Mister" is a symbolic name for the white Creole authority figure who preys on the bodies of young women and men in a historical reenactment that connects Theo to his foremothers.

Robber Talk: Voicing Woman Memory

Whereas trauma results in psychic and narrative chaos,[10] calypso's relationship to Carnival imbues the idiom with narrative and rhetorical masking techniques that allow "the wounded storyteller" the requisite distance to rise above chaos and to salvage and sound out his own memories as well as those of others. One of the chantwell's key linguistic masks is robber talk, the wordsmithery of the Carnival masquerade known as the Midnight Robber, among other appellations. As his name suggests, the Robber, whose narrative techniques evolved from both oral and written traditions, uses storytelling as a form of ransom. In one of his alternate iterations, the Robber adopts the wordsmithery of the courtly jester masquerade called Pierrot, or *nèg jardin*, whose hallmark is spelling out and improvising on archaic words from classic Western texts, newspapers, and oral tales. The capstone of robber talk is when the masquerade breaks apart a polysyllabic word, then either reassembles it in new ways or sounds it out whole after sounding it out in pieces (Wuest 44). This "syllabic method" demonstrates the Robber's virtuosity and is often part of his arsenal of humor. Pierrot's syllabic dismantling of colonial words finds contemporary iterations in Philip's literary memory work in *Zong!*, the lyrics of word artisans like Jamaican dub master Lee

"Scratch" Perry, or the Rastafarian language, Iyaric.[11] These linguistic innovations reclaim agency from the oppression and silence wrought by colonial language.

Robber talk finds its place in Theo's narrative arsenal. He forces Vincent and Madeleine awake with the insistence of his voice and holds them hostage with the horror of his story. Like Pierrot and traditional griots, he repeatedly demonstrates his erudition and wordsmithery with words from both written and oral sources and transduces colonizing literary texts into oral content. He breaks words and texts into component parts that he can reassemble into a new tale that more accurately conveys his history lesson. He then assuages his listeners' shock at his knowledge of sophisticated texts and "big words" despite his young age by showing that he has learned them "the syllabic way" (*NC* 220). The syllabic way tropes how Theo regains control over his dispossession and subverts the aphasia that trauma wrought. This technique empowers him to break "big words" and master texts in the way his psyche was broken by Mister and masters and to reassemble them into new sounds in a performance of wholeness. Theo's story, like the story of colonization writ large, is one of exploitation, robbery, and rape. Appropriating robber talk allows him to interrogate the colonial robbery of bodily autonomy and culture. Theo performs linguistic robbery; to tell the story of his numbing and dumbing wound, he robs the master's tool of language. Since "it's words that make me from small" (402), including the words Mister used to simultaneously comfort and violate him, at a young age, Theo mastered the art of turning words into tools to critique, commentate, and cure. His precocious facility with "big words" also registers the precocity that childhood sexual violence imprints on his psyche.

Deploying the robber's linguistic mask to safely narrate child sexual trauma, Theo thus goes beyond the humorous, timely sociopolitical commentary of the tradition to give voice to truths unspeakable even in calypso mode. In Nalo Hopkinson's *Midnight Robber* (2000), a comparable example of the narration of childhood trauma, it is only through the Robber mask that the narrator, Tan-Tan, can tell the community who impregnated her. To overcome the impossibility of speaking the horror and taboo of incest, Tan-Tan merges with the Robber Queen, who takes over the child's voice and, in rhyming couplets and calypso *picong* (insult) and *fateeg* (heckling), narrates Tan-Tan as a third-person character in her performed memory. By the end of the calypso, Tan-Tan unveils or "demasks" from third to first person so that the audience comes to terms with the truth behind the masquerade.[12] In order to tell this story that is "too nasty to be Carnival mako" in a way that will reveal it is precisely not play but truth, Tan-Tan has to make her psychic split visible and audible: "Rough with emotion, her cracked voice came out in two registers simultaneously. Tan-Tan the Robber Queen, the good and the bad." In only a few lines, she summarizes her rape and how "she kill she daddy dead. . . . Then Tan-Tan knew her body to be hers again, felt her own mouth stretching, stretching open in amazement at the words that had come out of it. Is she, speaking truth; is truth!" (Hopkinson 325–326). Like Tan-Tan, having used evasive mechanisms to survive the original trauma, Theo can only recount it using linguistic masking. He describes his mounted abuser as a "*borokeet*," the half-man, half-horse Carnival character, then "*jab molassi* [black devil] and red devil and *moco jumbie*" all at once (*NC* 378). It is as if he needs an excess of language with which to narrate this evil that consumes children as his occupation. Also like Tan-Tan, Theo employs a linguistic mask of double- and multivoicedness in order to tell a truth and deliver a history lesson that is "too nasty" for the supposedly playful calypso and Carnival, too horrible for his audience to hear and bear.

Although Theo has wounds of his own, his wounds repeat symbolically and narratively throughout history, place, and time in the traumas of others. Theo's calypso works by displacement: a deeply personal trauma is articulated by masking it in the voices of others. Not only is Theo transmitting his salvaged memory of the Dellacourt women's legacy of abuse; he also inhabits their voices to narrate their stories and to mask his own. Like Thérèse-Madeleine, whose displaced narration of the war ravaging France is enabled and disabled by the voices of others that possess her, Theo would often "[tell] it as he had heard it, rendering the tones of the voices which possessed him" (*NC* 151). Theo's voice often sounds "like many voices all at once" (92), as if there were "a multitude of voices in the boy's voice" (32). His is a collective ancestral voice that simultaneously sounds out layers of traumatic memory. Vincent is astonished to notice that, by evidence of the voice, "Theo was his great-grandmother" (154).

While griots usually inherit their art from the same-gender parent,[13] it is Theo's foremothers who pass on their sexual abjection and woman memory once there are "no more girl children" left in the line "to get take" (*NC* 286). Theo recalls that his "Mama, Emelda. . . . She have history lesson too. She give it to her boy. . . . She carry in herself a long memory" (149). This memory is passed on from great-grandmother to mother and from mother to son "when she not even know she telling me" (152–153). But although he is employing the calypso form, and while slave and neoslave narratives have long chronicled the horrors wrought by the plantation system on the bodies and psyches of women and men alike, Theo's ancestral woman memory is not typically conveyed in calypso.[14] Although in its earliest iterations the chanterelle was female, the modern calypso is predominantly a male form and the rhetorical devices of *picong*, *fateeg*, and *sans humanité* have taken on new meanings to embolden male performers for calypso tent competitions. As Tan-Tan's incredulous audience concludes, stories like hers, or like Theo's and the Dellacourt women's, are "too nasty to be Carnival mako" (Hopkinson 323). Theo's nighttime calypso, however, tells a different kind of story. He transcends the limits of the calypso traditions of his day to bring back the silenced voice of the original female chanterelle and allows his listeners to hear "women's voices surfacing" (Philip, *Zong!* 201). Dressed and speaking as women to remember and narrate woman memory, Theo is transgendered by his tale. Having inhabited the same abject sexual and subject positions as his foremothers, Theo is "umbilically connected" to their stories and carries their memories and voices in his own body (*NC* 155). Theo's wound connects him to the shared physical abjection that marks the Caribbean condition and allows him access to collective memory archives.

Scott's narrators usually transgress traditional gender categories; *Witchbroom*'s Lavren and Theo both take on female garb, voices, and subject positions in a bid to performatively remember suppressed memories. In both novels, transgressing and transdressing are rooted in "playing mas," not to entertain or provide social release but to make untold stories audible and visible.[15] Theo's use of costume and role-play goes beyond the calypsonian's typical deployment of costumes as a sartorial mask to embolden himself for performance; Theo's transdressing both distances and embodies historical trauma. Dressed as Ma Dellacourt, he is able to access in his own voice and body his great-grandmother's memories and to link them to his own testimony through the simultaneity of the performance. Theo's mas is a further innovation on Thérèse-Madeleine's use of the habit to slip in and out of iterations of her identity (*NC* 269). Whereas the nun's habit hides her sexual body and disguises her Jewish identity, Theo's inhabiting of his grandmother reveals the otherwise invisible and inaudible truth of his being and allows him to bridge personal and collective memory.

"All o' We Is One": Performing Collective Memory

Theo's use of costuming, role-play, and vocal transformations demonstrates how collective memory might be salvaged through "playing mas." Vincent calls Theo's dual linguistic and sartorial masking a kind of possession (*NC* 151). Although Theo has improvised his great-grandmother's outfit from towels and curtains and has taken on her mannerisms, Vincent suggests that masking goes beyond dress. Carnival masking assumes temporary, playful costuming and role-play that, as Gerard Aching theorizes, is less about disguising or concealing than making visible (6). Both European and Caribbean Carnival masquerades originate in subversive street parodies—the one to critique class and gender divisions, the other to upend racial and cultural hierarchies (Bakhtin, *Rabelais* 6). However, in ritual masking, the ancestor continues to live inside and with the celebrant. Aisha Beliso-De Jesús calls this "copresence," where the ancestor shares the living body of the host.[16] Theo's "possession" by the voice of his foremothers thus implies something beyond Carnival masquerade. Like Santería mounting, it makes visible and audible the connections between past and present in the voice and body of the mounted.

In Dennis Scott's play "An Echo in the Bone" (1985), a community of recently emancipated Afro-Jamaicans mourning the death of a father and husband, Crew, stages a Nine Night ceremony during which, with the aid of rum and drumming, congregants become possessed by ancestral spirits. What the performers retrieve is not only the recent past—what happened to Crew, how he died, that he killed the white planter and why—but the larger historical drama of slavery and oppression that continues to impact contemporary Jamaicans and the cycles of antiblack violence that finally led to Crew's retaliatory killing of Mr. Charles. Vocal transformation, posture change, and the touching of transitional props make visible and audible their transformation into the ancestors, both slaves and masters. Possessed by ancestors, the mourners retrieve and (re)play ancestral memories in the present through their voices that are the ancestors' voices, through their bodies that are now inhabited by the ancestors' spirits. On the register of visibility, the body of the mounted remains in view even as it is transformed by the copresence of the ancestor. On the register of aurality, those witnessing the mounting simultaneously hear the ancestor and the mounted, a double-voicedness where the past fissures the present to make itself heard. Vocal masking as spirit possession reveals history as temporally prismatic, layering past and present and incorporating individual and collective voices.

Night Calypso joins performative texts like "An Echo in the Bone" that index an epistemology of the voice that has resonance beyond the corporeal. Advertisements for early gramophones lauded the possibility of hearing the voices of the dead since recording technology separates voice from body (Sterne, *Audible Past* 287), while Walter Benjamin famously expressed anxiety over the presumed loss of aura ushered in when recording technologies cause the voice to be disembodied (220–223). As mounting traditions attest, however, in West African cosmogony, ancestors' voices are not completely lost; instead they linger and can become reembodied and revocalized through the griot or *santero*, individuals with appropriate receptive endowments for this kind of memory retrieval and transmission. Through Theo, then, Vincent and Madeleine can hear the *living* voices of his dead ancestors with remarkably high fidelity.

In the traditional Nine Night ceremony, the living celebrant is possessed by the ancestors so that the dead can deliver a final witness before returning to Dahomey. Such possession reveals the porous borders between living and dead, the final arc in African diaspora exile and return. However, Theo's possession concerns neither death nor return. Ancestor possession enables those living in the present to retrieve and replay otherwise inaccessible memories of black oppression and violation. In so doing, the possessed testifies and seeks justice on behalf of the dead and becomes empowered to tell her own personal and present stories with the aid of a community of cosufferers. Maureen Warner-Lewis has argued that spirit possession or *mayaal* (myal) is a curative ritual where ancestors inhabit descendants' bodies to impart to them knowledge to act in the present, particularly to counteract the effects of colonization (*Central Africa* 193). The communal aspect of these ancestor rituals resonates in Theo's own vocal possession to transmit collective memory and cure the ills of the present.

The Carnival refrain "all o' we is one," promulgated by Eric Williams, first prime minister of an independent Trinidad, is meant to capture how subversive masquerades break down the class and ethnic boundaries that plague society the rest of the year. But as Lovelace shows in his novelypso *The Dragon Can't Dance*, "all o' we is one" is only a platitude that allows revelers to pretend solidarity during Carnival. In *Night Calypso*, however, Scott reframes "all o' we is one" through the collective, even if differentiated, experience of trauma. As Emelda tells Theo, "All of we in the same thing. . . . This is how the place make. . . . This is what we make, and this is what they make of us" (*NC* 286). Possessed by voices of ancestors, Theo becomes a spokesperson for the collective and is empowered to deliver a history lesson to contemporary citizens that might replace collective amnesia. He tells the untold stories of race and place, inserting genealogies of trauma into the historical record of the nation. As such, Theo expands the calypsonian's role into an embodied Akashic record who speaks from the collective ancestral archives—he speaks as himself but possesses and is possessed by the memories of those who came before. Theo's night calypso attests to listeners that he has both heard their testimonies and shared in their experiences in his own body.

Lovelace has noted that "where chantwell and chorus combine to render a piece . . . I see expressed an awareness of self, of the I as well as a sense of the other. I and I" (Aiyejina, *Self-Portraits* 34). Lovelace's use of the phrase "I and I" alludes to the construction by which Rastafarians signify a collective psyche in which the speaker is copresent with the divine, Emperor Haile Selassie I (pronounced like the first-person pronoun). Subverting the singular "I" of the privileged Western individual subject, the "I and I" construction reinforces that it is through the voice of others that the story of the self, or individual memory, emerges. Scott's conception of Caribbean ontology illustrates Glissant's proposition that in the idealized authentic Caribbean novel, "the collective 'We' becomes . . . the true subject"; to work through collective trauma, the Caribbean writer must center on the collective consciousness, asking "Who are we?" rather than "Who am I?" (*Caribbean Discourse* 86, 149). Similarly, Theo's multivoiced narration makes audible the copresence of collective ancestral voices in the singular voice of the speaker. Unlike the traditional autobiographical "I," Theo's "autobiography" is a story of the "we" that (re)composes the fragments of the untold unspeakable stories of Caribbean trauma in order to tell them with his own voice and body and to testify obliquely to his own trauma. Since trauma shatters the survivor's sense of coherence and wholeness, it also fragments the cognitive and narrative "I" into what manifests in the novel as multiple voices. Theo's multivoiced "I" is thus both the seeing "eye" of witnessing and the first-person "I" of traumatic testimony, doubled and reverbed into the voice of the collective unconscious and collective memory.

That trauma ruptures the subject therefore becomes a productive problem in the novel. The multivoiced telling of the story of others displaces but helps Theo get to his own story. In the same way that Tan-Tan must become double and double-speak as both herself and the Robber Queen, since single-voicedness would be impossible and retraumatizing, Theo needs his ancestors to help him to bear witness. What Theo needs is what Glissant calls *relation* (*Poetics* 11), the recognition that he is precisely not alone—not in the present while he is connected to Vincent and Madeleine by their audition of his tale nor through time while he is related to his foremothers and other exploited women. For instance, while Emelda lamented that her mother's suicide left her alone to fend for herself, Theo himself is simultaneously alone and accompanied in his moments of assault. In his replay of his first violation, he reveals that he survived his own encounter with Mister by drawing on his memory of Alice's words and her survival techniques of playing dead (*NC* 151, 374). The double replay allows us to hear Alice's experience simultaneously with Theo's, even as it confuses who is experiencing violation in this moment. "All o' we is one" as a calypso replay technique thus registers the repetition of intersubjective violence, where different bodies are only shifting sites of subjection and memory.

Despite the vocal mask, however, this is Theo's own story: his voice and subject position almost always start the fragments, and during the tale, he often comments on the contemporary trigger for his remembering. Although in early fragments Theo often depicts "himself [as] a [third-person] character in his own story" (*NC* 93), as a result of his verbal mask, Theo's own voice and first-person memory eventually emerge. Like Tan-Tan, Theo's mask must eventually fall to reveal him and his own story underneath the story of others. This echoes the calypso tradition where, at a crucial point in the song, the listener witnesses a merging of the narrative persona. The chantwell's narrative mask falls, having served its purpose. In *Witchbroom*, Scott reveals that Lavren (whose first name riffs on the author's) is in fact the alter ego of the unnamed first-person narrator; this metafictional structure illuminates Lavren's historical record-keeping as a mask for the narrator's and author's own literary project: "These were stories I could not tell, and I hoped their voices in Lavren's preposterous narratives would speak out from where they stood . . . Can I have my own Carnival? Wear my own mask?" (110). It is only at the end of the novel that Lavren finally disrobes and de-masks into the triply articulated he/I/you. The ultimate dissolution of the "he" and "you" into the autobiographical "I" suggests that it is in "playing mas" that the history of self, family, and nation can be remembered and narrated.

Although in Scott's fiction the salvaging and sounding of traumatic memory are undertaken by a single individual gifted with special technologies and techniques, this task is enabled by and on behalf of the collective. Maurice Halbwachs has theorized that individual memory is in fact collective memory, memories of experiences that are recollected or narrated together within social frameworks (37). In "Fugues, Fragments and Fissures," Philip locates the construction of shared memories as the calypsonian's social function; she recounts the story of an Afro-Trinidadian woman who "hears a fragment of a calypso which reverberates within her. . . . [and] dislodges a memory of a former wholeness long forgotten" (79). *Night Calypso* also suggests that collective memory is publicly narrated memory, fixed and then circulated to the members of the collective through recording or performance. In this view, collective memory is not produced in the individual consciousness but rather *reproduced* there as it is circulated to redress cultural amnesia. This kind of memory work is always a constructed and mediated, if not secondary, process. The joint between individual and collective memory also raises questions of whose memories Theo recollects. As Philip frames it, if "calypso does remember" and enables us to remember, "what I doing in dis here dream—and who dreaming dis dream[?]" ("Fugues, Fragments" 80–81). In other words, calypso creates memories in her own psyche of experiences she did not personally live. This is the essence of Burning Spear's memory work in "Slavery Days," to expand recollection from the musician to the community.

Like the griot's song, the memories encoded in calypso become available to and incorporated into the experience and knowledge of listeners. The calypsonian's audience gains something akin to what Alison Landsberg calls "prosthetic memories," secondhand memories that become embedded in the witnesses' consciousness as if they had personally experienced them. As a human phonograph and apprentice chantwell, Theo's remembered and embodied tale creates an imagined community connected by shared memories; here, this community is not fostered by print media, as Benedict Anderson theorized of eighteenth-century Western nationalism in *Imagined Communities*, but through music and its transmission and audition on the radio and in live performance spaces like the Carnival tent. In his appropriation of Thérèse-Madeleine's father's letters, the question turns to whether these letters are the memory documents of her father the individual subject or her father as part of the collective of Jews being rounded up and killed. In his assertion that they are found objects to be reconstructed into a collective narrative, Theo disarticulates memory from individual consciousness and perception. He intimates that collective trauma consists of not only shared simultaneous experiences like the Holocaust or the Middle Passage but also individual experiences that an expert composer connects metonymically and makes part of the shared memory archive. Theo reconstructs memory and history as "all o' we" story, and he calls this appropriation, a provocative retort to contemporary anxieties over cultural appropriation or the extraction of cultural memory and markers from one (often subaltern) context to another (often a politically powerful one). He asserts that in his capacity as custodian of collective memory, he is entitled to appropriate other people's memories, and he makes them his own so that he can then tell them in the first-person mode of calypso.

Night Calypso suggests that it is the calypsonian who seeks out repressed memories and recollects or remembers them to allow others, including the person who first experienced the traumatic event, to remember in their turn. In so doing, the I-narrator becomes a surrogate for the trauma survivor. As the musician voices the experiences of others, the amnesiac hears her experiences narrated from someone else's perspective and in another's voice, which provides one mode of distance to enable her to grapple with the past. In this way, both the calypsonian and the survivor remember the event as a simultaneously personal ("I") and shared ("I and I") experience. This collective remembering underscores how shared abjection creates new categories of proximity and affinity. Transportation on slave and indenture ships forged new kinship ties beyond language—as the terms "ship brothers" and "ship sisters" indicate—since family and linguistic ties were broken on land and had to be reconstituted at sea and upon arrival in the New World. The chains that bound shipmates and enslaved laborers viscerally reinforced that mediated connection between their bodies. Forced proximity reconfigured the conceptualization of individuation: what I remember is repeatable; my sense of self is informed and transformed by the presence of so many others, similarly reduced and bound. It also anticipates the interconnectedness of performer and audience in the call-and-response mode that is a key characteristic of Caribbean music cultures.

Call-and-Response: Participatory Remembering

A key component of calypso's collective memory work is its compact between chantwell and audience. Although Theo has previously attempted to tell his story, only Vincent's mode of listening allows him to work through his trauma. In fact, the confessional mode of Father Dominic—his desire to uncover guilt and sin—sets the boy back into aphasia and disables his progress, and the inattention of the priests to his nightly violation under their very noses renders them complicit. The emergence of Theo's story, ruptured and truncated as it may be, requires the right kind of listener. Witnessing Theo's own witnessing, this secondary witness must hear, empathize, help him play out the past, and make sense of his need to tell by redirecting his feelings. The secondary witness is therefore as crucial to the memory work as the primary witness. But how can the secondary witness listen ethically, assisting remembering rather than retraumatizing the victim or becoming traumatized in the process? As a secondary witness to the trauma of others, Theo is himself impacted by the burden of remembering, such that he is unable to sleep and must compulsively tell. By extension, Theo's own memory work causes secondary trauma for Madeleine and Vincent, who must bear witness to Theo's insistent narration. The musician invites us to remember by his song and performance, but the call to remember must be heeded by the audience. Shifting the privileged mode of diagnosis, historiography, and memory from sight to listening thus foregrounds that this is not just a story that must be told; it is also a story that must be *heard*. As subsequent chapters affirm, the call-and-response mode of many Caribbean music idioms sets up a relationality between musician and audience, where remembering becomes a shared project.

In the same way that the stethoscope of both auscultator and sonar operator focuses and amplifies listening and immerses the listener in sound, Theo's robber talk is immersive and captivating; Vincent describes the boy's voice as "insistent," and Theo often climbs into the doctor's bed and whispers his story in his ear. While it is possible to close the eyes to foreclose sight, sound continues to penetrate the consciousness during sleep and is the first faculty to resume perception as one drifts into waking. If Madeleine's reaction to the tremendous toll of listening is to flee the bedroom, dozing is Vincent's only means of relief from Theo's voice, even as it penetrates his consciousness and forces him awake. Theo, however, critiques Vincent's dozing as a type of fugue; in addition to insisting on waking Vincent with his voice, among the first recorded words in his night calypso is the improvised lullaby, "Doctor, doctor. Sleep, sleep. *Do Do, petit popo*" (*NC* 34–35). His subverting the folk lullaby to awaken rather than put the doctor to sleep echoes his appropriation of the children's song "Frère Jacques" to comment on the complicity of the priests who remained sleeping and unconcerned while he was being violated. In contrast to Father Dominic, who, despite wanting to help Theo heal, is horrified by the illicit nature of the participatory listening Theo requires, it is when Vincent "play[s] for truth" (248), fully awake to and aware of the multiple layers of historical meaning and traumas embedded in Theo's tale that he can finally accomplish his role as healer.

Vincent has to jettison certain a priori of his medical training, including the clinical distance central to auscultation. Even though Vincent's ethnicity and class create social distance from his patients, Theo's treatment requires immersion, contact, and participation. Theo insists that it is not enough to listen and diagnose; salvaging traumatic memory requires *immediate* auscultation. Indeed, the mediated listening of the priest in the confessional, separated from the penitent by a lattice, is one reason Father Dominic's initial attempt to help Theo fails—the other is that confession presumes that the one speaking is guilty of a sin and needs repentance and forgiveness. Priestly listening is also mediated on at least two other registers: the priest only mediates on behalf of the one who will bring about redemption and restoration, and that ultimate intervention will be manifest in the heavenly rest to come. As a result, Father Dominic's listening does not offer Theo immediate relief by any measure. Theo in effect practices a kind of autoauscultation: "Turning the stethoscope back on themselves, [medical students] . . . encounter their own lived and experienced bodies . . . in new and potentially unsettling ways" (Rice 316). He displaces Vincent from privileged listener to secondary witness and participant observer as he transduces the sounds submerged in his subconscious into a narrative that others can hear. He also eventually turns auscultation onto Vincent; no longer outside of scrutiny, the one to examine and diagnose, Vincent is himself a patient, a part of what is wrong with society.

With his participatory practice, Theo shatters the boundary between storyteller and audience. On several occasions, Theo compels Vincent to pantomime the historical roles of master and servant as Theo reenacts his and his foremothers' violation, with Vincent in the roles of both Mister and the unnamed priest. Theo's recourse to dress and reenactment as part of his night calypso underscores the importance of mas in ritual healing for postcolonial peoples: redressing collective amnesia requires all participants to reenact their historical roles. By implicating Vincent as participant-listener, Theo enables Vincent to remember his preexilic life as the scion of a white French Creole planter family: "The boy's history lesson was . . . reminding him of something he did not like to remember . . . Vincent found his memories tumbling out an ancestry, a shared legacy, grounded in the source of the wealth of the creoles, much like Theo had described on the same hillsides" (*NC* 155–156). The novel interrogates Vincent's amnesia: he has forgotten about the colonial relics that he has brought with him from his family estate on mainland Sancta Trinidad,[17] and he has suppressed the memory of his own teenage sexual relationship with the daughter of his family's servant, resulting in a son he's never seen. Theo's memory work thus also facilitates Vincent's own work—he must acknowledge his complicity with the structures of patriarchal colonialism that traumatized Theo and his foremothers.

It is when Vincent acknowledges and performs his symbolic link to the role of Mister that Theo becomes exorcised—at least temporarily. But Vincent must also see himself in and through Theo to free them both from the cycle of compulsive repetition. Theo's ventriloquizing of Mister elicits Vincent's own memory, "almost forgotten," of a similar command by his own father before a beating and forges a connection between doctor and patient. Suturing his symbolic dual role as powerful and powerless into one moment of cathartic release, "Vincent stood with the switch in his hand and . . . cried for himself and Theo" (*NC* 406, 404). That Vincent is also able to extemporize the voice of Mister, to repeat the past but with a difference, suggests that Theo's calypso has created a memory text that is now available to Vincent's own consciousness and on which he can improvise in order to move Theo from acting out to working through—only "then he could assume his own self, Vincent, the Doctor" (410). The kind of listening required of the secondary witness is thus one that implicates his body and requires him to inhabit the other's point of view. Theo's working through cannot take place without Vincent's multiple masking and de-masking as listener, priest, doctor, and Carnival tent audience, as well as Mister and father figure.

A central theme running throughout Scott's oeuvre is that all members of society—including his fellow white Creole Trinidadians—must become implicated in order to effect social justice and political change.[18] The characters in the novel all begin as historical types because they are players in the social and political masquerade of Trinidadian history. Scott also implicates the reader-audience in the chantwell's history lesson and memory work; the night calypso's call-and-response form calls attention to the obligation of the reader-listener to bear witness in collaboration with the narrator and to undertake a kind of autoauscultation. It implies that the project of retrieving, recording, and curating Caribbean memory is not solitary but collective and collaborative. Scott's fiction thus models what I call an *ethics of remembering*. Reader, listener, and calypso tent audience are pressed into imperative listening and ethical response to the calypsonian's call. For instance, once *Witchbroom*'s narrator has accessed submerged collective memories, the novel itself simulates calypso's call-and-response mode; Lavren makes clear that calypso, whether sung, spoken, or written, "invites you to listen and to respond" (3). Scott ultimately proposes sound reading as an ethical and relational practice connecting author, narrator, character, and reader.

In proposing that repressed and fragmented Caribbean memory can be retrieved and reconstituted through the performative and mnemonic work of the musician who invites Caribbean auditors to listen and remember together, Scott envisages relationality as a tool for overcoming the traumas of amnesiac history. Here, Scott's version of relation is love, as indicated by the German sailor's love song, "*Die Liebe, die Liebe ist's allein*"—"it's love, it's love alone" (*NC* 73). While it is normally unethical to do so, it is not insignificant then that Vincent's ultimate healing technology is the love and family relationship he develops with his two most severely damaged patients. Later chapters will depict this intimate call-and-response connection between musician and audience through romantic and sexual congress, but here Scott uses a father-son love relationship; Vincent's love for his adoptive son inspires the trust and safety Theo needs to master his trauma and to school Vincent in the latter's own complicity in patriarchal colonialism.

J'Ouvert

By displacing the action of the novel to a miniature version of Trinidad off its shores, Scott creates a surrogate space where the traumatic events that occurred on the mainland in historical time can be reenacted at a distance and in fictional time in order to safely work through them. As Joseph Roach has theorized, performative surrogacy displaces the "real" to a new site so that it can be safely apprehended and worked through (2). The calypso song text and Theo's night calypso, like the leper colony, also serve as surrogate sites where traumatic memory can be safely confronted, performed, and narrated with the aim of the eventual reintegration of all the exiles on the mainland—the site of trauma. The epilogue, whose last lines return us to the novel's opening, suggests that "to live with himself and his body," Theo has to reenter "that time" and tell a "new story"—not the story of *what* happened to him but the story of how he *told* what happened to him; not the traumatic memory itself but the remembering and performance of the trauma (*NC* 458). This story, effectively the novel we have just read, is now not in the first person of the epilogue and prologue but in the third person of the historical narrative, with Theo not as the protagonist but as a character. In this "new story," Theo displaces himself as object rather than subject, mimicking the objectification and subjugation that caused his trauma. Through this third-person mask and double (re)telling, however, Theo adopts the objective distance of the historian as well as the perspectives of others, deploying them as vital tools in his own remembering. The mode of fiction is a key surrogate space for working through; as Richard Kearney explains, "The recounting of experience through the formal medium of plot, fiction or spectacle permits us to repeat the past forward so to speak. And this very act of creative repetition allows for a certain kind of pleasure or release" (51). The performative mode of the night calypso thus provides Theo, an exile from the mainland where the events took place, distance and a surrogate site from which to tell the untellable.

The displaced reenactments of calypso and Carnival offer Theo a language and form to safely confront the past—perhaps why Scott finds J'ouvert, the opening day of Carnival and a ritual rehearsal of Emancipation Day, such a fruitful metaphor throughout his fiction. Rather than Freudian repetition compulsion, J'ouvert turns on the deployment of Carnival play and surrogacy as tools for performing memory. In *Night Calypso*, repetition is not necessarily a sign of traumatic neurosis, or what Paul Ricoeur calls a "disturbance of memory" (127). Instead, it is often an outcropping of the normative working of memory in oral-dominant societies. Repetition provides pleasure through recognition and enhances the transmission and remembering of oral culture. Rather than a glitch in the memory system, repetition, even when obsessive, can also be a conscious choice to ward off or redress forgetting.

Going beyond the high-fidelity vocal replay I have described so far, Scott shows how Theo must deploy the full range of tools in calypso—linguistic, narrative, theatrical, and sartorial masquerade—to bypass the unspeakable; in other words, even calypso narration fails Theo in crucial moments. He therefore moves beyond voice to silent masquerade then to full performance, not playing mas as escape and entertainment from trauma but in order to work through trauma. The full reenactment—extending over hundreds of pages and several years—is graphic and horrid, profoundly traumatizing for Theo's listeners and for the novel's readers, yet Vincent realizes that "the boy needed to be doing what he was doing, and he, Vincent, needed to play this part, so that Theo could in turn play his. If he stopped it, he might prevent some important retrieval" (*NC* 283). With Theo repeatedly and forcefully assuming the posture of and inviting penetration, Vincent "had to discover the fine line between the acts the boy wanted performed, and the semblance of them which Vincent felt he had to use" (405). Theo's remembering techniques suggest that since intersubjective violence like rape has both psychic and physical implications, telling alone is insufficient in working through. To rise above psychic chaos and amnesia, the impacted body must be brought into service in the work of healing. Since to replay the recorded sound the needle has to retrace the grooves, likewise narrating trauma retraumatizes the wounded witness and repeats the original inscription, although with a difference.

Correspondingly, *Night Calypso* suggests that Caribbean traumatic remembering is not a mere vocal replay of an experience recorded on the memory but rather a reliving of a wound recorded on both mind and body. Theo's embodied retrievals recall Edward Casey's notion of a corporeal memory that "can be 'enacted' in the same manner as all the other modalities of habit . . . But the ordeals, illnesses, wounds, and traumas of the past invite corporeal memory to target precise instances that call in particular upon secondary memory, upon recollection, and invite a recounting" (Ricoeur 40). Having retained traces of memory even when the event has become unavailable to consciousness, Theo's wounded body instinctively replays and repeats what it has experienced. In the above scenes, he keeps resuming the posture of rape because only by doing so can he remember, tell, and evacuate the subconscious disturbance. Similarly, it is ultimately through corporeal remembering that Theo retrieves and vocalizes in plain, declarative statements the final traumatic memory: his first attempted flight back to Africa and the consequent fire that consumes the big house and his mother. In the same way that his wound memory insists on reproducing in his body the posture of repeated violation, it also repeats and reproduces the trauma of his mother's death. In its final iteration in the novel, Theo's fire destroys the leprosarium and the marine base. His repeated reenactment of the burning of the great house suggests that his body has also recorded the corporeal memory of enslaved ancestors who used fire to physically destroy the crops and masters' houses that justified their oppression. This too is the story of the scar.

The novel ends on the continued process of rehabilitation, how to let the past stay past while telling a new story that will lead to a new future. Theo's burning of the base and convent leads to the lepers' reintegration into mainland society, where the revolutionary leaders had not made headway. The historical narrative ends with the nascent labor movement and a hint that the social rupture of wartime has set the stage for the nation's independence and self-governance that would follow in the 1960s. In the closing lines of the historical narrative, Elroy, an inhabitant of the leper colony, muses that with the ousting of the Yankee marines, the new masters of the colony are "we self" (*NC* 441). Glissant has argued that enslavement dispossessed the enslaved of both speech and mastery over their own bodies (*Caribbean Discourse* 122). I read Elroy's statement as a provocative suggestion that Theo has achieved a measure of self-mastery and self-possession during the psychic upheavals he narrated during those war years. Through remembering and replaying the past, he is that much closer to an integrated self.

While Carnival and calypso appear to have become emptied of political power in the real world, *Night Calypso* suggests that calypso still holds the potential to enable the working through of the wounds of history.[19] Regardless of the real content and function of calypso songs in Trinidadian culture, writers like Scott, Lovelace, David Chariandy, and others affirm that the calypsonian's traditional function remains crucial to the continued working through of persistent cultural and social traumas. Novelypsos like *Night Calypso* continue to interrogate the benefits of the musical idiom as a model for Caribbean memory work, both actual and literary, and underscore that if both memory and the body record the violence of history, it is the calypsonian, if he is worth his salt, who is able to capture these experiences in song and on record and enable us to remember them down through time. In the same way that the wounds on the body and on the mind can become legible recordings of violent history and memory, calypso narratives—like phonograph technology—function as playback mechanisms, replaying these physically and psychically recorded narratives and transmuting their silence-inducing inscriptions into sound and meaning.

CHAPTER 2

"Record Your Memories"

THE BOLERO AESTHETIC IN OSCAR HIJUELOS'S *THE MAMBO KINGS PLAY SONGS OF LOVE*

With a flick of your wrist on your phonograph switch, the fiction of the rolling sea and a dance date on a Havana patio or in a smart super club will become reality. Certainly, if you cannot spare the time to go to Havana or want to revive the memories of a previous trip, this music will make it all possible.

—Oscar Hijuelos, *The Mambo Kings Play Songs of Love*

In the previous chapter, I showed how traumatized Caribbean peoples use music to access and replay repressed memories. In the pages that follow, I consider the role of recorded music as a portable memory device that disables the successful negotiation of traumatic memory. As Caribbean-based sound recording projects of American companies like RCA Victor and Okeh Records escalated in the first four decades of the twentieth century, phonograph records captured more than just the sounds of particular artists; compilation records also circulated early Cuban-originated idioms like the rumba, the bolero, and the mambo. Consequently, listening to a rumba record meant listening to what Cuba, or at least Havana, sounded like in the 1930s. As the epigraph above describes, "with [just] a flick of your wrist on your phonograph switch," the auditor can take a mental trip to Havana, to memories of either an actual past trip or an imagined future one. These discs of portable memories were central to the creation of a Cuba of the mind for American audiences. This was even truer for the growing Cuban exile communities in Miami, New York, and elsewhere, as Cuban records became time capsules of memories of an idealized Cuba. But the attraction of recorded music—its ability to replay the exact same sounds and associated memories each time—can also lead to obsessive listening and recollection, especially in the face of traumatic loss or when identity comes under threat.

For Cuban American novelist Oscar Hijuelos (1951–2013), the Cuban exile condition is one of terminal nostalgia, a paralyzing desire to return to a time and place that often can only be experienced through memory and recording technologies. As such, much of his oeuvre is concerned with how to remember and record the Cuban past. His Pulitzer-winning novel *The Mambo Kings Play Songs of Love* employs various musical and recording tropes to tell the story of two brothers, Cesar and Nestor Castillo, who in 1947 migrate from Cuba to New York to make their living as mambo musicians.[1] The brothers enjoy a brief period of musical success during the 1950s mambo era, which culminates in their full-length album *The Mambo Kings Play Songs of Love* and their appearance on an episode of the *I Love Lucy* show as guests of real-life Cuban American musician and actor Desi Arnaz.[2] Forever heartbroken over his lost Cuban love María, Nestor soon dies in a car accident, leaving Cesar to reminisce on their glory days. These memories unfold over the course of one night in 1980 as a terminally ill Cesar locks himself away in the Hotel Splendour—the name an ironic dig at his loss of flashiness, fame, and sexual attractiveness—and obsessively replays the records from The Mambo Kings' heyday, in particular the 33 rpm LP from which the novel takes its title and structure. Cesar's story is framed by a prologue and epilogue from the first-person perspective of Nestor's American-born son, Eugenio, who himself engages in repetitive reminiscences via reruns of the *I Love Lucy* episode that technologically resurrects his father and uncle. In contrast to the role of music in *Night Calypso*, in this novel, music and remembering can reanimate rather than work through trauma.

The Mambo Kings Play Songs of Love shows a deep engagement with reconstructing subjectivity out of fragments of memory and music. In particular, in its attention to record-playing and the mambo industry of the 1950s, the novel yields new insights into the mechanics of exilic memory. For the Castillos, memory is a record comprised of sonic, visual, and narrative fragments that together create a version of a past self that can be recalled, reencountered, and reconstructed in the present—but that can become warped the more it is replayed. As both William Luis and Gustavo Pérez Firmat have shown, the novel's phonotopes are indeed inseparable from their cultural contexts—to hear the mambo in the novel means to hear the specific context of 1950s New York City, when Cuban big band musicians recreated the sound of Havana with both Cuban and American instruments and for both Cuban and American audiences. Even as I build on previous scholarship on the novel's musicality, I juxtapose what I call the bolero aesthetic—the simultaneous romantic and nationalist nostalgia inherent in the "songs of love" of the novel's title—with the extant narrative of the Cuban exile condition.[3] The first sections of the chapter explore how the proliferation of technologies of recording, repetition, and recollection in the novel provides a fascinating case study into how recording technology might enable Caribbean exiles to relive an idealized past. Later sections of the chapter examine the novel's depiction of the exile's quest to retain Caribbean identity and memory as a constant tension between bolero nostalgia and mambo acculturation and between atavistic music and the forward-driven books that trumpet the "American way." I argue that the Castillos' obsession with Cuban music and the phonograph record allows them to repeat and replay the Caribbean in the new homeland; musical nostalgia simultaneously situates the auditor in multiple spatialities and temporalities even as music's mobility disrupts the locatedness of culture on which nostalgic memory work depends. In *The Mambo Kings*, nostalgia is both deadly and contagious. The chapter therefore traces how mediated nostalgia affects even second-generation exiles and opens up conceptions of memory and Caribbeanness as inherited alongside LPs, language, and cultural traits.

High Fidelity: "Record Your Memories"

In *The Mambo Kings*, various modes of recording function as portable tools for memory making and recuperation in the face of loss. As I argue throughout this book, sound recording technologies enable the preservation of memory in formats that allow it to be repeated with exactitude in new times and spaces. Music journalist Rob Sheffield has observed that "nothing connects to the moment like music. I count on music to bring me back—or, more precisely, to bring [my dead wife] forward" (7–8), while for Lars Nyre, recording "bring[s] [an] event into the future as something that can be experienced again and again" (7–8). This capacity of music and its technologies to bring forward a past event or a long-gone person "again and again" underscores Hijuelos's deployment of recorded music as a tool for what Michael Bull calls "auditory nostalgia" (87–89) and for mental time and space to travel back to an idealized Cuban past.

The novel borrows its structure from the LP record: in addition to being littered with icons of tiny LPs, it is divided into side A and side B.[4] The main section of the novel follows Cesar's memories of Nestor as conjured by the replay of the *Mambo Kings* LP. As memory on vinyl, this LP connects the English noun *record* with its Spanish false cognate *recuerdo* (memory). For his trip down memory lane, Cesar deploys this disc of frozen time, sounds, and memories to call forth memories of his dead brother. As the story begins, he puts the record on the turntable, and we follow him on the mental journey triggered by the songs. Each track on the *Mambo Kings* LP releases the specific memory sequence it has encoded. Daniel Levitin has explained that "the music that you have listened to at various times in your life is cross-coded with the events of those times. . . . as soon as we hear a song that we haven't heard since a particular time in our lives, the floodgates of memory open and we're immersed in memories. The song has acted as a unique cue, a key unlocking all the experiences associated with the memory for the song, its time and place" (166). Similarly, along with the songs themselves, the tracks on the *Mambo Kings* album have recorded a lost era that

Cesar can relive in any place and time. For instance, the opening track "Juventud" ("Youth") triggers Cesar's mental journey back to the Cuban foundations of his personality and musicianship, while hearing "the opening chords" of their "minor hit" "Bella María de Mi Alma" ("Beautiful María of My Soul") not only brings him back to his brother's suffering over the titular beautiful María but also creates a switch in point of view to Nestor (although he is by now dead) and to the story of the romance that inspired the song (*TMK* 101). Rather than chapters, the reader experiences the narrative transcription of characters' memories as evoked by the repeating record. The novel thus depicts memory as a recording of lived fragments that can be replayed, even out of order, in the present.

Beyond lending the novel its structural metaphor, the LP allows the auditor to return to the past "with a flick of your wrist on your phonograph switch." In its guise as a literary version of the LP, then, the novel displays a documentary impetus: from documenting real-life mambo kings like Damáso Pérez Prado, Machito, and Tito Puente, on whom Cesar and Nestor are modeled, to long descriptions of album covers, dress styles, dance styles, and car models, as well as extensive lists of mambo songs, groups, instruments, and definitions of everything from the LP to the rumba. Rather than what critics see as "Anglophilia" (Flores, *From Bomba* 167–169), the novel's obsessive recording of the details of the mambo era transforms the novel into an archival record in its own right. Since glossing is an act of cultural translation, the novel translates the past and chronicles the death of an era for contemporary readers for whom the 1950s and its familiar sounds, tropes, and lifestyles "are long gone" (*TMK* 442).

The following textual interlude encapsulates the function of the record as a portable time and memory machine and raises several issues I will return to throughout this chapter:

> And now this ten-cent 78 rpm metal disc recorded in a "Record Your Memories" booth in Coney Island, 1954:
>
> (Laughter) (Static) (Laughter) (A man's and a woman's voices, joking, whispering, the man's voice saying) Go ahead, go ahead . . .
>
> Okay. (Static) Ayyyyy! Don't grab me there! (Laughter) (In the background the roaring roller coaster as it makes a turn and a kid shouting in English) [. . .] *Bueno*, hello out there in radio land! (Laughter) This is Angie Pérez and I (Neck kisses and slurpy sounds) (Laughter) (Static) I . . . I . . . ayyyy! just want to say that I'm here with my new boyfriend, Cesar, that is, the famous Cesar Castillo, at Coney Island, July 10, 1954 [. . .] And . . . (Static) Oh, time's running out. The, the red light is flashing. We have to say goodbye. Goodbye! Good (Static and click). (*TMK* 132)

This transcript illustrates both what the phonograph record does on vinyl and how memories are engraved and retrieved. Here in 1980, Cesar replays an albeit staged conversation from 1954, with sonic representations of not just the foreground (Cesar and Angie) but also context: the roller coaster, the "kid shouting in English," and the romantic shenanigans of the couple. The entire sonic moment is brought *forward* to the present with remarkable fidelity. Anyone who picks up this record down through time would theoretically be able to relive this moment as if she were *back* there in time and in space, while for Cesar and Angie, hearing the recorded sounds would trigger not just the technologically preserved memories but also the surrounding details of their relationship, the context of the recording, who they were at the time, and so on. But such high-fidelity retrieval wholly depends on not just the preservation of the recording medium and recorded content but the preservation of the technologies of replay as well. Further, the storage capacity of the record-your-memories LP is limited. Despite wanting to continue recording, Cesar and Angie have to cut their performance short. In fact, the recording cuts off even before they can record their abridged sonic greeting, and their anxiety that "time's running out" underscores a key motivating factor in the development of recording technologies: to forestall incipient death or obsolescence.

Part of what drives the novel's obsession with documentary realism is the technology of recording and the mechanics of memory. Advancements in the sound reproduction industry in the past century have largely been driven by the quest for the highest quality audio recordings. Currently, the format most championed by high-fidelity enthusiasts is FLAC (Free Lossless Audio Codec), an open-source audio compression codec that comprises high-definition "lossless" digital audio. Highly prized by audio experts and sound aficionados, FLAC and the related ALAC (Apple Lossless Audio Codec) aim to avoid the loss of information that usually accompanies compression—the condensing of real-world audio into a format that can fit onto another medium. In comparison, an MP3 file is considered "lossy" because quite a bit of sonic information has to be stripped out in order to keep the file size small for easy digital storage and sharing (Sterne, *MP3* 2). Today, despite the premium placed on lossless audio, only a few hardware and streaming companies support the format—it is a key selling point for the otherwise failing TIDAL streaming service owned by hip-hop mogul Shawn "Jay-Z" Carter and a collective of his peers. Even if one could afford to buy and store lossless audio, one might not always have the requisite medium to play it. Although the pursuit of high fidelity remains the engine of advancements in sound reproduction technology, recording and forgetting remain inextricably linked.[5]

Although *The Mambo Kings* focuses on vinyl, the contemporary romanticizing of lossless media highlights some key characteristics of memory that will underpin my analysis. At the heart of the novel lies the following question: How do Cuban exiles attempt to encode and store cultural memory and identity in a lossless format, even as such a project is inherently futile? As Levitin has explained, the human brain records incomplete information—a kind of lossy

MP3 file, if you will—and each time one recalls the information from the brain's hard drive, it supplies the missing information culled from contextual cues it has stored about the world. The brain is not actually remembering but guessing and inventing memory from context cues (Levitin 99–100). In order for the brain to record information in a close to lossless format, it must be repeatedly exposed to the same cue so that it can write and rewrite the information to fill in as much detail as possible. In fact, the more one reexperiences the original material and the more familiar it becomes, the more attention the hippocampus can pay to encoding previously ignored detail. The encoding of memory thus relies on repetition, but by the same token, excessive repetition can distort the original memory "text." Each time one recalls the information, one runs an equal chance of increasing its fidelity as of corrupting the file. This simultaneous retrieval and distortion of replayed material is precisely the project and pitfall of nostalgia.

Music, Memory, *Cubanía*

The kind of nostalgic memory performed by Caribbean exiles in *The Mambo Kings* is particularly fraught territory. The brothers' music-making, listening, and remembering aim to replay the Cuban past or mambo era with the highest possible fidelity, exactly as it was back there or back then. I am using *nostalgia* here in both its etymological sense of homesickness—from the Greek *nostos*, or "home," and *algos*, "pain or longing"—and its more contemporary sense of longing to return to a past place or time.[6] The different valences of nostalgia align with the bolero, a romantic love song that originates in the *décima*, a Spanish epic *canción* (song) with French troubadour and gypsy roots that, according to ethnomusicologist Ed Morales, lend the form "a sense of nomadic loss" (xiv–xv). The Cuban variant grew out of the *décima*'s nineteenth-century interaction with African drum-based music in Oriente, Cuba's easternmost province, which was predominantly inhabited by Afro-Cubans and Afro-Haitians and served as the incubator for much of what would become Cuban (and later Latin) music. It is also the province from which the Castillo brothers, though white-identified, originate.

The typical bolero lyric is a meditation on the "*profundo dolor*," or deep pain of love lost, soured, or unrequited, as is evident in the first recorded example, José Pepe Sánchez's 1885 *Tristezas* (*Sadness*):

Tristezas me dan, tus quejas mujer	Woman, your complaints bring me sadness
Profundo dolor, que dudes de mí	Your doubt brings me deep pain
No hay prueba de amor, que deje entrever	There's no test of love that can show
Cuánto sufro y padezco por ti.	How I suffer and agonize because of you.

The bolero has since morphed into the staple love song of Latin pop, popularized as kitsch sentimentality in the American mainstream by Hispanic Caribbean acts like Julio Iglesias in the 1970s and 1980s, Miami Sound Machine in the 1980s and 1990s, and Ricky Martin in the late 1990s and early 2000s, all of whom exploited the form in English and Spanish. Boleros often narrate the bolerista's refusal to move on with a new lover. In Martin's "Casi Un Bolero," an almost perfect summary in song form of *The Mambo Kings*, the singer is locked in a physical and mental room:

Con tu recuerdo siempre	With your persistent memory
Como un fantasma que no se va	Like a ghost that doesn't leave me
[. . .]	[. . .]
Suena en mi corazón	[It] (re)sounds in my heart
Casi un bolero.	Almost [like] a bolero.[7]

Obsessed with his own broken heart and threatening to die if his lover does not return, he dwells in this space of brokenhearted solitude. Ironically, as the bolerista sings the chorus again for the second or third time, we realize that he is not actually retrieving pleasurable memories of the lost love but rather dwelling in the pain and repeating the hurt—sonically picking at a mental scab.

Unlike the largely romantic lyrics of contemporary Caribbean Latin lovers like Ricky Martin,[8] however, the early bolero alternated between romantic and nationalist lyrics often drawn from famous Cuban nationalist poems, such as the poetry of Cuban nationalist Jose Martí in the world-famous "Guantanamera." In *The Mambo Kings*, sugary bolero sentiments define Nestor's thoughts of María as he "lean[s] up against a small statue of the Cuban poet José Martí" (117). The conflation of references to Martí and María frame the bolero's romantic lyrics as a metaphor for love of country, with Cuba lamented as the woman left behind as the man travels. This tension between romantic and nationalist nostalgia—what I call the bolero aesthetic—renders the bolero an ideal form for narrating the "*profundo dolor*" of lost love and lost homeland. The novel depicts the recorded Latin music of the 1940s and 1950s as a time capsule of romanticized national identity, with Nestor's longing for María serving as a trope for Cuban exile.

Fidel Castro's 1959 communist revolution inaugurated more than half a century of flight from the island to the U.S. mainland and the exile condition that numerous scholars see as the defining characteristic of the Cuban American experience.[9] For those like the Castillo brothers, who were temporary workers or resident aliens in the United States when the Cuban Revolution ruptured the bridge between the two countries, as well as for those who fled in the aftermath, loss of access to their roots was shocking and unexpected. Unlike conventional migrants who consciously abandon their home country for another, the volatile political nature of the Cuban-U.S. standoff—from the Bay of Pigs to the Cuban

Missile Crisis to the Mariel Boatlift—meant that *cubanos* could not return to Cuba regardless of their initial intentions.[10] As I emphasize by the use of the term *ex-isled* throughout this book, the focus is on the trauma of separation (*ex*) from the island (*isle*) homeland. For postrevolution Cuban exiles, return to Cuba is forestalled and suspended in time; they are often depicted in exile literature and film in a state of cultural cryogenics, as if to say "wake me up when the Castro regime ends."[11] Consequently, many exiles live with angst over the prospect of acculturation to the United States and the potential loss of Cuban identity.

As a survival tactic, then, exiles often embrace markers of Cubanness, what Fernando Ortiz has called *cubanismos*, particularly the Spanish language and Cuban culture as expressed through music and food.[12] Pérez Firmat also characterizes the exile condition as a tension between nostalgia and acculturation symbolized by the hyphen that connects the "Cuban" to the "American." He contends that all immigrants go through three stages of adaptation to their new homeland, but in the case of traumatic expatriation, "the exile aspires to reproduce, rather than recast, native traditions" (6). This first substitutive stage (1960s and 1970s), in his view, is characterized by a feeling of pure nostalgia, or the "we are there" stage. The second stage (1980s) is one of destitution and loss—"we are nowhere"—characterized by a sense of disconnect from both sites (8–10). The third stage, which sees the move from "nowhere" to "now + here," is dominated by a generation of "one and a halfers"—"an intermediate immigrant generation" of people and cultural artifacts that are "born in Cuba but made in the USA" and are consequently torn between two competing forces: tradition and translation, the one "a homing device" and the other "a distancing mechanism" (3).

I reframe Pérez Firmat's conception of tradition as a pull *backward* in time to the past and in geography to the "home" and origins. For its part, I characterize translation as the push *forward* to the new culture and to acculturation, transculturation, or biculturation (Ortiz, *Cuban Counterpoint* 102–103). This dual temporal and spatial negotiation is in fact deeply connected to the son/rumba complex: Cesar remarks on the tempo of Afro-Cuban music as moving in "3/2 time, clave time" (*TMK* 255). As Njoroge Njoroge as argued, the clave is both the instrument and the temporal consciousness underlying Afro-Cuban music: "The 3/2–2/3 structure vacillates *backward and forward* through space and time" (64; emphasis added). For Cuban exiles, the proximity of Cuba and the suddenness of incipient or permanent loss of access to the homeland create a crisis of belonging that manifests in nostalgic memory. Modern notions of progress and contemporary construction of U.S. identity privilege acculturation as a process in which one culture is left *behind* to move *forward*, and in circumstances of cultural hegemony, the immigrant is put under pressure to make haste into assimilation. One-and-a-halfers like Nestor's and Delores's American-born son, Eugenio, thus often display a *forward-backward* negotiation of the "life on the hyphen" between Cuban and American. The "we are there" generation (Pérez Firmat 9) to which Cesar and Nestor belong, on the other hand, often struggles with spatial and temporal disorientation.

I consider nostalgia in the novel, particularly nostalgia facilitated by recorded music, as a manifestation of a fixation on the lost past and lost home, an attempt to use recording to bring not only the past forward in time but the Caribbean homeland across the ocean to the new place. Nostalgic memory work in *The Mambo Kings* creates a version of Cuba in the here and now; the record repeats the music and the memories as well as an idealized version of the homeland. The trauma of crossing from Cuba(n) to America(n) along the axis of the hyphen engenders the conscious or unconscious repression of Cubanness and manifests as something akin to what Freud calls repetition compulsion; since the affected subject "cannot remember the whole of what is repressed in him, and what he cannot remember may be the essential part of it . . . he is obliged to *repeat* the repressed material as a contemporary experience, instead of . . . *remembering* it as something belonging to the past" ("Beyond the Pleasure Principle" 32). He distinguishes repetition from remembering; the one is the subconscious reproduction of the past, the other the conscious reencounter with the past (18). But while Freud sees repetition compulsion as a manifestation of trauma, for Antonio Benítez-Rojo, repetition is a defining characteristic of Caribbeanness and, as I posited in the first chapter, a feature of Caribbean memory. The product of the plantation machinery, which provided the engine to the Industrial Revolution and the impetus for uprootings and transplantations, the Caribbean's physical and psychological neuroses manifest in the discontinuity, disorder, and disruption that repeat throughout the region (Benítez-Rojo 11). In *Cities of the Dead*, Joseph Roach elaborates on these ideas and proposes the term *surrogation* to explain the ways that Caribbean peoples use repetition with a difference to performatively work through repressed trauma. With this notion of surrogation in view, I read the nostalgia in *The Mambo Kings* as a manifestation of the urge to repeat and replay the Caribbean in the new homeland, which functions as a surrogate for the island. Spaces like Little Havana are not so much a diminutive "copy" of the "real" Havana (Pérez Firmat 7), as they are the repetitive replay of this record of *cubanía* in another time and place; since mambo and bolero records encode Cuban identity and Cuban memories, their repeated audition in the United States enables the exile to repeat and translate Caribbeanness in a new time and space—to bring the Caribbean past forward in time or to imaginatively transpose it across the ocean to the new place. This "Cuba" is not the "real" Cuba located at 23° north and 82° west but the Cuba of the mind.

Given that they were adults upon migration, Cesar and Nestor are first-generation migrants, but like Desi Arnaz and the other prerevolution musicians and cultural migrants on whom the brothers are based, their trajectory does not perfectly align with the Miami-based, revolution-initiated exile narrative that dominates Cuban American discourse. The brothers arrive in New York in 1949—a full decade before the revolution—due to a combination of push and pull factors: Cesar, who wants to make it as a mambo king in the footsteps of Arnaz, drags Nestor out of Cuba to protect him from the fury of María's new husband and from his own melancholy. Moving to New York's Spanish Harlem in a time well before Little Havana and the Cuban exile community in Miami (or anywhere else, for that matter) were established, neither planned on permanent migration; they came with their musicianship and could make Cuban music that incorporated American instruments and styles without much anxiety. Cuba was close by, and Cuban music could flow back and forth across the sea carrying strains of Americanness and new developments from Havana as it circulated. It is only later when Nestor anchors himself in New York by marrying the Cuban American Delores and when Castro's revolution cuts Cesar off from the home he never expected to lose that the reality of permanent disconnection from Cuba and Cuban identity throws Nestor and Cesar, in turn, into the pathological nostalgia that has come to define the Cuban exile experience. Their different reasons for moving to the United States determine the difference in the brothers' initial attitudes and exile experiences as well: while Nestor remains mostly Cuba-focused and nostalgic like the bolero, Cesar is open to acculturation and Americanness like the mambo. According to Gema Guevara, "In the case of Cuban exile community, it is music, in particular the internal dialogue between the musical genres and a discourse of nationalism that links the exile community to its 'authentic' cultural roots" (38). As the next section will show, this obsession with origins and roots can result in a tug of war between forward-moving acculturation, represented in the novel by mambo music and American print narratives, and backward-looking nostalgia, represented by the bolero.

Mambo Memories, Bolero Nostalgia

While the *Mambo Kings* LP replays the mambo era and the zeitgeist just before the revolution, the "Beautiful María" bolero soundtracks the brothers' obsession with their past loves and lives. In other words, whereas the bolero is the *form* of memory and nostalgia, the mambo era is the *site* of nostalgia. The mambo era represents a time when Cuban culture was on the ascendancy and signaled cultural and geographic exchange between the two countries. The United States' World War II–era Good Neighbor policy public relations blitz included featuring Latin music in Hollywood films—many starring original "Latin lover" Desi Arnaz—and a wave of New York City recording missions for Latin American musicians spearheaded by RCA Victor. As a result, after the war, the mambo craze swept the nation's airwaves and dance floors, but it soon waned in the wake of the revolution.

The mambo is often described as an urban story told by a big-band orchestra of Afro-Cuban percussion instruments with a clave base, driven by virtuoso piano playing and high-energy improvisational breaks that feed its eponymous dance style.[13] At its heights, the era centered on the recordings and performances of music maestros like Machito and his Afro-Cubans, Beny Moré, Damaso Pérez Prado, Tito Rodriguez, and Tito Puente, with its locus at New York City's Palladium Club in the 1950s and 1960s. These mambo kings appear as characters in the novel, and the fictional Castillo brothers perform in many historic mambo clubs like the Palladium. A Cuban-originated cultural form with arms wide open to American culture, the mambo had no qualms incorporating American instruments and jazz stylings in its otherwise Afro-Cuban music and band structure. Pérez Prado, one of the musical models for Cesar, is considered the key player in bringing Afro-Cuban mambo to a mainstream American audience with major crossover hits including "*Que rico el mambo*" and "Mambo No. 5" (Morales 45). The mambo thus arguably represents what it means to be Cuban in America: a trend toward transculturation from which Cesar eventually retreats, turning instead to backward-looking nostalgia.

Cesar's—and by extension, the novel's—exuberant obsession with music, women, and sexual prowess reflects the mambo era with which his memories are concerned. Originating from a Bantu term for spiritual possession, the word *mambo* initially referred to the high-intensity, percussion-based improvisation break or *descarga* at the climax of earlier, more extensive musical arrangements in standard nineteenth-century Cuban music forms like the *danzon* and *son guaracha*. Often translated as "jam," *descarga* literally means "to discharge" in all its verbal, performative, and sexual connotations. The mambo quickly gained a reputation as "uninhibited," "libidinal," and "barbaric" due to "what one writer called its 'high sex quotient'" (Pérez Firmat 93)—terms strikingly similar to readers' descriptions of the novel's style.[14] The first half of *The Mambo Kings* is fast-paced, jam-packed with long descriptions of music, fashion, and Latinx culture and teeming with extensive and graphic sex scenes. The prose often devolves into *descarga* mode, extended and dizzying textual mambos or musical interludes: "And now nothing but drums, a battery of drums, the conga drums jamming out in a *descarga*, and the drummers lifting their heads and shaking under some kind of spell . . . and the slamming-the-door drums and dropping-the-bucket drums, kicking-the-fender drums . . . and Benny on the congas for a little ten-second interlude in the middle of one of those old Mambo Kings songs" (278–279). Here, as throughout the first section of the novel, the mambo form mirrors the mambo content, particularly linking the music to Cesar's mind-set during the mambo era before his brother's death. The sexual-musical tension in the term *descarga* also connects the mambo and machismo, as illustrated by Cesar's obsession with women's anatomy and his own sexual prowess across innumerable erotic passages; his life ends while he is drinking, listening to music, and dreaming about Vanna's "pretty mouth . . . struggl[ing] with the thick and cumbersome proportions of his sexual apparatus" (435). Cesar's compositions consist of "an infinite variety of dance numbers . . . capturing moments of youthful cockiness ('A thousand women have I continually satisfied, because I am an amorous man!'). Songs about flirtation, magic, blushing brides, cheating husbands, cuckolds and the cuckolded, flirtatious beauties, humiliation" (43).

The libidinal excess of the mambo and Cesar's obsession with wine, women, and song echoes Freud's conception of an ego-libido preoccupied with erotic pleasure, sexual discharge, and reproduction of the species ("Beyond the Pleasure Principle" 52). Freud's juxtaposition of this sex instinct with the death instinct seems to mirror the dualism of the brothers as expressed through music: Cesar embodies mambo sexual energy, Nestor the deadly "urge . . . to restore an early state of things [he] has been obliged to abandon" (34). Quiet, somber, and soulful like the traditional bolerista, Nestor thinks of love in naively romantic and overly dramatic tones. In contrast to Cesar's exuberant promiscuity, "in those days, [Nestor's] heart filled with an unbearable pain" (*TMK* 43). With its minor chords, "melancholic tone," and lyrics expressing the "torment beyond all sorrow" that characterizes the genre, the bolero "Beautiful María" is Nestor's musical meditation on leaving both María and Cuba (43). Whereas Cesar and mambo are defined by sexual prowess, movement, and infidelity, Nestor and the bolero embody romantic longing, stasis, and faithfulness, although the novel takes pains to show that he is just as well-endowed as his brother. The novel in fact invests as much energy in sustaining as in collapsing the binary opposition between the brothers: Nestor's only "moments of release occur when his penis exploded with sperm and obliterated his personality, throwing him into a blue- and red-lit heaven of floating space, and when he played the trumpet and got lost in melody" (113). It is in sexual and musical pleasure that Nestor approaches Cesar's affinity for mambo *descarga*, but whereas Cesar's sexual and musical prowess is life-affirming, Nestor seeks mental obliteration, a release from the body and eventually from the constraints of time.

Nestor's alignment with the bolero imbues him with some of the classic characteristics of the Miami exiles who comprise the "we are there" generation. He obsesses about returning to the past, and his nostalgia makes it difficult for him to acculturate despite all that seems to be in his favor—a wife, Delores, a New York–born Cuban who represents the incipient Hispanic American identity; children; marginal success in music; and a self-help book on the American dream. For his brief life in the United States, and even during his marriage, Nestor remains caught up in the obsessive replay of his mental record of his brief romance with María.[15] Fittingly, Nestor externalizes this *mental* record into a *musical* record that he can replay in order to relive the past with sonic, if not marital, fidelity: "He relived their life over again so often that he sometimes had the sensation of being buried by the past, as if the details of this shattered love . . . had been turned into stone, weeds, and dirt and thrown over him" (*TMK* 45). His melancholy becomes a death drive when he cannot fulfill his desire to return to María and Cuba. By living in the past, he becomes zombified; when the novel opens, he is already dead, although he immediately reappears in the rerun of the *I Love Lucy* episode and as Cesar resurrects him by replaying the *Mambo Kings* LP. We are always aware that Nestor's appearance in the novel is technologically staged and that sometime soon he will actually die, again, for the first time.

Death in *The Mambo Kings* takes on a carnivalesque, machinic quality that recalls Benítez-Rojo's figuration of a Caribbean temporality defined by alternating interruption and flow: if the story of a life is a linear narrative from birth to death, premature death such as Nestor's interrupts the narrative as much as it ruptures the novel's plot. Nestor's death stalls Cesar's progress and prevents the novel from progressing in a linear fashion. Instead, the novel's structure comprises spurts of forward narrative constantly interrupted by flashbacks. Unexpected death, like traumatic memory, realigns time, narrative, and teleology. The bildungsroman form and normative chronology become impossible; beginnings and endings collapse into each other, and the narration of one character's memory intersects and overlaps with another's. Nestor's interruptive death further suggests that repetition is in fact stasis even as it gives the illusion of movement, and this repetition is deadly. Constantly seesawing back and forth along the hyphen, the exile is neither fully in Cuba nor in the United States. Likewise, nostalgic memory is a parenthesis between past and present, not an actual return to the original event, since that is both temporally and physically impossible.

Boleristas have for centuries threatened their imminent death by heartbreak, the *profundo dolor* of the *corazón* of classic boleros from Sánchez's *Tristezas* to Marc Anthony's 1997 "Como Duele"; Nestor is the first on record to have actually taken this threat to heart. Minutes before he dies, "while he was onstage and playing the solo to 'Beautiful María,' a bad sensation had started. . . . It was the simple feeling that his desires somehow contradicted his purpose in life, to write sad boleros, to lie sick in bed, to mourn long-past loves, to crave what he could never have.[. . .] He had dreamed about *undoing things* [. . .] of somehow going to Cuba again and into the arms of María" (*TMK* 197–199; emphasis added). Nestor's desire to return to a prior state of imagined coherence is literally unsustainable and fatal. By "looking backwards" to the motherland, Nestor's "instinct to return to the past . . . bring[s] about death" (Freud, "Beyond the Pleasure Principle" 38, 39). But where Freud sees the sex instinct as a marker of self-preservation, Hijuelos depicts the self-preservation instinct of the Caribbean exile as the drive to preserve the premigratory self.

With its imbrication of the romantic and the nationalistic, the bolero is central to Nestor's nostalgic remembering. For Ortiz, the term *Cubanness* has multiple meanings; it often refers to clichés of cultural authenticity that can be performed or consumed by anyone wanting to be affiliated with the island. Portable and external, non-Cuban citizens or nationals can perform or adopt these *cubanismos*—which undercuts the assumptions of authenticity that attend discourses around them—and Cubans can turn to them when ex-isled in order to reinforce their national identity. *Cubanidad*, on the other hand, is the broad category of citizenship evinced by "official documents" (Ortiz, "Human Factors" 458). But Ortiz takes pains to distinguish these external markers from "real" Cubanness and his neologism "Cubanía, which is consciousness, will, and root in the native land, [and which] emerged first among people born and raised here [as opposed to the first arrivants], with no return or retirement, *with the soul rooted in the land*" (478). Ortiz's definition of "real" Cubanness as a rooting of the soul in the land lends new valences to the title of Nestor's bolero. "Beautiful María of my Soul" records Nestor's nostalgic longing for the site where his soul is rooted. And if *cubanía* is a rooting of the soul, the *up*rooting of migration and exile thus makes one's soul sick for another place than where one is presently transplanted. Unable to return to Cuba or to the relationship with María that would (re)vivify and complicate the memories he holds of them, both Cuba and María become "mythic" and distorted in his mind (56). Nestor's death by obsessive memory replay thus reveals that remembering does not provide access to an intact, anterior self or experience. Rather, the very act of remembering not only re-creates but also distorts the original event, making its retrieval even more impossible and the replay of those memories the more addictive.

The subtitle of Hijuelos's 2002 novel, *A Simple Habana Melody*, suggests that nostalgia for Cuba is bound up in a romanticized notion of returning to "when the world was good." *The Mambo Kings* is explicitly oriented to the past: the Cuba of the past and the New York mambo era of yesteryear. In Hijuelos's early drafts for a musical version of the novel, Cuba is also ever-present: the story begins in a Havana music club and extensively develops the Nestor-María relationship in Cuba before the brothers leave for New York. Later drafts written by Arne Glimcher reduce and ultimately cut the Cuban scenes, leaving an entirely America-located story. In the staged version of the musical, performed in San Francisco in May 2005, both Cuba and María are completely excised; only the music remains to evoke the repressed island.[16] Even in a key scene when Nestor experiences a night of tormented dreams of María, the Cuban lover is embodied by the same actress who plays Delores—"Dolores" in the stage version, from the Spanish for "pain," a key trope in boleros. To the American theater audience, indeed for Nestor himself, neither Cuba nor María is visible or accessible. Instead, in the same way that Dolores is a repetition of the absent María in a new place, Cuban music repeats and replays the inaccessible Cuba in the United States. The novel's journey to the American stage also depicts becoming American as repressing and excising Cubanness—or in musical terms, compression; only the clichéd or outdated musical influences are allowed. The "lossy" versioning of the novel and musical illuminates that for the exile, "Cuba" is only a memory, a trope, and a melody. "Cuba" is what is lost and repressed en route to Americanness, the ghost that haunts the text as much as Nestor and memories of him haunt Cesar and Eugenio.

In this way, *The Mambo Kings* reveals that it is precisely because exiles cannot return to yesterday that they turn to mediated memory and technologies of replay. The past, having passed, is irretrievable. But since the past can be captured by recording technologies, the only access the Castillos have to the past is mediated by the LP, the TV episode, and performative reenactments of *cubanismos*. Repeated listening and viewing might create a sense of having brought the past forward in time and place, but it is a repetition with a difference that highlights the surrogate nature of the retrieval and creates an even more fervent desire to replay the past. Regardless of the high-fidelity quality of the medium—even as technological advancements allow for the capture of audio information with increased fidelity—access to the "original" is always mediated via a copy or performance. Despite the pursuit of lossless media, recording is predicated on the loss of the thing being recorded. Nestor's bolero emerges precisely because Cuba and María are lost, while Cesar's later repetitive audition of the *Mambo Kings* LP stems from losing his brother, fame, and access to Cuba.

To complicate matters, the music-mediated flashbacks reveal that Nestor's melancholia resulted from a trauma even anterior to forced migration and loss of his lover. The existence of the repressed primal memory of a childhood near-death experience certainly problematizes a reading of Nestor's melancholy as purely due to exile. Nestor himself admits this, albeit in a parenthetical, doubly interiorized thought: "(*Mamá*, I wanted María the way I wanted you when I was a baby feeling helpless in that bed, with welts covering my chest, and lungs stuffed with thick cotton)" (*TMK* 56). Finding love with María symbolized for Nestor the retrieval of the peace of the mother, also named María. María is not only the object of his romantic and sexual desire; María is also mother and motherland. María, mother, and Cuba are thus collapsed into a single signifier, accessible postexile only through phonographic memories. *The Mambo Kings* describes both a traumatic rupture in the normative development of sexual identity and, ironically, the normative development of *cubanía*.

This follows from Freud's association of repetition compulsion with the oedipal complex, which he sees as a normative stage in heterosexual childhood development where the male child fixates on the mother as an object of desire. Using a reel attached to a string to surrogate and compensate for his departing mother, Freud's young patient sublimates his separation anxiety through repetition and ritual. Freud explains that "these reproductions, which emerge with such unwished-for exactitude, always have as their subject some portion of infantile sexual life" ("Beyond the Pleasure Principle" 18). Ortiz expresses a similar idea when he theorizes that *cubanía* "comes from the entrails of the native land

and envelops and penetrates us like the breath of creation that springs from our Mother Earth after she has been made fecund by the rain sent to her by Father sun.... It is something that attracts us and draws us to love, like a woman who is one in three persons: mother, wife, and daughter" ("Human Factors" 459). Ortiz locates *cubanía* in an oedipal attachment to mother and motherland; creolizing the biblical trinity of Father, Son, and Holy Ghost, he further collapses the object of hybrid romantic and nationalist desire into a feminine trinity that both "envelops and penetrates."

Underlying the trauma of Cuban exile—in fact, the original trauma that is repressed and repeated in the trauma of exile—is the trauma of separation from the mother. This anterior mother trauma possibly evinces a sublimation of mother Africa in the production of the white-identified Creole Cuban identity the brothers embrace despite their origins in Oriente and their investment in Afro-Cuban music. It is also the source of pathological machismo that manifests differently for the brothers, outwardly in mambo libidinal excess for Cesar and inwardly in bolero nostalgia for Nestor.[17] Nestor's angst is increasingly distanced from the root cause; weaned from his mother's breasts, his fixation on the mother becomes displaced as a fixation on María the lover. Wrenched from his lover's body, he becomes fixated on Cuba as lost lover and motherland. Adrift without mother María, lover María, or mother country in an updating of Ortiz's national trinity, Nestor dies of *profundo dolor*.

If Nestor's nostalgia existed even before migration, then it is quite ironic that Eugenio perceives Nestor's pained and lost expression as essentially "'Cuban': melancholic, longing. Arnaz had it, his Uncle Cesar had it [after Nestor's death], Frankie, Manny, and most of the Cubans who walked into the household, jitterbug and all, had it" (*TMK* 403). The prevalence of this prerevolution nostalgia in the musical men, all of whom came to the United States before the first wave of exiles, undercuts the traditional exile narrative, revealing rather that bolero nostalgia indexes a primal mother-son trauma exacerbated by later traumas such as loss and exile. By clinging to the irretrievable past, whether of returning to the mother's womb or to a motherland that only exists in memory, the novel's America-based Cuban men, regardless of place of birth, find themselves in a state akin to what Pérez Firmat calls "destitution," mourning the impossibility of returning to the memorialized version of Cuba as much as the impossibility of the reunion with the mother's body. They eventually awaken from their fiction with the realization that the world has moved on, which delivers a tremendous shock to their system. Pérez Firmat concludes that "the exile is someone who thinks imagination is a place . . . The problem is, imagination is *not* a place. You can't live there . . . Sooner or later reality crashes though, and the exile loses the place that never was. His or her reaction to the substitution is vertigo, disorientation.... If you aren't there, where are you?" (8–10). This disorientation in time and space leads to the death of both Nestor and Cesar in their turn. To return to the mother's womb—either through regression or through surrogation via sexual partners—would shatter teleology and ontology.

When Nestor dies in 1957, halfway through the novel, the formerly forward-moving Cesar, an America(n)-loving mambonick, becomes melancholic and atavistic, clinging to the mambo era even though the decade, the music, and everyone else seem to be moving on. Although Cesar willingly moves to the United States as a temporary migrant rather than an exile, the revolution, coinciding with the death of his brother and soon thereafter the death of the mother, forestalls travel to Cuba and seeing his daughter, Mariela. Soon the rest of his family there either dies or migrates to the United States. Retreating from mambo-fueled transculturation, Cesar becomes a custodian of memory, collecting and repairing the refuse and cast-off mementos of other people's lives (*TMK* 257). His descent into basement living surrounded by the trappings of modernity and music is only an early phase of his final days in the Hotel Splendour where he spends his time "stoking the dying larvae of embers" (258). Despite their mambo beginnings, then, both the novel and its characters eventually retreat into bolero nostalgia in order "to be somewhere else" (258). Cesar's transformation from forward-looking to backward-looking suggests perhaps that all Cubans in diaspora became nostalgic exiles once the revolution rendered return impossible.

The novel emphasizes the futility of attempting to retrieve the past as it once was. Nostalgic remembering is always a present-tense activity; the mind has traveled elsewhere, but the body is still rooted in place, and the present context for the project of remembering likely contaminates or inflects the retrieval of the past. For example, listening to the recorded sounds encoded on the *Mambo Kings* LP is inseparable from the room where Cesar plays the record, the technology that enables its replay—including considerations of fidelity and obsolescence—or other sonic presences that interfere with complete immersion, including the loudly copulating couple in the adjacent room. Cesar's eventual death evinces the pitfalls of nostalgia. He has lost touch with the present and future, symbolized by the jaunty progression of Latin dance idioms: "the *pachanga* in 1960. The bossa nova in 1962. The Mozambique and the bugaloo in 1965. After that, he couldn't figure out what was happening" (*TMK* 323). Central to Cesar's willful self-imposed exile—first in his basement and then in the Hotel Splendour with his suitcase of memory aids—is his sense of incipient irrelevance; his nascent fame has vanished, and the new generation of musicians and Latin music lovers has already forgotten who he is.[18] His only weapon against erasure is to replay the *Mambo Kings* record and its associated memories.

However, in the same way that excessive play warps wax and vinyl records, excessive reminiscences warp memory, and the warped performance paradoxically becomes fixed *in* and *as* memory. Mourning his former Latin music colleagues, Cesar eulogizes "Puente, Eddie Palmieri, Ray Barretto, Pérez Prado. I knew a lot of guys going back a long time. Talented guys with style and good musical ideas who vanished into thin air. . . . Most of them are where now? A friend of mine, a really good *conguero*, watches the dinosaur bones over at the Museum of Natural History" (*TMK* 381). His meditation on the demise of mambo greats suggests that bygone music can become a sonic museum of Cuban history. It is dinosaur music; it goes extinct if it does not move forward with the times. Because he has chosen to remain in a mummified past, Cesar's self-willed death while listening to repeating memories ultimately serves as a cautionary check to obsessive memory work, but as the next section shows, the Castillos have few other resources outside of music to access the "American way."

Forward (in) America!

In its juxtaposition of records and books, *The Mambo Kings* depicts the American dream as more easily achievable for Caribbean immigrants by musical literacy.[19] A trope for the contrasting access of sonic and print media, the fictional D. D. Vanderbilt book *Forward America!* (*TMK* 130), with its exclamation point, imperative case, and italic font that strains inexorably forward, encapsulates the progressive bent of modernity and the American dream. The jacket copy, reproduced with a font change in the novel's text, announces a self-help book detailing the author's transformation from a man "plagued with self-doubt" to one who found "happiness the *American Way!*" (130). Already, just reading the flap, Nestor is "momentarily uplifted," and he buys the book and produces it at key moments of despair. He mines it for its "practical principles" such as the following: "Ally yourselves with progress and tomorrow! The confident, self-assured man looks to the future and never backwards to the past. The heart of every success is a plan that takes you forward" (162). This forward-looking imperative mirrors Cesar's mambo-like desire "to look forward and never back into his past" in order to stave off overwhelming loss with motion and music (48). Despite Nestor's diligence, however, these principles never seem to work for him.

Forward America! depicts migrant nostalgia and nostalgic music as fundamentally at odds with the forward march of progress; it is the American way versus the immigrant's way. The book traffics in clichés of upward and forward mobility, an American dream that often excludes and eludes people of color. As Ralph Ellison's invisible man's retreat to his own basement of light and music shows (7), articulations of modernity through American ideals of progress have been complicit in the erasure of black and brown bodies, rendering the bootstrap narrative a mere illusion. Luis concurs that "Cesar cannot become a Vanderbilt. . . . Just as Vanderbilt's book failed Nestor, it will remind Cesar that there is a lacuna between his life and the one Vanderbilt lived and wrote about" (207). Despite its progressive title and ethos, *Forward America!* fails to counteract the pull of bolero nostalgia for the musical men. The inutility of the self-help book for even American-born characters like Eugenio suggests that unlike the (fictional and real) Vanderbilts, they do not have the requisite rootedness that comes from knowing one's lineage that would enable them to be forward-looking rather than backward-looking Americans.[20]

Cesar does get a late forward push from Celia, a Puerto Rican whom he dates in the 1970s, the era of the ascendancy of Nuyorican culture: "She was known locally as something of a clairvoyant and was always sensing presences in the house—his mother, his dead brother—and wanted to take charge of his life, *push him forward*, play up his nearly glorious musical past, and encourage him to cultivate people in power like Machito and Desi Arnaz" (*TMK* 331; emphasis added). After she ties him up to keep him from philandering, he lashes out in anger, calling her actions humiliating and unforgivable (332). Beyond her presumable gender forwardness against which Cesar rebels, Celia robustly attempts to propel Cesar forward through her "clairvoyant" understanding of the past, but Cesar insists on clinging to ghosts and adhering to backward views about women. It is not insignificant, then, that for Celia (and ultimately for Nuyorican salsa music, which I discuss in the final section), moving forward and getting ahead requires embracing the past, whether past musical styles and achievements or past memories and identities.

Music and writing and their attendant sensibilities are also juxtaposed in the opposition between Nestor and his wife Delores, who is defined by her love for reading and self-improvement. In contrast to the male-dominated Cuban music world, the world of American books provides her an escape from domesticity and insulates her from her husband's mental infidelity. Her books awaken in her an interiority not afforded her by the fast-paced, oral, mambo culture—although her interiority is doubly framed by music-mediated male narratives. We learn of the "course of terrified learning," including being beaten on the head with an English dictionary at Catholic school in the Bronx, despite which she "endured, studied and excelled . . . becoming one of those *latinas* who . . . could speak English as well as anyone" (*TMK* 100). Later, as Nestor's wife, reading provides her the introspection to begin to resent and question the circumscribed role of a mambo wife: a domesticated sex kitten and massager of musician's feelings and sexual instruments. The sight of Columbia University students going to classes stirs in her jealousy and outrage: "Why were they students, and not she? . . . Why was it that when mambo time came around, when the house filled with musicians and their wives and the record player was turned up, why did she act willingly like a slave, attending to all the men . . . ?" (188–189). Two things happen after Nestor dies: first, Delores immerses herself in books, which, I argue, allows her to avoid the trap of grief that plagues Cesar and eventually Eugenio: "She liked to spend two or three hours a day with [her] books, *propelled forward* by a dictionary and the simple desire to possess more knowledge" (213; emphasis added). Fascinating here is that reading using a dictionary—the process of translation, an act of transculturation—propels her forward. The second development is her remarriage to a bookkeeper, Pedro—boring, thoroughly unmacho, with an unstimulating "long fish-headed penis" (404), "a non-musician, reliable and steady, whose instruments were not congas, or guitars, or trumpets, but rather, ledger books, rulers, and mechanical pencils" (241). Pedro symbolizes Delores's rejection of the regressive world of music—although she still desires and fantasizes about it—while she decidedly forges forward through the acquisition of book knowledge. The novel's juxtaposition of music and books provides a fascinating counterpoint to models of acculturation and resistance experienced by real-life Miami-based *cubanos*. On the one hand is the backward-looking tragic figure of Nestor and other musical men; on the other is the forward-looking hopeful figure of Delores and other reading and writing women. In between are Janus-faced characters like Cesar and Eugenio, stuck in the groove between the *phonic* and *graphic*. It is to the reconciliation of that forward-backward tension that I now turn.

Repeating Records

Nestor's son, Eugenio, belongs to a generation of Cubans who feel cut off from the kind of lineage and homeland that would enable them to move "*Forward [in] America*." Consequently, the novel ends with various repeated records. In addition to the *Mambo Kings* LP and Cesar's rewriting of the bolero, the novel also repeatedly performs a narrative rerun of the TV show, itself a repeating episode in its own right, reexperienced by Cesar, who was in it, and Eugenio, who has seen it numerous times before (*TMK* 4–6). Then in the novel's epilogue, the show's transcript is repeated verbatim for more than two pages, except now the song lyrics are in English although the brothers sang in Spanish—a discrepancy perhaps explained by the perspectival shift to the anglophone Eugenio. Watching the episode, this time beside the aging Arnaz who now stands in (sits in, as it were) for the Cuban father, Eugenio "walked over and sat on the couch and wrapped [his] arms around [his] father. Expected to find air but hit on solid flesh. And his [father's] neck was warm. His expression pained and timid, like a hick off the boat. He was alive!" (444). Eugenio's traumatized reviewing of the episode is only—at least temporarily—resolved when he "hit[s] on solid flesh"; his lifelong motive for turning to recordings is a physical resurrection of the father, a move beyond the father of the imagination to a real one.

Like the *Mambo Kings* record, the *I Love Lucy* episode repeatedly resurrects Nestor and brings his body and spirit into the present. Eugenio recalls that "the first time I saw a rerun of [the episode], I could remember other things about [Nestor] . . . so many things simultaneously that it was like watching something momentous, say the Resurrection . . . because my father was newly alive and could take off his hat and sit down on the couch in Ricky's living room, resting his black instrument case on his lap" (*TMK* 5). The trope of resurrection connects the first-generation nostalgia over María, the name of the Virgin Mother, and the second-generation nostalgia over the father. If Christological resurrection replaced the inanimate, crucified body with a living but absent body, then Nestor's televisual resurrection likewise both resolves and reemphasizes his absence. Nestor's technological resurrection also reveals that modernity—here in the form of the television in particular or, as I have discussed so far, sound recording technology in general—does not always signal progress and forward motion. In *The Mambo Kings*, characters often use modern technology for atavism. In fact, the novel's frame suggests that it is Eugenio who reconstructs his father's and uncle's past out of the scraps of music and memories.

In *Thoughts without Cigarettes* (2011), Hijuelos the memoirist constructs the fictional Eugenio as his best friend and source, which installs Eugenio as a generational stand-in for the author. Eugenio's lifelong quest to reconnect with Nestor and Cubanness certainly connects with a repeated primal memory in Hijuelos's oeuvre of how he "lost" his Spanish and his Cubanness.[21] In a traumatic replay of this origin tale, Hijuelos's "too Anglo" characters use Cuban music to retrieve and replay memories of an anterior, Cuban self, including *inherited* selves. As José Van Dijck argues, personal and individual music memories can become collective through intergenerational transfer and the narratives that we craft about what these recordings mean (111). Despite, or perhaps due to, not having lived through the original sonic experience, auditors in later generations can nevertheless travel back in time and space "with a flick of your wrist on your phonograph switch" and experience auditory nostalgia as if they were the original "earwitnesses."[22] Auditors in Hijuelos's and Eugenio's generation ironically become trapped in terminal nostalgia in their turn.

Despite being born in a *Forward!* generation, Eugenio is nevertheless weighed down by the baggage—the memento-laden suitcase—of culture and identity that he must constantly mimic and perform in the present. Achy Obejas, in her own musical novel, calls this the "memory mambo," where the second-generation Cuban exile with little or no memory of her parents' island, language, or culture finds it impossible to thrive in the American present, always taking two steps back for every step forward, as the idiom's 3/2 timing suggests. To be sure, *The Mambo Kings* reveals itself to be the transcript of Eugenio's narrative recomposition of memories that are not his own. Ironically, this American-born son of a first-generation Cuban migrant and a New York–born Cuban comes to display classic signs of bolero nostalgia: "Although he was not consciously aware of it, Eugenio had by now acquired the same expression he forever associated with his father, the same shattered expression of Nestor Castillo in his role as Alfonso Reyes" (*TMK* 403). Most tragic here is not only Eugenio's attempt to perform his memory of his father by reproducing his father's expression and posture in his own body but the fact that the record on which Nestor's, and by extension, Eugenio's *cubanía* is modeled is actually a performance—specifically, Nestor's performance of a trope of Cubanness circulated by Arnaz and others. There is no stable point of origin to which Eugenio can return; the memory only points to a performance, itself a repetition of an anterior performance.

The novel thus illuminates how recording and memory necessarily index multiple layers of loss. Eugenio becomes addicted to the rerun because he no longer has real access to Nestor. Worse, unlike Cesar, who owns musical recordings of Nestor's voice, Eugenio lacks his own personal recording of his father and thus cannot replay the memory of his own volition; he is subject to memory triggers cued by others. The happenstance of Eugenio's technological recollection means that he is not in control of his own autobiographical archive and subject to life passing him by as he sits in front of the TV, waiting for his father to appear. The novel thus illustrates what Jonathan Sterne has called "the preservation paradox": by pressing "record" on a device, we not only outsource memory; we also let go of the necessity to remember without mediation. The majority of human experience has never been and can never be recorded; there is simply not enough storage space for the astronomical amount of data such a complete recording would require ("Preservation Paradox" 57–58). Much of human experience thus exists nowhere: not in memory, not in written records (empirical or creative), not in monuments or middens, neither in media nor in human mediums. It is simply gone. Human experience, I argue, is ultimately a lossy format, and despite our best efforts, memory and memory media record our lives only partially, selectively, and poorly.

The rerun of the TV episode, like the repeating LP record, indexes an obsessive recourse to the past that results in the auditor becoming stuck in a temporal groove. When listening to an LP, the stylus will progress through the tracks in concentric clockwise circles unless interrupted deliberately or inadvertently. The latter often happens when the stylus encounters a scratch that causes the needle to fixate on a moment in the groove, replaying and distorting that sonic moment and inhibiting "progress" to the end of the track and album. The only way to exit a scratch is to lift the tonearm and position it elsewhere. For the Castillo men, the needle of their lives has encountered a sediment or artifact that causes a narrative scratch and interrupts any possibility of linear development. They fixate on earlier moments of their lives, replaying and further distorting them as they do so.[23] Purposeful record-scratching such as in hip-hop and dub entails "backcueing" the record on the turntable: quickly spinning it counterclockwise—in other words, the "wrong" way—and holding it still so it can be synced in timing with another record when it is returned to the "proper" clockwise motion. The scratch, whether as a fixation or a conscious backward rotation, thus ruptures temporality and interrupts narrative and biological time.

Eugenio's obsessive rewatching of the TV episode and Cesar's terminal fixation on the record as a way of repeating the past are foreshadowed by Nestor's spending his brief life in the United States writing and rewriting the one song that would become the Mambo Kings' lone hit. He wrote twenty-two versions of it before fixing it on record; it is remade by numerous other artists, and even Cesar rewrites the song at the end of the novel, which itself ends with juxtaposed repeated iterations of both the *I Love Lucy* episode and the song: "The next morning . . . they found him [dead], with a drink in his hand and a tranquil smile on his face, this slip of paper, just a song, lying on the desk by his elbow. Just one of the songs he had written out himself" (*TMK* 435). Flipping over the page and expecting to find the text of a new song, the reader finds instead the handwritten text of "Bella María de Mi Alma." There is little to clarify whether this is the "original" record—if this recorded lyric is Cesar's or Nestor's version. The Spanish lyrics here seem to be roughly equivalent to the English snippets recorded in the early parts of the novel.[24] We are left to wonder what it means that Cesar dies having (re)written the song.

As Delores's experience shows, the laconic male musical world refuses interiority, including that of women. Indeed, in mambo mode, Cesar privileges the quickly passing present in an attempt to stave off the consuming memories of the past. Walter J. Ong has theorized that a key aspect of oral-dominant cultures is an orientation to the present that is incompatible with introspection. Introspection, he argues, is only afforded by writing, which encourages past and future consciousness, delay, and distance (32). Whereas in live music mode Cesar is consumed with self, sensuality, and the present, recorded music allows him to slow down and develop introspection—making novelistic narration possible—and a nascent sensibility that eventually leads to his epiphany. Like Ellison's invisible man for whom descent into his basement means a retreat into the mechanical reproduction of Louis Armstrong's voice (7–8), Cesar's retreat to a solitary space to listen to the phonograph record affords him the distance and introspection to hear the multiple narratives that underpin the musical tracks. The mambo era during which María and Cuba become lost to the Castillo brothers is the site of trauma where language is fragmented and narration becomes possible. The laconic mambo contrasts with the inherent narrative excess of the bolero with its surfeit of words and emotions. In contrast, in the retrospective sonic space created by the repeating LP and the rewritten bolero, both memory and its narration become possible: Cesar realizes the influence of the past, particularly his father's philandering and physical abuse as roots of his own mambo machismo and infidelity. Cesar also re-members—pieces together through the work of (re)memory—the root of his inability to love: he cannot have normal relationships with women because of his abnormal connection to his mother; likewise, he cannot have a normal connection to another land because of an unhealthy connection to his native Cuba.

It is in this recognition that Cesar comes closest to an epiphany; memories of learning music for the first time reveal that real love for a woman is the true source of Afro-Cuban music, and this takes him on a litany of the names of women he had spurned but to whom he now confesses his love in a sequence reminiscent of Prado's "Mambo No. 5": "And I loved you, Ana. . . . I loved you, Miriam . . . And I loved you, Margarita." Then in his memory, Nestor "sings this new song, this fucking new song he had been working on for a long, long time, and when he's done, he says, 'That's how I feel about María'" (*TMK* 433). Finally connecting his past to his present, then, an introspection afforded by the doubly recorded bolero, Cesar realizes that the bolero is a song for the mother, the daughter, the brother, and Cuba. Even more than introspection, this moment illustrates what I would term *stereospection*—a dual consciousness that allows him to look both forward and backward in the same way that properly aligned sound audio allows one to hear both left and right channels.[25] It is at this juncture when he simultaneously recognizes love and rewrites the bolero that he is finally released from melancholy and from biological and narrative time. Although his epiphany coincides with the *Mambo Kings* LP reaching the end, having previously set the record to repeat on its own, replay is now rote and inescapable; with the tonearm returning to the first song (435), the obsessive musical remembering is set to be inherited by a new generation.

Cesar's rewriting the bolero, his leaving behind a written record of himself alongside all the mementos he brought with him to the hotel, suggests not only that the song and its associated memories are impossible to escape but that every rewriting and replaying of the record is only an attempt at a faithful repetition of the original recording. In the ongoing fidelity debate in sound theory, questions remain about whether the record captures an original sound event that recordings aim to reproduce with the highest fidelity possible or the recording can actually *produce* the original.[26] *The Mambo Kings* suggests that recordings do not refer to any "pure" original outside of or anterior to itself. The "original" is created in the studio or on a portable device like a smartphone or tablet; it is always already technological and constructed. Although Nestor alone writes the lyrics of "Bella María," Cesar has significant input in its recorded version and the song is constantly remade and rerecorded by other artists throughout the novel. The proliferation of versions and copies of both the lyrics and the sound recording suggests that the "text"—whether the song text or the memory-text—is always in flux and never final. Neither the music nor the memory record is a faithful reproduction of a singular original event, just as "Beautiful María" is not a faithful record of the relationship between Nestor and María but rather a constantly reworked, revised, and reproduced document. Writing the song is depicted as an ongoing process; even after it is recorded for posterity, it is constantly being revised and remade.

With the presence of a sequel, *Beautiful Maria of My Soul* (2010)—the Americanized, unaccented Maria's rewriting of the novel—a musical version with its libretto cowritten by Hijuelos and a movie version that (as movie versions often do) takes liberties with the story and characters, the novel's versions also mutate, challenging conceptions of memory and records as stable documents. Rather, the novel suggests that memories, like records, are merely versions of experience that produce their own original in the moment of creation. As such, the repeating records and texts problematize the possibility of recuperating an original home and identity or recovering original memory. Neither the Cuba of the bolero nor the mambo era of the 1950s can really be recovered; Eugenio cannot literally touch his father despite Nestor's technological resurrection. As a result, the only recourse is to continually replay and rewrite these memories and records in order to temporarily live in the desired moment. The four versions of the story all tell the story differently, not merely as four discrete texts but as competing versions, with the Maria of the second novel challenging her representation in both the movie and the film in a fictional encounter with a fictionalized version of the author (Hijuelos, *Beautiful Maria* 318). Likewise, we assume that Cesar hears the same songs as he replays the record, but does it release the same memory every time, or does the unchanging record produce changing memories? And what memories are elicited for Eugenio as he listens to these records and "remembers" and narrates events he himself did not live and could not know?

With these repetitions and reruns, *The Mambo Kings* explores what happens when exiles become stuck between the contradictory pulls of backward-facing music and the *Forward!* impetus of modern writing. But the materiality of the phonograph and the experience of music and sound problematize the West's predominantly linear and visual metaphors for memory and identity and offer one way out of the deadly forward-backward binary. The phonograph record itself is circular, with two sides existing in a contrapuntal relationship. Progress through the tracks in the record does not describe a linear but a concentric motion, going deeper and deeper on the physical surface from the outer rim in, as into the work. Knowing where you are in sonic time and place visually comprises where you were before, and there need not be an end to the experience; instead the audition could continue ad infinitum. In Benítez-Rojo's construction, instead of a "punto final" (final period), there is a "punto redondo" (roughly, a circular ending), and this recursivity is a feature, not a bug, of Caribbeanness. He argues that "the dramatic structure of the Caribbean text [does not] ordinarily conclude with the phallic orgasm of climax, but rather with a kind of coda which, for example, would be interpreted in the Cuban popular theater by a rumba danced by the entire cast. If we look at the Caribbean's most representative novels we see that their narrative discourse is constantly disrupted, and at times almost annulled, by heteroclitic, fractal, baroque, or arboreal forms" (Benítez-Rojo 25). In true Caribbean fashion, then, *The Mambo Kings* refuses a climactic, phallic ending. Like the increasingly impotent Cesar, the novel flails to multiple anticlimactic endings. The "record" of the novel sprouts a third "side," subverting the side A / side B form it previously set up and gesturing to the limits of the LP format for the long durée of Cuban exile.[27] There are at least three putative "endings"—the end of Cesar's tale that reprises with the handwritten text of "Bella María," then reprises again, as in Benítez-Rojo's formulation, "with a kind of coda" staged as an all-out mambo *descarga* in the streets of New York. The novel's end is simply the fade out at the end of a musical number. Despite the fact that Cesar has died, the novel's fractal endings preserve his memory and resurrect him again in the final rerun of the TV episode.

The Salsa Revolution, or the Return of the Repressed

Although the novel is set in 1980, the heyday of the salsa revolution, characters never mention salsa, the main Latin music form that emerged in the 1970s after the Cuban-dominated mambo-mania ended and Latin music's influence went underground. As Willie Colón and other Latin musicians suggest in the 2009 PBS documentary *Latin Music USA*, after Afro-Cuban rhythms permeated the American psyche, they seemed to disappear as rock and rhythm and blues took hold in the 1960s and 1970s (episode 2, 43:04). What really happened, they say, is that Afro-Cuban music became acculturated—it did not go away; it was just integrated into the emerging "American" music forms as its "difference" disappeared. With the waning popularity of the Latin *conjunto* and the closing of the Palladium, former mambonicks joined emergent rock bands or became music producers and executives, carrying within them the seeds of cultural exchange fostered by the interracial, intercultural dance and music scene of mambo dance halls. According to Jimmy Smits, the documentary's narrator, "The riffs and rhythms of Latin music became part of the rock arsenal" (episode 7, 3:05). Songs like the Beatles' "Day Tripper" and "Twist and Shout" were sonic reruns of mambo and *cha-cha-cha* rhythmic structures from Machito and others. Without a musical homeland, young English-speaking *cubanos* and Latinos growing up in Spanish Harlem latched on to rock and roll and the Beatles. When "Latin music" reemerged in the 1970s, it was as a rugged, English-speaking (later bilingual) music form called salsa, dominated by New York Puerto Ricans, or Nuyoricans—not immigrants but American citizens due to Puerto Rico's commonwealth status.

Salsa unearthed some of the foundations of Afro-Cuban music and combined them with the rhythms and sounds of multicultural New York. Although salsa gestures toward a discrete Latinx culture, it is inherently American, urban, New York music. At the foreground of this evolution from Cuban-dominated mambo to Nuyorican-dominated salsa were musicians like Tito Puente, former mambo king, who unlike the fictional Cesar followed the forward march of the music, keeping in time with changes in rhythms and culture and, as a result, remaining present when the new generation needed a maestro to connect their musical past, present, and future. What Puente represents for the salsa generation is a bridge, a functional hyphen between generations, and this is what the terminally ill and terminally nostalgic Cesar fails to represent for Eugenio. Nestor's and Cesar's legacy to Eugenio is a mediated, second-generation nostalgia for a Cubanness removed from its source, which the novel reveals as a dangerous and deadly business.

Opening and fading out with Eugenio's framing memory work of making sense of the fragments and mementos his uncle left behind, the novel illuminates the complexities of negotiating an ex-isle Caribbean identity informed by memories of both Cuba and America: a thoroughly "made in America" identity but with deep Cuban resonances. Like the mambo and salsa, Caribbeanness is creolized and mutating. It is vibrant and vital, playful, and promiscuous. It is not terrified of movement and mutation; rather, secure in its roots—the fodder for its Creole and creolizing stew—it has the grounding to accommodate new ingredients. *The Mambo Kings* thus stages the dialectic of Caribbean ex-isle identity; rather than Ortiz's notion of the contrapuntal play that characterizes transculturated Cuban and Caribbean identity, the characters struggle with the loss associated with acculturation into hegemonic Americanness—the obsolescence and disappearance of Cubanness into iconically American rock music—and as such, (re)turn to phonographic memories and technologies of nostalgia in order to (re)turn to a Cuban past that is no longer accessible and perhaps never was.

Music composition relies on the repetition of motifs that build our anticipation for the return of a previously iterated compositional element (Negus 483–486). The return of an earlier motif does not cause trauma but elicits pleasure—what we call recognition. I would redefine this type of *re*cognition as the cognitive pleasure and catharsis experienced by the return of something we presumed past or lost, the resolution of auditory separation anxiety. Repetition and return are thus not structural failures. A phonographic model of memory does not necessarily mean a return to a past that is "back there," somewhere other than where we are now, but it signals a reintroduction into the present of an earlier state. In this paradigm, Cubanness and Americanness—Cuban memories and the American present—can coexist; one does not need to relinquish Cuba to the past to thrive in the American present. Instead, they can be mutually constitutive—not *ad*culturation but *trans*culturation: transitory, transgressive, transactional, transmissible. Similarly, foregrounding a sound, Caribbean epistemology makes possible a conception of Cubanness as not "back there" but "here" as well, resonating and vibrating in the same space as "America," with sonic "progress" redefined by simultaneity and heterogeneity.

Hijuelos ultimately broadens the contours of Caribbeanness—and not as an outpost of mainland America. Of course, various U.S. administrations have tried to annex Cuba throughout its history, with the prison enclave of Guantanamo Bay a visceral reminder of American hegemony in the region. Instead, the mass migrations of Cubans and other Caribbean peoples have made an American state like Florida and neighborhoods like Spanish Harlem as Caribbean as they are American. Caribbean migrations and cultural vibrancy have claimed territory in the mainland United States as much as from places like Costa Rica, Columbia, and Belize—much to the chagrin of American ethnonationalists. The same story repeats itself in New York and Toronto, Brixton and Birmingham, and Nantes and Marseille, where Caribbean peoples have turned on its head neocolonial encroachments on Caribbean territory. Cuba is prime territory for this, given its historical role as the port for circum-Caribbean exchange—of the music that would become jazz, of tobacco and sugar, of slaves and freedmen. Hijuelos suggests that the Cuban homeland is mutable; Cuba is Havana and Spanish Harlem and Little Havana simultaneously, and the movement of Cuban music and peoples repeats the homeland—with a difference—in a new space, in tandem with the parabolic curve of nostalgic memory that aims to repeat the past in a new time. Return and retreat, if possible, would not bring the exile to a stable a priori, since the Caribbean homeland is constantly shifting under one's feet, even the feet of those who remain in the region. Indeed, the past and the homeland only remain unchanging in nostalgic imaginations.

CHAPTER 3

Re-membering "Body and Soul"

GENDER, JAZZ, AND GWOKA IN DANIEL MAXIMIN'S *LONE SUN*

> *What you see in my early work is an alternative music giving me an alternative riddim, as it were, but as I get to know more about the Caribbean the emphasis shifts from jazz to the Caribbean to calypso, to reggae, to our folk music.*
>
> —Kamau Brathwaite, "Travelling Miles"

Outside of the Holocaust, few moments have become so enshrined in Western collective memory as the terrorist attacks of September 11, 2001. Global audiences tuned in to televised images of two jetliners flying into the World Trade Center in Manhattan, the Twin Towers billowing black smoke and crumbling into the ground, carrying with them the incinerated and disintegrated bodies of thousands. Faced with this spectacular tragedy that defied reason and language, Barbadian poet Kamau Brathwaite turned to a recording of a September 11, 1967, performance by Coleman Hawkins at Ronnie Scott's club in London. In the resulting poem, "Hawk's Last Body & Soul" (*Born to Slow Horses* 92–115), Brathwaite forges a connection between the targeted violence of 9/11 and broader systemic violence that has seared and shattered innumerable black bodies throughout history and suggests that, in its specular horror, the repeated broadcast of images of charred body parts becomes a visceral replay of embodied violence throughout the African diaspora.[1] Inspired and soundtracked by the jazz recording, the poem narrates the salvific role of improvisational black music in enabling those dismembered black bodies to become "remember[ed] . . . whole & powerful again" (96). It is the jazzman's performance that heals "the black the blurr(ed) the burn(ed) the bomb(ed) the scarr(ed)" as "only he cd" [*sic*] (98, 94). "Hawk's Last Body & Soul" thus depicts two forms of memory work: the psychological retrieval of a past experience through the mediation of recorded music, and the physical reassembly of broken body fragments mediated through musical improvisation. But since such physical healing is only imaginary, it is really the writer who accomplishes remembering by recomposing fragments of sounds, histories, images, and text into narrative.

This chapter explores the connections between remembrance—the repeated *psychological* reassembling of memories—and re-membering—the *physical* reassembling of the disarticulated or shattered members of the female body—and how they are enabled by the mnemonic and improvisational ethos of black music. Like Brathwaite, characters in Daniel Maximin's *L'Isolé soleil* (1981; *Lone Sun*, 1989) also turn to a recording of "Body and Soul" to work through embodied violence and fragmented memories. Both the vinyl recording and the song title become nodes through which women negotiate physical violence and its psychological effects. My reading centers on three female characters who experience various forms of psychic and physical trauma and traces their provisional re-membering enabled by listening and dancing to various versions of "Body and Soul," including a creolized performance of the song that brings together jazz clarinet and gwoka drums. In contrast to previous critics' framing of *Lone Sun* as a jazz novel based on its improvisatory mode and the recurring motif of this jazz standard throughout its pages,[2] I take an ethnomusicological rather than formalist approach to foreground the improvisational and mnemonic ethos of *both* jazz and gwoka. With a focus on the power of the saxophone, clarinet, and drum to, in Wil Cartey's words, "resurrect memories . . . awaken emotions, [and] . . . infuse vitality and movement into lifeless form" (21), I consider the viability of improvisation-based African diaspora musical practices as countercultural Creole alternatives to European literary and political models that aim to reclaim Antilleans from the cultural exile and psychological shattering wrought by departmentalization.

Lone Sun seems to illustrate Brathwaite's initial proposition that jazz might model for Caribbean novelists an "alternative" to European literary forms (*Roots* 55–110). But why choose an African American and not a Caribbean music idiom? As Brathwaite indicated in an interview with Donette Francis, "What you see in my early work is an alternative music giving me an alternative riddim" (Francis, "Travelling Miles" 149). Due to its early-twentieth-century global cachet and the denigration of local music in the preindependence Caribbean, jazz was available to a certain class of cosmopolitan Caribbean auditors seeking anti- and decolonial artistic and political models. Just as Brathwaite first turned to jazz to develop an authentic local, critical, and creative tool, so too in *Lone Sun* does Maximin reroute African American jazz to and through Guadeloupean gwoka music, even as his characters (writers, musicians, and anti*département* dissidents) negotiate the shift from assimilation to a liberated national consciousness. The novel's trajectory from jazz, to gwoka, to what contemporary Guadeloupean musicians call "jazz-ka" is similar to Brathwaite's own trajectory, where "as I get to know more about the Caribbean the emphasis shifts from jazz to the Caribbean to calypso, to reggae, to our folk music" (qtd. in Francis, "Travelling Miles" 149).

This shift from African diasporic to Caribbean music also tracks with the liberationist trajectory championed by Guadeloupean separatists in the 1970s to 1980s as a means of rectifying the cultural amnesia caused by colonization: from French to Creole language, identity, and culture. It therefore situates *Lone Sun* within coterminous conversations about Guadeloupean sovereignty and the role of Creole and gwoka therein. Unlike other Caribbean islands that would gain independence from various European colonial powers throughout the 1960s, Guadeloupe and Martinique became overseas *départements*, or administrative regions of France, in 1946 with the consequence of a continued economically dependent relationship to the metropole. That the opening pages locate the novel's present in relationship to waves of independence throughout the rest of the Caribbean frames its memory work as a quest both for literary and political sovereignty and for a cultural awakening. Given Guadeloupe's unique political reality, while much of this book explores the ways that nation music reorients mobile Caribbean peoples to national homelands and national identities, the subsequent analysis explores how citizens of countries that are not autonomous nations often look elsewhere in the wider African diaspora, at least initially, for musical models that might inform an eventual nationalist project. Thus, even as characters gain provisional remembering from music while in exile, the novel ultimately turns to the musical remembering practices specific to the Caribbean place.

By crafting a novel that reassembles fragments of herstory and memory, Maximin charts a poetics of remembering. He structures the novel as a mise en abyme around several self-reflexive narrative threads radiating from the exploded epistolary frame. These concentric threads mark the repetitive and ruptured nature of Guadeloupean history, where moments of incredible possibility in the struggle for independence result in impotent eruptions and the reinstatement of the colonial regime. The frame narrative relates the story of three young Guadeloupeans who, in the summer of 1962, exchange letters and novel drafts across the ocean. Adrien, the author surrogate, is recently "ex-isled" to Paris aboard the liner "Antilles," its name indexing Antillean mobility.[3] Back in Guadeloupe are Antoine, a young jazz-ka musician and dissident, and the protagonist Marie-Gabriel, whose father died in the real-life Air France explosion near La Soufrière on her seventeenth birthday, June 22, 1962. The plane's is only one of many "unnatural" explosions that draw attention to the somnambulant and perpetually unexploded volcano, the symbol of a dormant populace whose revolutionary potential has been repressed since Guadeloupe became a *département d'outre mer* (DOM) in 1946. Sending shockwaves backward and forward through Guadeloupean history and imploding narrative and historical time-space, the plane's explosion supplies both the narrative genesis of the novel and the psychological genesis for Marie-Gabriel as she reassembles her parents' memory from textual and sonic fragments. With both parents dead, she is cut off from biographical and narrative lineage; the airplane explosion results in the loss of her father's musical and literary records: his music notebook that chronicled his attempt at a musical history of the new world and a second notebook consisting of pages torn from history books, letters, and written records of the island's struggles for self-governance over the centuries.

At the heart of both Marie-Gabriel's novel and the one we are reading is her mother's story and her "mother's song," the jazz standard "Body and Soul" that Siméa listens to live in Paris in 1939 and that Marie-Gabriel listens to on vinyl as she writes her memory text. Bereft of the source texts—memories and historical documents—that would enable her to craft a proper historical account, Marie-Gabriel turns to the sound recording to reawaken "memories" of her parents and Guadeloupean history—in other words, experiences she did not personally witness and thus must create rather than retrieve. My attention to the novel's phonotopes thus highlights how both jazz and gwoka enable psychic, physical, and literary remembering: characters use music to recollect shattered pasts and body fragments as a prelude to literary (re)composition. I therefore attend equally to Marie-Gabriel's authorship practices as to the musical strategies of her father, Louis-Gabriel, who discovers in gwoka an emancipatory practice that enables women to restore bodies and psyches shattered by French colonization, cultural assimilation, and physical violence.

Maximin joins numerous other male writers across the circum-Caribbean who embody female narrative voice in sensitive, ethically minded ways in order to perform woman memory.[4] In so doing, he interrogates the marginalization of women in literary, political, and cultural movements and recenters women in gwoka and nation-making. I read his deployment of woman-centered Caribbean poetics as a form of narrative allyship; this mode metafictionally depicts male authors and musicians who decenter their own voices and perspectives to collaborate with women's own creative and political projects. For Maximin's female characters, healing, writing, and political action emerge from an embodied feminist Creole poetics, even as they are inspired by and dialogue with fathers, male lovers, and male musicians. As the latter sections of the chapter show, the turn from lone male jazzman to male-female collaboration undercuts the early nods to "*l'écriture féminine*."[5] Consonant with his reorientation from his initial inspiration in French feminist Hélène Cixous to the Antillean feminist Suzanne Césaire, Maximin roots the novel's intergender allyship in *liyannaj*, a Guadeloupean Creole term for forming alliances to accomplish a common goal, ultimately creating a new entity from the linkages (Bonilla 152–153). *Liyannaj* connects to the novel's focus on synthesis, whether in the form of sexual coupling, rejoining broken bodies and instruments, or collaborative authorship. Thus, while the novel's improvisational form at first seems to mirror jazz, it in fact stages the return to musical, narrative, and mnemonic practices specific to Guadeloupe. Improvisation and *liyannaj* offer alternate modalities of narration and figure memory as collaborative rather than the project of a solitary subject—the "lone" male author of the novel's title.

Le Corps Morcélé: Dis-Membered Bodies and Souls

Lone Sun establishes physical and psychological dismembering as the result of compound factors with roots in colonization and patriarchy. "Siméa's Journal," one of the texts Marie-Gabriel reconstructs by listening to music, is set in 1939, squarely in the moment that gives rise to negritude and the literary revolutions that accompanied the publication of seminal texts like Léon Damas's *Pigments-Névralgies* (1937) and Aimé Césaire's *Cahier d'un retour au pays natal* (1939). This is also the moment when Guadeloupe and Martinique first weighed the choice between independence and departmentalization. The latter course was led by Césaire, communist mayor of Fort-de-France, who saw departmentalization as a route to decolonization.[6] Given France's political ideology of erasing racial and cultural specificity in favor of a "universal" Frenchness, departmentalization in effect cemented colonization and resulted in an assimilationist spirit in the mulatto class and educated *nègres* who celebrated "[their] ancestors-the-Gauls" and dismissed their own black skins as "just a touch of sunburn" (*LS* 152–153). It is not incidental, then, that Marie-Gabriel's mother, Siméa, has gotten pregnant by a white Frenchman, Ariel, while a student in Paris, as it signals her *doudouiste* mind-set at this stage in the novel.[7] The tragic figure of the *doudou* has been disparaged throughout Antillean literature and folk culture as the embodiment of assimilation and racial self-hatred (Hill 20–23). In one of the Antilles' earliest folk songs, "Adieu madras, adieu foulard," the Creole woman stands on the quay pleading after a departed French sailor, her *doudou* (sweetie), who has provided her with scarves, madrass headwraps, and gold necklaces—the trappings of colonial consumption that mask her own status as consumable and disposable.

If her pregnancy by her Frenchman signifies her ultimate *doudouiste* false consciousness and the source of her cultural amnesia, Siméa's abortion while a student in Paris engenders a crisis that eventually triggers her racial and cultural memory. In a journal rendered as a lament written from the mother to her aborted fetus, Siméa describes her forced abortion as violence against her body: "The house of my womb turned upside down, its heart gutted, my streets cluttered with every kind of debris, my arteries uprooted. My whole land devastated. . . . Your corpse ripped out of my ruins" (*LS* 111). The language here is natural, the abortion calling to her mind the unprecedented destruction caused by Okeechobee, the Category 4 hurricane that devastated Guadeloupe on September 12, 1928, leaving at least 1,200 dead in its wake; however, the abortion is *un*natural, imposed on Siméa by her mulatto mother who wants to restore her daughter to respectability. Siméa's traumatic rememory of her child being "aerated" and its "corpse ripped out of [her] ruins" likely indicates a near-term dilation and extraction. Dangerous, rare, and at the time punishable by death in France, in this third-trimester termination procedure, the fully formed fetus is pulled feet first through the cervix and its brain aspirated via a catheter to allow its skull to collapse and its remains to be removed from the mother's body.[8] The novel stages this experience as physically and psychologically traumatic for both mother and fetus, even as it uses repetition, stream of consciousness, and the metaphor of natural disasters to displace and grapple with its effects.

Recent studies indicate that women who undergo abortion can experience long-term post-traumatic stress disorder even decades later and that clandestine abortions conducted with dilation and curettage can increase the risk of complications, including uterine perforations (Rousset et al.; Nkwabong and Fomulu). In Siméa's case, not only is she emotionally shattered by her experience, but her uterus is also damaged, leading to her postpartum death after giving birth to Marie-Gabriel more than six years later. As I demonstrated in the first chapter, trauma often leaves a wound on both body and mind, and these wounds can function as a type of body language, a record of the unspeakable that allows for later replay with the right technology. Roberta Culbertson, for her part, has shown how wounding unravels the self and undoes the psychic wholeness on which narration and subjectivity rely (179). Siméa's insistence on re-membering her aerated fetus through writing is all the more striking given the novel's particular focus on the deleterious effects of maternal wounds. Ti-Carole, Marie-Gabriel's great-grandmother, demonstrates in her Creole storytelling and musical practice a poetics of womb memory. As she transmits to her daughters deep racial and cultural memory in the form of the Creole proverbs, stories, and songs that would be left out of French historiography, she enjoins them to "let [their] womb and heart and ears remember" (*LS* 74). Womb and wound memory, in their ability to tap into submerged memories, are even more vital when written documents and official historical records can be ripped up, falsified, jettisoned, or destroyed in hurricanes or explosions. In the same way that Maximin shifts the narrative center from the male to the female conarrator, womb memory likewise shifts the burden of historical transmission from revolutionary men to wounded women. It is through Siméa's wounded womb that Marie-Gabriel is physically and narratively birthed. It is also through her own sexually quickened womb that Marie-Gabriel discovers a lineage to her mother and is able to re-member her parents in writing.

In her post-traumatic haze, Siméa oscillates between referring to her child as "daughter," "son," and "son-daughter," symbolizing the loss of the compound possibility of future generations and reflecting a connection between the maternal body and the body politic. Maggie Allison has described how the severe penalties and rhetoric around the 1942 abortion laws of the Vichy regime focused on constructing the act as an offense against the state (225). In the wake of the mass loss of life during the Second World War, abortion was criminalized in order to ensure rapid nation-building. The notion that women in their childbearing capacity enable the reproduction of the nation means that abortion laws and policing women's wombs (including policing interracial reproduction) are often central pillars of nationalist regimes. By naturalizing Siméa's abortion through the language of the land and its devastation by the hurricane, Maximin frames the nation itself as a womb and the novel as an extended allegory on the repeated abortive struggles for Guadeloupean sovereignty.

In the same way that Brathwaite fashions a poetics of seeing and writing wholeness from fragmentation and trauma, Maximin charts Siméa's psychic and bodily restoration through music and writing. Siméa's abortion unwittingly enables the emergence of a new sensibility from her shattered body that allows her to reject the false consciousness of assimilation as well as the tyranny of white paternity and paternalism, especially as symbolized by French intellectual traditions. Mourning the loss of bodily integrity, Siméa first uses journaling to begin to deconstruct whiteness and reconstruct her body in a process Jason Herbeck likens to jazz improvisation (167) and Ronnie Scharfman to "signifyin'" (240). Siméa's trauma makes her receptive to the words of black revolutionary Antillean poets *entre-deux-guerres*, particularly the poetry of her friend, a fictionalized Damas. Mouthing but personalizing lines from some of Damas's most iconic poems, Siméa reveals her growing awareness of the role of her studies in her colonization: she declares, "I vomit you, white poetry" (*LS* 116), rendering Damas's hiccup in "Hoquet" even more violent and thorough. Having thus cleared space, she adds, "Give me back my black poets and black body" (118). In this nod to Damas's "Limbé," which begins with "Give me back my black dolls / so they dispel / the image of pale whores" (*Pigments-Névralgies* 117), Siméa figures assimilation as a source of psychic fragmentation, the antidote to which is the recovery of black bodies and poetry and eventually a Guadeloupean identity rooted in a reawakened racial memory.

Siméa's allusion to Damas also allows for a figuration of memory as not merely a psychological rediscovery but a *physical* recovery of what was stolen. Indeed, Damas's black dolls are not merely artistic creations that Europeans robbed from Africa even as they justified the falsehood that Africa had no art or civilization; rather, they are an imagistic reminder of a self that existed prior to colonial dismembering. Seeing the beautiful black dolls is a graphical and graphic wake-up call to the black subject's present fragmentation. Consequently, reclaiming their associated *africanité* allows the poet to "become [him]self once again [him]self once more / out of what [he] was Yesterday" (Damas 118). Siméa, however, skips past dolls and calls instead for black poets: living, adult subjects who agitate for a black New World present and future rather than lifeless child-size relics of an African past.

Even as she affirms the value of black male artists in her healing, Siméa's trauma also sensitizes her to the segmentation of women's bodies via male poetry and song. Sitting in the Cuban Cabana music club postabortion, she internally revolts against the misogyny of both André Bréton's poetry and the bolero lyrics that dissect her into fetishized body parts "debited, subtracted, tracked, analyzed, synthesized, poetized, automatized" (*LS* 127). Siméa's critique of the psychological effects of her colonialist and patriarchal literary training echoes Lacan's theorization of the belated sense of fragmentation that a child experiences postmirror stage—ironically, the moment when she recognizes her own image as separate from others. As Deborah Harter elaborates, the child's recognition of her wholeness "launches a memory of a body in its bits and pieces—a '*corps morcelé*'—a memory that is suddenly frightening and that is in large part the mark of a retrospectively imagined lack of totality" (68). If such a psychic state attends childhood, not womanhood, then Siméa's epiphany here reveals that male texts are not only dismembering but also infantilizing.

Her critique is not limited to white male poets; even as she draws strength from Guillén, Damas, and Césaire, she interrogates their tendency to romanticize black women as muses to male heroes rather than heroines in their own right (*LS* 135). Maximin therefore revises the mirror stage to express the effects of patriarchy on women and expands W. E. B. Du Bois's conception of double consciousness to figure the continued sense of fragmentation experienced by Afro-Caribbean subjects of what Yarimar Bonilla calls "non-sovereign states." In tandem with Siméa's recognition of the universal male objectification of women, then, the novel inserts black womanhood not only into white feminism but also into the masculinist negritude discourse that effectively erased the contributions of Paulette and Jane Nardal, in whose Parisian salons the would-be fathers of negritude met and whose intellectual work provided the foundation and nourishment for what would become a male-centered movement.[9] It is this erasure and shattering of black and female bodies and psyches that animates the novel's deployment of "Body and Soul" as both a female lament and an assertion of embodied racial trauma.

Re-membering "Body and Soul"

In *Lone Sun*, Maximin imagines a Guadeloupean society fully anchored in an African diasporic community and as part of the circum-Caribbean flow of peoples and culture instead of one oriented to France,[10] a Guadeloupe that is open to music, writings, and political events from beyond its linguistic and virtual boundaries, whether the Haitian revolution or the Haitian merengue, Martinican dissidence or Cuban bolero, the African American civil rights movement or African American jazz. Siméa's trajectory mirrors the birth of negritude in the Parisian transnational exchanges of the Césaires, Senghors, and Nardals and the development of jazz in the transnational encounters of various displaced Caribbean music styles in Cuba. It also matches but predates by at least two decades the origins of separatist politics, which fomented among Guadeloupean students as they experienced racial awákening in late-1960s Paris. That all of this section takes place as Siméa, an "ex-isled" Guadeloupean, is sitting in the Cuban Cabana music club in Paris, first listening to and then playing Afro-Cuban music, highlights the role of Cuba in fostering diasporic connections and the circulation of Caribbean music throughout the black Atlantic world. Cuba is central to the development of what would become "American" jazz; it was via Cuba that Afro-Haitian music circulated to New Orleans in the mid to late nineteenth century as the generic "Latin tinge" and the raggy style that feeds ragtime, jazz's precursor.[11] *Lone Sun* likewise shows how, before the entrance of the jazzmen onto the stage, it is Malhia, the Cuban bolero singer, who first affirms Siméa's womanhood and who allows her to center black radical poetics on the black female body as whole and restored, not fetishized, dissected, or erased.

Just as Siméa comes to realize how black radical poetics and politics often erase or sideline women, the novel's deployment of "Body and Soul" as a motif illuminates a similar elision of the female voice in traditionally male-centered conceptions of jazz. Although Hawkins's rendition is the most well-known version of the standard, "Body and Soul" was originally written for and performed by British actress and singer Gertrude Lawrence in 1930; Hawkins only happened to cut the recording in a one-off session for Bluebird. Indeed, the unheard lyrics of the (un)heard melody in Hawkins's canonical rendition simultaneously call to mind and erase the first-person testimony of a woman pining for requited love:

> I spend my days in longing,
> And wondering why it's me you're wronging.
> Why haven't you seen it?
> I'm all for you—body and soul.

In her 1967 live performance of the standard on the NBC special *Frank Sinatra: A Man and His Music*, blues singer Ella Fitzgerald rends the word *body* in each verse such that her "body" is rarely whole until the end of the song. The speaker's desertion by her lover has so devastated her sense of self that even as she declares that she is "all for [him] body and soul," her torn "body" belies her statement. After a series of rending tonal center shifts and scatting every other word, the final "body" is sung normatively in two discrete notes. It is as if Fitzgerald has put everything she has into producing this sonically whole "body" by the end of the performance. The song's lyrics and performance, particularly when foregrounding the woman's voice and embodied experience, model the provisional physical and psychological restoration of the rent female body and contextualize its significance for Maximin's female characters. Even as Maximin locates musical improvisation as the domain of men and focuses on jazzmen performing "Body and Soul," he stages Marie-Gabriel's recuperation of the song as female testimony. As a blues lament that narrates a woman's weariness, the song is sonically and historically connected to the spiritual, the hope of rest in the great beyond for the slave's tortured body. "Body and Soul" resounds the continued experience of weariness and relative lack of freedoms that freed blacks are even now negotiating in urban spaces. Fitzgerald's performance further attests that it is in her body that the contestation and performance of the still-future freedom is enacted; for black women then, as for black Antilleans now, the "improvisational élan of freedom" that characterizes both jazz and gwoka is crucial to their present and future restoration (*LS* 211).

Jazz interrogates and subverts Western traditions and foregrounds black vernacular culture. This is precisely why, in 1967, during the period immediately following independence across the anglophone Caribbean and the setting of the novel's frame, Brathwaite hailed African American jazz as the only extant standard for a truly authentic, alternative, and liberatory Caribbean poetics that creates "some- / thing torn / and new" from mnemonic and historical fragments (*Arrivants* 270). While Brathwaite would soon revise his privileging of jazz at the expense of Caribbean musical forms, it seems to me that what he was looking for was not jazz per se but rather "an alternative to the English Romantic/Victorian cultural tradition which still operates among and on us . . . despite the presence among us of a folk tradition which in itself . . . is the basis of an alternative" (*Roots* 196). In other words, Brathwaite's jazz aesthetic was really shorthand for a Creole way of seeing, a West Indian vernacular aesthetic rooted in Afro-Caribbean folk culture but routed through the African diaspora. During the 1930s and 1940s in which "Siméa's Journal" and "Mother's Song" are set, however, there was no Guadeloupean counterpart to jazz. Traditional gwoka, the collective drum-based practices of Guadeloupe, was still denigrated by the French-oriented Guadeloupean bourgeoisie as *mizik vyè nèg*, or "old niagger music." Until gwoka descends from the *morne* to the city and moves from rural folk music to urbanized, modern, "emancipated Negro's music" (Brathwaite, *Roots* 196), cosmopolitan Antillean auditors and musicians would need look to the broader African diaspora for a music that met Brathwaite's conditions for an "alternative" form.[12]

Maximin depicts jazz enabling both re-membering—provisional embodied relief—and remembrance—the resuscitation of cultural memory. Listening to Hawkins's improvisation of this female lament while dancing with Ariel in the

Parisian club, Siméa discovers: "I'm happy that I restored my body . . . I am full and whole . . . melodious and improvised, I feel good, *body and soul*" (*LS* 142). Siméa's embodied experience of the jazz standard in Paris echoes Brathwaite's poetic treatment of Hawkins's performance of the same song in London thirty years later. Thanks to the balm of Hawkins's improvisation, Siméa's shattered "body body body bodies" is, like those of the victims of the World Trade Center attack, now "remember[ed]" and en route to "becoming whole & powerful again" (Brathwaite, *Born to Slow Horses* 97, 96). Significantly, while Brathwaite compares Hawkins's jazz performance to a sonic "cure" comprised of "myrrh & anegeda salt & cinnamon upon our / flesh" (94), and even though Siméa refers to her body as "restored" and "whole," her physical re-membering remains imaginary and performative; restoration and cure reside purely in the psychological effects of listening and dancing to jazz.

The language of bodily re-membering also calls to mind Jan Assmann's description of Egyptian embalming rites. In these rites, the priest uses song and invocations to physically reconstruct the dismembered body in order to restore its biographical memory in a ritual called limb deification (Assmann 52). For her part, Gabriele Brandstetter connects the Latin root of *limb* or *extremity* with *limbo*, the liminal space between death and life for children who die unbaptized (108).[13] In a reversal of the dismembering tendencies of white male texts and the maternally mandated abortion, jazz music provides Siméa a temporary balm to reconstitute her first child's limbs and limbo state into a verbal text as well as to re-member her own way to psychic and narrative wholeness. Siméa's writing to her aborted fetus is both a form of re-membering and a prophecy: while the aerated fetus cannot physically be recovered, its bodily recovery will eventually come to fruition in and as Marie-Gabriel.

In her statement that "I restored my body . . . I am full and whole . . . melodious and improvised" (*LS* 142), Siméa conceives of improvisation as an act of creative rememory that draws together the shards of broken black bodies, memories, and culture, echoing Brathwaite's notion of creolization as the creation of "some- / thing torn / and new" from fragmentation (*Arrivants* 270). This figuration of bodily remembering echoes in the case of little Angela, a young ward at the insane asylum back in Guadeloupe where Siméa becomes a teacher a few years later during the occupation of the southern Caribbean by French troops. Angela's case underscores the physical component of re-membering: if black (female) bodies have been broken, violated, and devastated, then in order for them to be restored to society and equipped to participate in Guadeloupe's emancipatory future, their bodies will need to be re-membered. At a 1943 Carnival ball, Siméa hears a solo improvisation of "Body and Soul" on alto clarinet, in which Louis-Gabriel "delivers up the hidden richness around a melody turned and returned to the very limits of improvisation" (*LS* 166). While the song stirs Siméa's embodied rememory of Hawkins's performance in Paris, something in the music proves too disturbing for little Angela, who breaks the ebony clarinet on the ground (167).

Throughout *Lone Sun*, *ebony* is used to symbolize the black body, likely an allusion to the term *bois d'ébène*, slave traders' code name for captive Africans. During her time in Paris, Siméa writes to her aborted fetus, "My child, you should know this well-kept secret: there are many suicides among the colonized in Paris. Pieces of ebony in the bottom of the Seine" (*LS* 124). The preferred instruments of the jazz soloists she so favors are ebony clarinets that they "warm up" in the course of their improvisations. In the same way that the explosive death of the musician father opens up space for Marie-Gabriel to craft a female-centered historiography, Angela's breaking the ebony clarinet shatters the phallic male instrument from which Louis-Gabriel has produced this sound that "penetrate[s] body and soul" (166) and alerts him to the need for a performative practice that gives attention to women's trauma. Angela's reaction to the ebony clarinet points to her subliminal understanding of the connection between African diaspora embodied trauma and black music. But the wholeness of the ebony clarinet is retraumatizing for Angela even as it testifies to the rent black body and psyche. In other words, a poetics attuned to race is not enough if it privileges men at the expense of women.

Angela witnessed her father drown during a surprise attack by a German submarine that swallowed the fishing boat carrying him and the dissidents he was smuggling to Dominica (*LS* 161). Although she loses the ability to speak, she is drawn to performative reminders of her trauma, notably Lafcadio Hearn's Creole tale of Pélamanlou that Siméa often recounts to her. On one such occasion, she reacts viscerally to the power relations depicted in the tale, connecting Hearn's fabular "Armor'd Fish" with the German submarine and all other representatives of colonial power that victimize and destroy black Antillean bodies. Apart from the lullabies her father used to sing to her, the only word Angela can as yet utter is the name of this boy "who abandoned his mother to go back and look for his instrument lost in the forest, and who, caught by nightfall, manages to charm with his music first the horned horse and then the zombi-dragon before being swallowed whole by the seven-headed beast" (164). That the music-wielding boy inspires little Angela even though he does not survive repeated attacks by stronger animals is an early indication that she recognizes something about the power of "music as the antidote to death" (180).

Unlike her father's folk songs that put children to sleep with the myth of the "docile Negro," Louis-Gabriel's rendition of the jazz standard "awaken[s]" Angela out of passivity and produces "the shock of healing" (*LS* 173). Siméa's Creole language teacher suggests that compared to the *doudouiste* lullabies of the drowned father, "I think it was your jazz there that excited her too much" (187). Angela affirms her recognition of the power of Louis-Gabriel's work by presenting him with the broken halves of the instrument: "In her hoarse voice, coming up from the depths of the waters, she lets two words escape from her throat like the debris of a shipwreck: *Pélamanli/Pélamanlou*" (193). In offering the jazzman the doubled and broken word and the two halves of the broken ebony, Angela symbolically offers her father's missing, broken body for the musician to reassemble. In keeping with the salutary role of improvisatory black music and musicians throughout the novel and Hawkins's musical balm for dismembered bodies in Brathwaite's poem, already Angela's gesture reveals her understanding that healing is forestalled until the "pieces of dead wood" can be made whole again. But rather than reassemble the *broken* clarinet, Louis-Gabriel instead "assembles [Siméa's] father's clarinet as an incredulous Angela watches him. . . . The first notes have a hard time coming forth from the cold instrument; he blows one very soft long breath to warm up the ebony without making the high notes squeak" (194).

The magic of Louis-Gabriel's work here is in recognizing that, unlike Siméa's body, figuratively re-membered when she hears Hawkins's song, Angela's father's broken body, lost in the Caribbean Sea, can never be restored. Indeed, even if one were to retrieve and reassemble all the fragments of the 9/11 dead or as in *Zong!* to locate and surface the bodies of Africans drowned in the Atlantic, there is no current technology to bring them back to life. Louis-Gabriel must use his artistry to improvise a *different* body to replace the missing one and to awaken the voice from the cold ebony. I want to draw attention to the fact that this awakened voice is not the drowned father's but Angela's. If trauma theory posits the emergence of the voice from the secondary wound—not the violence that initiated the trauma but the shattering that accompanies its recollection and narration (Caruth 3)—here Maximin suggests that even as the *physical* injury impacts the father, the *psychological* injury is Angela's. It is therefore Angela, not the father, whose trauma must be attended to by the musician.

The doubling of clarinets and bodies also echoes Brathwaite's use of the expression "body body bodies" to describe the way that violent trauma, such as the World Trade Center explosion, fragments the body into multiple units. It is also reminiscent of the communal experience of embodied trauma and ultimately of the need for a communal rather than individual approach to defeating the Armor'd Fishes that trouble the waters of Caribbean history. The communal nature of black brokenness is reflected in the positioning of the improvising soloist in relation to the rest of the group. *Lone Sun* shows how talented individual jazzmen enable the working through of not just individual but collective trauma, effectively linking individual broken bodies to each other to create a collective record of colonial violence. Angela intuits that through "Body and Soul" the jazzman bears witness to the brokenness of black minds and bodies. Louis-Gabriel's assembly of the replacement ebony body also presages how Marie-Gábriel's body, emerging from Siméa's own at birth, replaces the irretrievable body of the aerated fetus: a whole body for a broken one.[14]

In addition to revealing its capacity to re-member broken bodies, *Lone Sun* draws on improvisation's unique properties to reawaken and consolidate Siméa's racial and cultural memory so that she can return to her native land. Contrary to popular usage, musical improvisation is not a matter of "picking notes out of thin air"; rather, it results from years of training, immersion, and practice, of repetition, mimicry, and precision that are not jettisoned but audibly sublimated during the performance (Berliner 1). Improvisation is extemporized commentary, invention, and revision; it is also a performative dialogue with and departure from what has gone before. Given jazz's origins in oral-dominant subcultures, the entire performance relies on musicians learning and performing an arrangement from memory and highlights "the paradox of the (intentional) forgetting" of the archives of the performative vocabulary (Brandstetter 128). The band lays out the theme at the beginning of the performance and then successive soloists take turns riffing on and teasing out the theme in sonic flights. For Brathwaite, "Each successful improvisation is a true creation and is an expression not only of the individual artist or artists, but of the *group* of which the artists are part" (*Roots* 57). Jazz improvisation thus affords numerous multidirectional mnemonic threads—remembering the individual performer's place in sonic space and time in relation to the group, engaging in the conversation with other improvising instruments and with previous iterations of the standard, and calling on sonic memories and song fragments from the entire repertoire of African diaspora and Euro-American songs and sounds in an ever-widening field of signification.[15]

Part of the aesthetic pleasure a jazz listener experiences is the anticipated challenge to her auditory memory as the skilled jazz musician overwrites previous mental recordings of a song with each new act of improvisation, even if the auditor has heard that particular song before. This is true particularly in the age of recording and radio, when fixed recordings of performances reinscribe sound events as long-term memories that we can retrieve and replay with fidelity. Jazz has now been hailed as high art precisely because it relies on sophisticated memory recall on the part of listeners and performers. Heard music becomes encoded in long-term memories through a process of repeated exposure to the stimulus that allows for its movement from short-term memory for immediate recollection to storage in the annals of our unconscious for embedding into our knowledge systems (Snyder 72, 23). It is from the storehouse of long-term memories that listeners "recognize" and "understand" music as entire pieces or genres and from whence musicians derive the tools to improvise even without prior rehearsal.

Hawkins's improvisation reconnects Siméa to her racial and cultural memory and activates a musical *décalage*, to use Brent Hayes Edwards's term (13–15)—a sonic lag that resuscitates her repressed Guadeloupean "yesterday," as it does for the speaker of Damas's "Limbé." This belated resurgence of "yesterday" highlights the reverb that imbues most African diaspora music forms with their seemingly anachronistic notions of time and temporality.[16] Connecting to Hawkins's "warmed-up ebony clarinet," she experiences a "renaissance" that empowers her to resist the allure of whiteness and Frenchness, represented in the novel by Paul Éluard's *Capitale de la douleur*, which she rejects in favor of Césaire's *Cahier* (*LS* 142). Her reawakened memory inspires her to effectively reject the fragmentation she experiences in Paris, her own "capital of pain," to instead "return to [her] native land" to reconnect with the Creole culture her assimilated upbringing encouraged her to suppress and disavow—the original source of her psychic brokenness.

Although Nick Nesbitt reads the novel as drawing on free jazz's relationship to the American civil rights movement and thus makes a parallel between musical dissonance and political dissidence, I want to emphasize that Hawkins's "Body and Soul" never soundtracks the dissidence movement. Rather, the performance of the song inspires and replays the memory of Siméa's journey from *disiecta membra* to whole body and soul, from *blanchie* (whitened) to embracing her broken ebony body, and from translating what she calls "Harlemican" male poetry in Paris to interrogating Caribbean feminist texts back home in Guadeloupe. The subsequent section of the novel, "Mother's Song," set in World War II–era Guadeloupe, recounts her participation in the independence movement alongside a group of Antillean dissidents agitating both in writing and in political action.[17] But as I show in the next section, the novel does not merely drop jazz into the Caribbean space; even as it shows the jazz standard's almost universal appeal for and impact on traumatized black women, it also foregrounds how the dissidents' quest for a political model that will lend itself to large-scale cultural awakening requires jazz's (re)creolization. For both Louis-Gabriel and Siméa, African American jazz not only models liberatory and revolutionary poetics but also leads to the realization that these already existed in some form in Guadeloupean culture. Transnational jazz functions as the route to Caribbean cultural remembering; it leads physically and psychologically ex-isled Antilleans back to their native land, the site of their memories—back to Creoleness and to their own folk culture, particularly gwoka, which was still, at the time of Maximin's writing, folkloric music. Thanks to jazz's re-membering of devastated or dead bodies, the characters reconnect to the gwoka drums that hold the power to create new bodies and lives.

Gwoka: Remembering *Créolité*

Whereas in Paris it is male music and writing that inspires female rememory and healing, Siméa's story shifts to Guadeloupe as the novel opens out to a more explicit feminist and Creole perspective. Siméa's preliminary healing empowers her to not only participate in the dissident movement but partner with and inspire the awakening of male musicians. Louis-Gabriel is politically green when Angela's break occasions his meeting Siméa. Wrongheaded and idealistic, he thinks music should be free but not in any way that relates to any "big political idea" (*LS* 170), and he thinks Hearn's stories are just meaningless tales. However, his instinctual improvisation at the Carnival ball becomes enriched by his encounter with the newly re-membered Siméa. Beyond Louis-Gabriel's role in Angela's working through, the novel takes pains to show Angela's and Siméa's effect in awakening *his* memory: reading Siméa's critique of Suzanne Césaire scribbled in the margins of *Tropiques* inspires his rememory of his mother's black feminist Creole storytelling practices (191–192). Siméa's marginalia and Angela's insistence that Louis-Gabriel perform the miracle of physical re-membering nudge him forward from a talented jazzman to an emancipatory Creole musician who masters the combined art of Damasian dissidence and Hawkins-like healing.

Armed with Siméa's advocacy for folk culture as the site of resistance and his foremothers' Creole storytelling practice, Louis-Gabriel improvises a rememory of the Pélamanlou tale that turns on the trick of the twins (*LS* 195), a motif that runs throughout the novel in the form of the carnivalesque double. Her own name doubled as both Marie-Gabriel's and Adrien's mothers', Siméa also seems to be a fictionalization of Suzanne Césaire.[18] There are two fictional Angelas, two pairs of twins named Jonathan and Georges, two Gertys, several Louis and Gabriels, and various reassemblages of their names in Marie-Gabriel's family tree, and this is not counting their proliferation in the two subsequent novels that, with *Lone Sun*, constitute a single narrative of Marie-Gabriel's life.[19] Fictional characters also rub against both their historical doubles and historical figures, from Anaïs Nin to Richard Wright. More to the point, in response to "the invasion of Vichy's armored-fish battleships [that] transformed Martinique and Guadeloupe into two old-fashioned plantations" (149–150), Maximin's Guadeloupean characters are almost all fictional doubles of Martinican dissidents, a technique that frames the two islands as twins. Early in *Lone Sun*, the characters realize that they are connected to each other through the act of writing despite the seemingly *isolé* (isolated) nature of islands (12). The motif of the twins in *Lone Sun*, particularly as it evokes both male-female alliances and what Daniel Brant sees as "cross-island solidarity in the face of cataclysm" (221), foregrounds *liyannaj* in order to bypass the limits of isolation and individual heroism in favor of a collaborative effort. As Bonilla has explained, Guadeloupean dissidents since the 1970s have promoted certain Creole forms as alternatives to both French domination and the models of sovereignty and nationalism practiced in neighboring states. Guadeloupean activists have reframed sovereignty in the wake of departmentalization and in keen observation of how independence in the rest of the Caribbean has not yielded the freedoms from Euro-American hegemony that the postcolonial movements envisioned. *Liyannaj*, one of these "native categories," "evokes a new model of community and collective possibility outside of the traditional categories of citizenship and nation" (Bonilla 152, 177).

It is this spirit of *liyannaj* that animates Louis-Gabriel's version of the Hearn tale. With Creole trickery, music, and a doubled body, Pélamanli and Pélamanlou—their names differing where they join like the shards of the broken clarinet—outwit the beast, itself multiple with its seven heads. When one twin is tired and would be conquered as in the original version, the other takes over, leading to an endless musical performance that exhausts the beast to death (*LS* 196). In "Hawk's Last Body and Soul," Brathwaite also turns to the trope of twins; he inserts the inky serrated glyph of two black children holding hands and footnotes a directive for the performance of the piece to include "two murals corresponding in spirit to the *marassa* (twins) of the twin towers of the World Trade Center. (1) of sound . . . and (2) [of] names of the beloved dead. . . . [to allow] this double column of the ancestors [to] occur" (*Born to Slow Horses* 110, 115). Mirroring Brathwaite's sense that being doubled and twinned is a kind of spiritual reinforcement in the face of embodied violence, Louis-Gabriel tells Siméa that the magic of the twins "was the best thing I could find on the spur of the moment to kill the nasty seven-headed beast in your little girl's mind . . . According to what I read a few minutes ago in your *Tropiques* . . . tales are our prophecy of a better future" (*LS* 196). The "better future" than one where oppressive systems represented by the fabular Armor'd Fish thrive is one in which the beast "vomit[s] out all the children it had swallowed . . . all those children who had been waiting to be saved by a human being generous enough to carry two hearts in a single body" (196). Armed with both Caribbean Creole and African American jazz practices, Louis-Gabriel is that human being. He not only saves the twins but, by overcoming the beast, also restores to life numerous other children. Bodies multiply: from singular body to twinned flute-playing bodies, to innumerable children's resurrected bodies in a further reprise of Damas's culture-reviving hiccup and Siméa's cultural upchuck that clears the path for her Creole identity to reemerge. Unlike with Hawkins's "Body and Soul," however, these bodies retrieved via Creole improvisation are living rather than dead and are retrieved whole rather than fragmented or even re-membered.

Although its appearance in the novel seems fleeting, gwoka is central not only to Siméa's bodily restoration but also to Maximin's thesis of an emancipatory, collaborative, Creole literary aesthetic. *Gwoka* (alternately *gros-ka*), from the Creole term for "big drum," refers to a set dance centered on multivocal responsorial drumming and singing. It likely derives from West African drumming traditions—possibly with some influences from the French quadrille—that survived the Middle Passage and was practiced during slavery in the rural hinterlands of Basse-Terre, the lower half of mainland Guadeloupe.[20] Since emancipation, the practice has continued as popular entertainment among rural cane field workers, who answer the call of the drums and gather in a hidden location where they form circles to play music and dance away their weekly cares. Traditional gwoka is performed during outdoor gatherings called *swaré léwòz*, or simply *léwòz*, also simultaneously the general term for all gwoka rhythms and one of its seven rhythms. A typical gwoka ensemble is comprised of three barrel-shaped drums: a high-pitched *makè* responsible for improvisation and two low-pitched *boula* that play the rhythmic ostinati from a stock of traditional rhythms. Each of these seven rhythms has specific meanings and accompanying dance styles and thus requires deep training and mastery. During the *léwòz*, the *chantè*, or lead singer, raises a song in a key and tempo of his choice, and the *repondè*, or chorus, arranged in a semicircle around the drummers, engages him in call-and-response; after a couple bars, the *makè* sets the tempo and drumming style for the two *boularyen* to follow. Soon, the three drummers all play in tandem, and any one of the performers can break off in an improvised solo. The pinnacle of each performance is when a dancer enters the circle and engages the *makè* in a two-way improvisation, united by the rhythm and intense eye contact until one of them gives the signal to break off. This can go on and on as new dancers take the floor to continue the "conversation."

For many practitioners and proponents, gwoka is a record of collective African memory suppressed in favor of French assimilation. Local priest and gwoka advocate Chérubin Célèste has connected the repression of gwoka during French colonization and departmentalization with the repression of Creole language and culture, of mother tongue as of mother Africa (*Gwoka* 30:45–31:40). Dominique Cyrille has also traced how in the postemancipation period, newly freed Guadeloupeans rejected the "crude," "shameful," and "African" drum dances of black peasants in favor of European-derived music and dances like the biguine and the quadrille ("Sa Ki Ta Nou" 224). Introduced by French planters in the eighteenth and nineteenth centuries, the quadrille signaled urbanity, gentility, and the embodied embrace of assimilation for those lighter-skinned Guadeloupeans who could mimic in their bodies and steps the airs and bodily markers of Frenchness by performing the quadrille "just as it is done at court." She notes that many Antilleans viewed respectability as "expressed in the restrained movements of the hips and lower torso, which seemed to play no part in the European court dances" ("Creole Quadrilles" 205). In its associations with the *vyè nèg*, "old Negro," and "pure" blackness, gwoka thus represents resistance in musical form, the survival and persistence of the suppressed and disavowed—all that must be reclaimed and re-membered to scaffold a truly emancipated nation.

It is unsurprising, then, that following the 1967 protest against French state violence and the renewed agitations for independence described in the novel's present-tense frame, Guadeloupe's nationalist movement—spearheaded by the GONG (Groupe d'Organisation Nationale de la Guadeloupe) in concert with the AGEG (l'Association Générale des Étudiants Guadeloupéens)—co-opted gwoka as an alternative to French culture and advocated for gwoka's revitalization and modernization as part of their platform for a national identity. These separatist organizations advocated the abandonment of French music and culture and the embrace of gwoka and Creole language as the foundations of a subaltern, oppositional national culture. The formerly denigrated gwoka became the sonic marker of Guadeloupean national identity,[21] echoing Brathwaite's definition of creolization as a marker of Caribbean cultural autonomy. In its updated articulation as *gwoka modènn* (modern gwoka), which combines traditional *ka* drums with jazz instruments, gwoka becomes operationalized to revivify national Creole-centered culture: Creole is taught in schools, institutes of dance transmit and modernize gwoka dance steps, and Père Célèste himself even makes it central to his practice to conduct Catholic communion to the sound of gwoka drumming and singing in Creole (*Gwoka* 25:48). The once repressed, hidden, and hill-bound gwoka music is now played at all kinds of occasions: at parties, at national events, at funeral wakes, and even during strikes, the latter underscoring its position as the soundtrack of resistance against systemic injustice and oppression. This latter point is brought into relief in the predepartmentalization dissidence section of *Lone Sun* when gwoka is played in the town square where Siméa's friend Toussaint uses the cover of Carnival and robber talk to shout words of revolt and to weaponize Damas's already explosive poetry by wrapping stones in pages torn from *Pigments* and throwing them at both colonizer and colonized (202–203).

It is thus noteworthy that the turn to gwoka in the novel soundtracks Siméa's own turn to Creole, a feminist negritude, and the nationalist movement. As she argues in her margin critique of the writings of the *Tropiques* group and in a passage that reads almost verbatim like the later treatise of the *Créolistes*, true liberation comes when Antilleans reject assimilation—especially in the insidious forms of culture and ideology—and forge thoroughly Creole cultural and identitarian models even as "we adapt, not adopt" foreign models (*LS* 191, 197). This reflects the trajectory of identitarian discourse in the Antilles, from the Africanist orientation of negritude, a "true" racial consciousness that replaces a French-oriented false consciousness, to the Caribbean orientation of *créolité* and *antillanité* (Caribbeanness), rooted and grounded in a consciousness of place.[22] It also reflects Siméa's own journey, beginning with her racial awakening in Paris that disconnects her from assimilation and reconnects her to her black body, native land, language, and culture. Even further, it anticipates the novel's movement from jazz to gwoka, then to an adaptation—not a mere adoption—of jazz to the local reality.

At this stage in the novel, gwoka and jazz are still separate music forms; the one is considered "old Negro" music of the mountains and the preliterate black masses, and the other is the privileged choice for cosmopolitan New Negro Guadeloupeans. But Jerome Camal has highlighted how the positioning of gwoka as a pure and authentic alternative to assimilation runs contrary to Glissant's relational definition of creolization and in contrast to the type of transnational mutual interplay that I have been describing here.[23] Indeed, the novel's and the music's transnational influences show an alignment with Glissant's notion of Creole identity as an open specificity rather than the ethnonationalism toward which the dissidents tended. Although this is mostly suppressed in the later romance of the nation, Gérard Lockel, whose 1969 treatise on *gwoka modènn* influenced many nationalists and musicians in their views on gwoka, came to an awareness of the liberatory potential of traditional gwoka during his time as a jazz guitarist in Paris in the 1950s, and he incorporated many jazz instruments and compositional elements into the music (Camal, "DestiNation" 222–223).

In the same way that jazz's black sonic modernity awakens the poetic consciousness of Antilleans like Brathwaite and the fictional Siméa, so too did Lockel find in jazz a model for what *gwoka traditionnel* could become, thus providing him and the nationalism movement with the soundtrack to and symbol for their political ends. In fact, Siméa's journey—from an assimilated Guadeloupean student in Paris, to one who gains racial and cultural awareness via African American jazz, then returns to Guadeloupe during the separatist movement to influence the modernization of gwoka—mirrors Lockel's trajectory some thirty years later. In keeping with the novel's feminization of the nationalist narrative, however, instead of the later AGEG and the official underground student movements in Paris, Siméa's burgeoning solidarity is with a fellow female Antillean student, her "sister-friend" Gerty—a fictional double of the feminist lawyer who represented the Guadeloupean communist party (PCG) in the French National Assembly from 1946 to 1951. Further, the constant interplay between Guadeloupean and African American, and between Guadeloupean and Martinican, foregrounds a *créolité* that is both localized in Guadeloupe and formed by transnational flows of peoples and culture.

There are numerous similarities between traditional gwoka and jazz as (alter) native music forms. Both are rooted in improvisation and a call-and-response format, and both are protest idioms born of anticolonial resistance during slavery. Jazz's modernist and postmodern reworking of black cultural memory into an assertion of being and (non)belonging is the record of the African American quest for nationalism and citizenship within a free nation. With its roots in the Caribbean slave plantations and maroon hills, gwoka reawakens collective, embodied black cultural memory and the emancipatory resistance of the African drums, and it sounds out the Guadeloupean quest for citizenship within and independence from France. Both jazz and gwoka aim to counteract silencing and erasure by giving expression to black suffering and selfhood. Both gwoka and jazz inherit and transmit what Nesbitt calls "the determinate experience of the suffering, unfree individual in society within the construct of an equally real and actual creative freedom" (155). The complex political condition of the Caribbean DOMs means that they are not quite emancipated and not independent, leading to what Glissant saw as a type of neurosis (*Caribbean Discourse* 65). For Antilleans, musical expressions of liberation could not wait for actual independence but would be its engine.

Both history and the novel reveal that it is when the music descends from the *morne* (rural hills) and comes into contact with other cultural and political forces that its potential for a modern project of nation-building can be realized. But although *gwoka modènn* is the music of the historical dissidence movement of the 1970s and 1980s, the novel always refers to traditional gwoka; it is to the rhythm of the *tambour-ka* that the novel opens. Despite writing at the time of gwoka's modernization, Maximin apparently did not yet see traditional gwoka as a viable Caribbean literary model, in the same way that Brathwaite initially advocated for a jazz aesthetic while calypso, ska, and early reggae were already extant. Instead, Maximin invests his radical energies in a *liyannaj* of *vyè nèg* local music and diasporic New Negro music as the apotheosis of political and cultural revolution. This fusion of "free-jazz delirium and the well-structured rhythms of the gros-ka drum" (*LS* 281) has been called "jazz-ka" by contemporary musicians. Albums like David Murray's *Gwotet* and Jacques Schwarz-Bart's *Soné-Ka-Là* attempt a hybrid jazz-ka sensibility—neither an exoticizing of jazz through dabbling in Caribbean music forms nor a modernization of Caribbean music through sonic interactions with jazz but a thinking together of the synergies and shared projects of both jazz and gwoka that transforms them both in the process. In other words, far from privileging jazz, *Lone Sun* in fact performs a *liyannaj* between jazz and gwoka in the same way that it proffers a strategic alliance between black men and women, and Guadeloupe and Martinique, in order to be able to confront powerful enemies as a stronger unit.

At an impromptu *léwòz*, Louis-Gabriel has the occasion to ground jazz in the gwoka practice from which his and Siméa's "civilized childhood" marooned them and they are now "rediscover[ing] together" (*LS* 211). The "nourishing soil" of Siméa's and Louis-Gabriel's native land provides the ground and grounding that inspires all the gwoka performers: the *chantè* goes "into an endless stretch of improvisations" (210) while the lead drum breaks into "ardent solos" that sound out "an improvised élan of freedom" (211). Notice that already, before the introduction of Louis-Gabriel's jazz clarinet, these *vyè nèg* gwoka performers from the rural hinterlands of Basse-Terre are performing amazing feats of improvisation, dispelling the assumption that it is the meeting of jazz clarinet and gwoka drums that enables Louis-Gabriel "to infuse Caribbean music with some of the improvisational élan of jazz" (Munro 179). As this scene reveals, traditional gwoka is always already improvisational music; these peasant singers, drummers, and dancers are all improvising with their voices, bodies, and drums in a performance of African cultural memory.

Back in the Cabana club in Paris, Siméa, a drummer in her own right, had conceived of the conga drum as having a body, heart, lungs, and skin; now, witnessing this gwoka *léwòz* session, she describes the *makè*'s drum as "plant and animal united in skin, chords, and body" (*LS* 211)—which is apt considering the drum's origins from the skin of animals, where the animal's body has to be mutilated to produce the drum's membrane or head. In his poem "The Making of the Drum" (*Arrivants* 94–97), Brathwaite describes how the craftsman must do violence to—dis-member and destroy—the goat to produce this drum that is vital to the survival of the African's voice in diaspora. For Brathwaite, the drum's voice derives from violence and death. It is thus doubly significant that the gwoka performance transitions from human voice to the voice of the drum, as the instrument sounds out missing black voices and testifies about traumatized black bodies. The relationship between body and drum sheds light on why this music is so crucial to the project of restoring women's traumatized bodies and psyches. Just as the broken ebony clarinet both testifies to Angela's psychic brokenness and is the key to her re-membering, so too the drum created by embodied violence is central to African diaspora embodied rememory. Louis-Gabriel himself notes that "one good beat on [the] skin [of Siméa's conga] is enough to bear witness to your combats with a force that revitalizes the memory of conch shells'" (*LS* 182). He thus illuminates the role of the drum in performing racial memory and providing alternate historiography and archives.

Whereas in both Brathwaite and *Lone Sun*, jazz is used to re-member but not reanimate fragmented and dead bodies, Wil Cartey's claim that the drum is able to "resurrect memories" and "has the power to infuse vitality and movement into lifeless form" (21) suggests that gwoka's power stems from its ability, rooted in African drum practices, to give life to the lifeless, resurrecting not only memory but dis-membered bodies. This is perhaps why the *bouyanjel* gwoka rhythm is played during wakes, signaling the faith that gwoka affords a re-membering after death and calls to mind the belief during and after slavery that those who die in the New World would live again upon transportation back to Africa. In his reading of Brathwaite's "Atumpan," Kofi Anyidoho suggests that "the single drumbeat is often an echo of the past, a record of the present, a dream of the future. It activates the memory of humankind and calls up visions of future time" (49). The ability of the gwoka drums to (re)activate memory so as to inspire present and future realities is akin to what Rastafarian drumming and Garveyist ideology lend to roots reggae, which I discuss in the next chapter. Gwoka drumming is thus intricately connected to a liberationist ideology rooted in a vision of a black future, and for the islands of the French Antilles, the possibilities awakened by a rememory of the past scaffold realities not yet in existence.

Lone Sun nevertheless demonstrates that drumming in itself is not necessarily emancipatory. Before meeting Louis-Gabriel, Siméa translates a Hearn fable about the attempts by the Lawd to steal the drum, "the sole possession of 'niggers'" (*LS* 162). In Hearn's figuration, the folk drum can be co-opted to disarm black folk by putting them to sleep so they can be physically attacked by the likes of Armor'd Fish; however, when Louis-Gabriel integrates it into his retelling of the Pélamanlou tale, he reorients the role of music and drumming in service of liberation from oppression. It is in dancing, which connects the drum to the body in another way, that this liberation is often, if temporarily, enacted. Most black music forms are tied to dancing, and dance—the embodied response to music—is often a means of performing identity and resisting the constraints of enslavement in its historical and contemporary articulations. That the contestation of French assimilation takes place through dance music aligns with the fact that "dance was meant to express what the French called '*bon goût*,' or refined taste" (Cyrille, "Creole Quadrilles" 196). As such, when newly freed and enslaved peoples learned and practiced the French court dances, *contredanse* and quadrille, they subverted the hierarchical system of social and racial difference on which the colonial system in the Antilles relied. Yvonne Daniel has likewise argued that "within Caribbean popular dance, liberation is personal; it is felt, experienced, stored, and remembered bodily. Dancers' . . . daily struggles are muted temporarily and replaced by body freedom and rhythmic connectedness" (106–107). The freedom to and practice of dance are thus integrally connected to asserting and reclaiming bodily integrity for African diaspora peoples whose bodies have often borne the marks of physical trauma. Dance is both embodied freedom and embodied memory.

In response to the improvisational virtuosity of the *makè* during the *léwòz* that Louis-Gabriel and Siméa are witnessing, a young boy starts to engage the drummer in a responsorial dance (*LS* 211). The little boy's "violently syncopated steps" describe the gwoka dance style called the *bigidi*, which I consider a type of "break" dancing—not the popular dance of the 1980s but a dance style defined as much by its breaks as its flow, dancing that features stops, pauses, staggers, stutters, and other fancy footwork. The "violently syncopated steps" of the bigidi testify to the fact that these dancing black bodies are precisely not free; this is how one dances when one's feet are shackled, when one's body is racked by pain, when one's body is laden by burdens visible and invisible. At the same time, with its roots in temporary reprieve from slave labor, dancing in this way is an assertion of a future freedom and a protest: *despite my present condition, I will dance.* It is not surprising, then, that many gwoka rhythms and dance styles refer to liberation amid suffering; Konket claims that the *toumblak* expresses the breaking of chains, while the *léwòz* expresses the sweat and misery of enslavement, "the suffering of the human flesh" (*Gwoka* 6:00–6:20).

The relationship between black dancing, freedom, and futurity explains the popularity of social dancing across the Caribbean and the diaspora, particularly among the poor and oppressed—the *passa passa* street dances in the ghettos of Kingston, where, to the chagrin of the middle and upper classes, the black, the unemployed, the disenfranchised, and the underclass leave behind their troubles—and often young children—and invest thousands of dollars in weaves, wigs, and shiny outfits to dance the night away (Stanley Niaah 82). The extensive focus on the black underclass cramming into Jazz-era clubs at night to dance and find sexual partners in *Home to Harlem*, a jazz novel by Jamaican cosmopolitan Claude McKay, caused untold chagrin to respectability-conscious Du Bois, who famously wanted to take a bath after reading the novel (202). But for McKay, the ability and insistence of black folk to dance while suffering and oppressed was a way to assert their humanity, and this is central to the renaissance of all black folk, not just Du Boisian "Talented Tenth" types. In fact, McKay overturns the notion that the New Negro must necessarily be the reading Negro like his bookish character Ray, who repudiates his body in favor of cultivating his mind and anticipates the way that the black middle class would turn jazz into cerebral music. For McKay, the black revolution would be embodied.

Given gwoka's preservation of the ancestral memory of the submerged African voice and its grounding in Creole language and culture, Louis-Gabriel's encounter with rooted gwoka, I argue, connects him to the drum's primal voice and ancestral body as well as to Siméa's body. At this impromptu *léwòz*, Louis-Gabriel, who has been searching for a way to express freedom in his music, is "so moved" by the virtuosity of the improvisational gwoka drumming, singing, and dancing that he takes up an alto saxophone and "starts to improvise a dizzying suite of calls in rhythm with the beating hearts of earth and drummers, like a bird flying over a forest . . . music that he carries unawares, into [Siméa's] open throat and body" (*LS* 211). Maximin underscores the revolutionary nature of Louis-Gabriel's performance by having Siméa laud his music shortly thereafter in the midst of her extended critique of Antillean identity and history, to which their fellow dissident Toussaint replies, "You translate Damas into English, I translate him into Creole. But Gaby plays him on the saxophone! And I don't know anything more revolutionary than his music" (226). The freedom and revolution that their generation would unsuccessfully fight and die for are awakened and performed in Louis-Gabriel's hybrid jazz-ka improvisation, highlighting the shared project of both music forms.

Having moved mother, song, and story to Guadeloupean soil and to the context of literary, musical, and political dissidence and the quest for autonomy, Maximin thus (re)creolizes Hawkins's African American jazz, infusing it with gwoka to continue the work of racial memory and gendered re-membering begun by listening to jazz in Paris. Further, if gwoka is "the soul of Guadeloupe," as the subtitle of 1995 documentary *Gwoka* proposes, then this removes the temptation to privilege jazz as re-membering the soul while gwoka re-members the body. Gwoka, like jazz, re-members *both* body and soul. Gwoka provides a crucial connection to the body—the body of the goat that must be dismembered to make the drums, which when beaten, call the human body to dance. But since to dance is to perform memory, gwoka simultaneously re-members the soul. Undercutting any temptation to imagine improvisation and dissidence as the sole or privileged purview of jazz, I emphasize that it is when jazz moves to Guadeloupe and interfaces with Creole music and storytelling practices that we see the fullness of the novel's quest for a revolutionary poetics. The novel's trajectory mirrors how during the dissidence movement of the 1970s and 1980s, transnational Guadeloupean students and militants in Paris took jazz's inspiration to rethink local music and politics; however, in order to port to the artistic and political specificity of the Caribbean, jazz, like the historical militants and the novel's characters, has to (re)turn to the Caribbean. The novel, characters, and phonotopes thus move from diasporic to local, with jazz providing the routes to Guadeloupean nationalism and gwoka providing a grounding in Guadeloupean memory and specificity.

While Munro reads the novel as foregrounding an "idea of a transnational community of musicians, singer and dancers" and "a means of bypassing nationalism, and of not having to belong to one single country" (181), I argue that the arc of the novel precisely reorients the transnational characters *to* nation and nationalism. The diasporic is a route to the local, a placeholder as it were, until the discovery or invention of a comparative local *poétique* or *politique*, in the same way that jazz provided Brathwaite a diasporic model that would in time orient him back to "calypso, to reggae, to our folk music" (qtd. in Francis, "Travelling Miles" 149). Louis-Gabriel's later rootless travels and interactions with Afro-Caribbean and African American musicians, leftist writers, and civil rights activists occur partly because his, Siméa's, and Toussaint's agitation for a free Guadeloupean nation in the 1940s fails. He notably dies in the plane explosion above Guadeloupe, as if history and the narrative engine must reconcile him to his native land. As such, the novel's reorientation to gwoka, Creoleness, and Guadeloupe reveals that for the characters, as for Brathwaite before them, jazz is merely the model, and—given the repression and denigration of Afro-Caribbean folk culture in the pursuit of respectability—the form that is readily available to cosmopolitan Antilleans. Instead of being merely ported to the Caribbean, jazz functions as a portal back to Caribbean memory and poetics, resuscitating the memory of the local and providing a model for the transformation of the local into a modern form for an eventual free modern nation. Without the recovery of the repressed Creole language and culture signaled by gwoka, however, the project of re-membering is at best incomplete and provisional.

Echoing the *liyannaj* between jazz and gwoka and anticipating the imbrication of women's sexual pleasure and cultural memory discussed in the next chapter, the collaborative nature of Siméa's and Louis-Gabriel's lovemaking that follows the inspired musical intercourse of the *léwòz* calls to mind another connection to gwoka and dancing. While gwoka performances are male dominated (Managan 93–95), it is most often in singing and dancing that women traditionally participate in the *léwòz*—but in a role that is integral to the performance; at the heart of the *léwòz* is the duet, the embodied and synchronized dialogue between male *makè* and female dancer. Mirroring the integrated jazz-ka and the intergender collaboration between drummer and *danseuse*, beyond merely passive listening and active dancing, Louis-Gabriel enables Siméa to take a joint and active role in her own restoration. The repetition of the phrase "body and soul" and their entangled body parts mark the unraveling of the components of Siméa's being only to have them reassembled in the couple's bodily union.

Whereas the volcano symbolizes impotent male explosions and revolutions, the fusion of Louis-Gabriel's and Siméa's bodies and souls privileges both jouissance and feminine "implosure" as the site and source of radical poetics and politics without sidelining men. The one is defined as female orgasm and bodily pleasure oriented inward rather than outward, while the other is Brathwaite's neologism for "a firm but subtile feeding to the stem of origins" (*Contradictory Omens* 61). That Siméa's story and Marie-Gabriel's novel culminate in Siméa's jouissance becomes even more significant in this light, especially as it follows on the heels of gwoka drumming and dancing. In *Lone Sun*, both dancing and sex provide bodily enjoyment, particularly for women. Siméa's attunement to the sensuality of Hawkins's saxophone, which she refers to as "his . . . big deep-voiced sex" (*LS* 141), calls attention to what Nesbitt refers to as the libidinal pleasure of jazz (50). Rather than essentialism, however, I consider the libidinal as crucial to Siméa's full revitalization as woman, mother, and sexual being. For women for whom bodily pleasure was never in view—black women who are hypersexualized while constrained by respectability politics—reconnecting to both body and soul is a vital project.[24] If listening and dancing to "Body and Soul" begins the work of reconnecting her to the sexuality, womanness, and motherhood that were violated by her abortion, it is in her sexual union with Louis-Gabriel, which connects them both to her womb memory (*LS* 239), that her restoration and re-membering is completed.

In the same way that jazz-ka *liyannaj* foregrounds the rememory of a collaborative, Creole, and feminist practice drawn from foremothers like Ti-Carole, so too the uniting of male and female bodies and souls is reminiscent of Louis-Gabriel's suturing of the halves of the broken ebony clarinet, transmuting them from cold to warm, from broken to whole. Although the union of their two bodies and the shared bodily pleasure enables Siméa to fall asleep fully "remembered" (*LS* 251), evincing the full restoration of her psychic integrity, her "remembering" does not ensure her physical survival; the original wound of her punctured womb already guarantees her future postpartum death. Ultimately, then, Maximin goes beyond—or perhaps retreats from—both the masculinist traditions of political heroism and jazz exceptionalism and the radical feminism of *l'écriture féminine*. Neither solitary self-pleasuring nor a female- and lip-centered plurality, this passage emphasizes the synthesis of male and female bodies, twinned, like the interlocked male drummer and the female dancer, like Pelanmanli and -lou. Maximin's vision of a revolutionary poetics and politics is neither the male-centered action of the failed 1802 Delgrès historical revolt nor the tragic failure of Toussaint's fictional one but one that incorporates newly re-membered women's voices, bodies, and stories. Likewise, instead of the lone male jazz soloist, the return to native land means resuscitating the memory and practice of women as repositories of Creole culture; the masterful solos of Louis-Gabriel and Hawkins work in tandem with the revelation of women as master drummers and keepers of memory that is consolidated in Marie-Gabriel's project of literary remembering. It is only through male-female *liyannaj* and the male musician's awakening to mother-memory that he is able to participate in the emancipatory projects that animate the 1940s dissident movement. Maximin reorients the novel to a gwoka and Creole culture that privileges multiple bodies, collaboration, and fusion—the choral "we" of the gwoka *léwòz* party rather than the individual "I" of the jazz solo—and centers women in a feminist and ethical practice that collects and recollects all that was previously missing.

Writing as Re-membering

As the survivor of her mother's postpartum death and father's explosion, Marie-Gabriel is the revolutionary possibility in vitro—the fruit of their dissidence. It is she who inherits the revolutionary improvisational spirit of Louis-Gabriel's jazz-ka, the dissident feminist writing of her mother—the texts and records the two leave behind—and synthesizes their fragments into a creolized feminist novel that sutures its sonic and literary, French and Antillean, "Harlemican" routes and Guadeloupean roots into "some- / thing torn / and new" (Brathwaite, *Arrivants* 270). The novel's opening pages record fragments of Marie-Gabriel's writing journal, describing how she chooses the names that her own parents will bear in her fictional narrative as well as a form for her imaginative reconstruction of their lives. Her journal is written in the second person in an oddly displaced and displacing narrative subjectivity. She decides, "YOU will take care never to write I" (*LS* 11), and she sustains this stance throughout the entire novel-within-a-novel; even her recreated mother's journal is written in the second person, making Siméa the object of her own journal. In the scene where Siméa dances to "Body and Soul" and composes her journal to her "aerated" child, she does not speak her words aloud. Rather, they are rendered in either reported speech or parenthesis; Siméa is textually silent and silenced. Indeed, it is perhaps more accurate to say that Siméa's journal is actually the record of Marie-Gabriel writing *herself* into being. She is the journal's displaced and missing "I," the restored body that emerges from the objectified and shattered body of the mother, the replacement ebony body for the irretrievable body of the "aerated" child. She is the one who is born from the maternal wound that eventually takes Siméa's life.

It is significant, then, that at the moment when her parents' "bodies [are] squeezed together to bursting fusion" (*LS* 234), Marie-Gabriel's first-person narration begins to emerge and finds its full manifestation; she writes her birth into being and narrates the emergence of her living body from her mother's dying one: "my synthesis torn from your debris" (247). At the moment of twinned death-birth, Marie-Gabriel realizes that her quest was not really for the father but the mother—or, more accurately, the self: "To be able to finally say YOU and I equals us, Siméa and Marie-Gabriel, she and she equals you and me, because I found you, recognized you, situated you in this spot in my womb that was like a huge emptiness of years" (248). Situating Siméa in *her* own womb suggests that, in writing this story, Marie-Gabriel has also given birth to her own mother; the bodies of mother-child and child-mother are textualized here as "two distinct grammatical subjects which form yet a third, founded in a relation of equality." As Scharfman argues, Maximin makes himself and his text a "daughter" of the "architexts" of the Césaires, Damases, and their ilk (244, 236).[25] Marie-Gabriel effectively reverses "Siméa's Journal"; now the child journals to the dying mother and narrates for herself a present and a future indexed in the construction "I am . . . I will be" in place of her failed quest for a paternal past (*LS* 246). Like the novel's reversed chronology,[26] this reversed ontology constructs memory as reversal and reversion, undoing being in order to become reborn as more fully constituted.

The connections I have teased out between jazz and gwoka and the interconnection of rememory and remembrance highlight that recollection is not only a psychological or narrative assemblage of the fragments of memory but also an ethical project of embodied care, of putting the self and the body back together—hence the novel's deployment of the "Body and Soul" record as trope, motif, and soundtrack. *L'écriture féminine*, often used to describe Maximin's style in *Lone Sun*, is premised on the idea that "to write from the body is to re-create the world," a process that requires the writing woman to shatter and fragment master narratives (A. Jones 374), even though such an investment in essentialist notions of women's bodies as the vital energy for art seems out of sync with the evolution of Western feminism away from the foundational thinking of Cixous, Irigaray, and others. But black feminist and womanist scholars like bell hooks and Patricia Hill Collins continue to affirm the importance of embodiment and an attention to the impact of systemic oppression and violence on women's psyches and bodies and on centering the body in liberatory poetics. Embodiment is key for women working through trauma, and writing the body is both restorative for the shattered woman and central to her subversion of the phallogocentric texts and structures that traumatized her in the first place. Maximin takes this even further to show how racially marked women write their way to wholeness using a form facilitated, soundtracked, and modeled by the embodied improvisational ethos of black music. The novel thus depicts writing as re-membering, with both European language and the Western novel form serving as master narratives that need to be dis-membered, re-membered, creolized, and feminized.

In "Siméa's Journal," the chapter titles are taken from anagrams using each letter of Siméa's name; in one sense, she is being dissected, but in another, she is being re-membered by her daughter's writing. Brathwaite defines his neologism *nommo* as "the atomic core of language" and distinguishes his conception of *nam* from our English concept "name" (*Roots* 236). Like Philip, who in *Zong!* disassembles the master text of slave traders in order to resurrect and re-member the drowned Africans from its textual fragments, and Brathwaite, who disarticulates English words to re-member submerged African languages and weaponize them like Toussaint's *Pigments*-wrapped stones for a radical poetic and political possibility, in their numerous name games, Maximin's characters break and reassemble the syllables of their names into component parts, improvising new assemblages and inventing a grammar as a mechanism of self-composition. The name games index Antillean fragmentation on the one hand while also articulating the Pélamanlic doubling and multiplication of the *nam* through which identities are no longer singular, much less stable. From Siméa's dissection, the discrete sounds that (de)compose the mother can be sounded and recomposed to give birth to the daughter: mother past, daughter present. "Language," Brathwaite concludes, "may be conceived as having the power to affect life" (*Roots* 241). Inspired by the life-giving power of the gwoka drums, stripping language to its "atomic core" in order to re-member it in radical new ways allows for not just the healing of body and soul but the improvisation of new language that, Logos-like, brings light and life into being.

Notably, the mother is reborn in *Soufrières*, the sequel to *Lone Sun*, as "a living and new Siméa—born of Gerty's desire to one day have a daughter of this Siméa of Marie-Gabriel's *Siméa's Journal*—laid in a cradle next to a bed of manuscript pages, themselves written with [the ink of] as much blood, flesh, love, and ruptures as needed" (*Soufrières* 160–161, translation mine). Gerty admits that Marie-Gabriel's improvisational reconstruction of her mother's memory and narrative engenders an embodied "living" daughter. Moreover, this Siméa "living and new" is simultaneously the child and the manuscript pages produced by the labor of memory work. In the aforementioned discussion of limb deification as textual reassembly, Aleida and Jan Assmann reveal that the outcome of the recollected and re-membered body is the book: "The word 'scatter' took on a positive sound in the era of book printing, as the printing press guaranteed an entirely new form of reproduction and dissemination of literature and, along with this, helped spread truth" (94). This illuminates that textual scattering is not necessarily negative but can be a technique that allows for reproduction.[27] The motif of print reproduction corresponds with Siméa's biological reproduction. As we have seen, the explosion of bodies results in the doubling, scattering, and (re)production of texts, or in Aldo Rossi's term, the creation of a *frammento*, "a small chip which has broken out of a larger body" (qtd. in Brandstetter 106). From Louis-Gabriel's exploded body emerge the fragments of his tattered notebooks; from Louis-Gabriel and Siméa's united bodies and from their collective music and writings emerge Marie-Gabriel's body and her book, whose pages are themselves extracted and dissected to enable her to share them with Adrien, Antoine, and Eve. It is unclear from the novel whether Marie-Gabriel sends them copies or originals of her manuscript pages and writing notebook. In any case, in order to get feedback, Marie-Gabriel has to experience loss. On the flip side of the broken-off bodily and textual fragment is the concept of incorporation, with the Latinate *corps*, or body, at its root. Marie-Gabriel's project is one of re-corporating her parents, gathering and suturing their exploded bodies so that she can incorporate them into her work of literary and self-authoring. Like the revivifying memory work enabled by gwoka music, literary re-membering "undo[es] the work of death" (Cixous 883) and enables not just the resurrection and rebirth of her parents in memory as in narrative but also Marie-Gabriel to live fully.

If the remembered jazz-ka practice that leads to her parents' union and her emergence underscores the futurity of Antillean memory, Marie-Gabriel's writing practice suggests not a mere recovery of the past—a task that would be impossible as the past itself is dis-membered—but the invention of a narrative future. Since Marie-Gabriel's writing and remembering are inspired and soundtracked by "listen[ing] ten times over to every version [Antoine has] of *Body and Soul*" (*LS* 268), she is listening to different versions of the song each time. As a result, her narrative "facts" keep changing. The instability of plot points—as both Marie-Gabriel and Adrien revise and edit on the fly the very story we are reading—undoes notions of the fidelity of recall and, by extension, exposes historiography and memory work as a creative rather than a recuperative act. This mutability subverts the key advantage of the advent of recording technology; whereas the live performer's improvisation makes the song text unstable, recording fixes an instance of the performance and allows auditors to replay it the same way every time. Recording enables auditors to learn and therefore remember a particular performance with fidelity. As I argued in the previous chapter, this is the central appeal of recorded music for memory work: the auditor imagines that by musical replay she too will reexperience the past the same way every time as well.

But in the same way that improvisation reinforces and challenges memory, since each performance is both familiar and unfamiliar, likewise Marie-Gabriel's listening to different versions of the same song inhibits exact recall and constantly changes what is remembered on each relisten. In the mode of fiction, the novel renders these changeable "memories" as errors and edits; in their letters, Adrien and Marie-Gabriel recognize that they have gotten facts wrong, and the reverse chronology of the novel and the trope of receiving and sending letters means that information the reader accepted in early sections is undercut, rewritten, and revised in later sections. The focus on improvisation as a mode of memory and historiography thus foregrounds the inventedness of remembering. And if improvised memory is changeable, one retrieves not facts but the truth of experience. This approach to memory also anticipates the notion of the "version," a key aspect of Jamaican dub music that I discuss in the final chapter. In this way, Maximin sustains the tension between live and recorded music; even as he seems to displace the frame recording to privilege various live performances, he makes clear that both Louis-Gabriel and Marie-Gabriel can improvise "live" *because* they have access to recorded music.

Further, since Marie-Gabriel has no access to her mother's memories nor her father's records, her novel consists of her imagined reconstruction of their memories from her own experience. The abortive nature of Adrien's writing notebooks and novel drafts, which purport to recover and narrate unrecorded histories, reminds us of the impossibility of such a project. It is thus in Marie-Gabriel's sections that the tools for postcolonial historiography are modeled: her narrative frames the story we are reading as her own remembering—the "I" birthed from literary remembering. Yet this suggests not her own psychological retrieval of experiences she herself has had but a remembering on behalf of others. At the same time, her work does have a psychological and autobiographical effect: the impetus for her narrative work is her own present-tense crisis—grappling with her loss of her father and his records and the lingering trauma of never knowing her mother. The effect of her writing is ultimately to compose her own subjectivity from the recollection of her parents' narratives.

This chapter has explored the importance of centering women's romantic and sexual restoration in postcolonial Caribbean nation-making. It has articulated a figuration of Caribbean memory as localized in the body and rooted in the Caribbean space and a conception of remembering as a *liyannaj* between musician and audience. The next chapter shows how these themes repeat in other music forms and other parts of the Caribbean as well. In Maximin, the *liyannaj* between jazz and gwoka models for Louis-Gabriel's novelist daughter a Caribbean literary aesthetic and reframes memory work as collaborative rather than individual. Although Marie-Gabriel's writing mimics her father's jazz-ka aesthetic, she arrives at it through her mother's body, and her aesthetic must incorporate both their bodies, recollected along with the research, comments, voices, and experiences of her friends Adrien, Eve, and Antoine. By reinserting women into the narrative of negritude and placing women front and center in gwoka and the Guadeloupean independence movement, Maximin reveals that the poetics of re-membering is thus ultimately a feminist practice even when practiced by male authors and musicians. *Lone Sun* illuminates how an ethical and feminist poetics lies at the heart of truly emancipatory Caribbean musical and literary aesthetics. Such a poetics is attentive to the soundness of women's bodies as much as the soundness of historical records of the nation, even as it holds the record of the sutures and scars in view.

CHAPTER 4

Roots, Romance, Reggae

(DIS)PLACING MEMORY IN COLIN CHANNER'S *WAITING IN VAIN*

I shall return
To hear the fiddle and fife [. . .]
Stray melodies of dim remembered runes.

—Claude McKay, "I Shall Return"

I am a born Jamaican
A son of the soil [. . .]
No matter where I roam
Jamaica is my home.

—The Astronauts, "Born Jamaican"

The writings of Claude McKay offer an interesting case study into the migrant's negotiation of place and cultural memory. After migrating to the United States as a young man, McKay soon became a poster child for the Harlem Renaissance. While his ballads and poems often evoke the rural landscape of his native Jamaica, his first two novels focus on New York City and Marseille respectively; the very title of *Home to Harlem* (1928) suggests an orientation toward the metropole. Yet in *Banana Bottom* (1933), his protagonist Bita Plant returns to her rural Jamaican village and becomes rooted there. The vagrancy of the nationless black men in McKay's two previous works gives way to the rootedness of the traveled black woman. It is Bita who fulfills the promise of the speaker in "I Shall Return" who yearns to return to Jamaica "to hear the fiddle and fife / . . . Stray melodies of dim remembered runes" (*Harlem Shadows* 33). This poem's placement in the 1922 collection *Harlem Shadows* between meditations on racial oppression ("Enslaved") and immigrant nostalgia ("Flame Heart") reveals that it is because the speaker is now far from his roots and living in a hostile "White City" where the "runes" are "dim remembered" that he so intensely desires to return to Jamaica. "I Shall Return" depicts this desire for repatriation as a manifestation of diasporic crisis: the degraded artifacts of memory, the "dim remembered runes," can be recovered and reconstituted only if the speaker returns to his birthplace. McKay figures memory work as not merely a psychological process, a desire to return to a past time or an anterior self—the remembering undertaken by Scott's Theo or the nostalgia experienced by the Castillos in Hijuelos—but rather a necessarily physical one, a quest to physically return, like Maximin's Siméa, to geographic origins. To recover memory, the exile must return to the site of memory.

Bita's return and subsequent rooting anticipate the postindependence romanticizing of Jamaica through its Festival Song Competition, an annual showcase of patriotic songs that broadcast a celebratory narrative of Jamaican cultural heritage. Winning songs often locate citizenship and birthright in place, this now free land that native Jamaicans inherited on August 6, 1962. Many songwriters boast that "No Whey Nuh Betta Dan Yard" (Stewart), a patriotic claim that is all the more radical given the scale of Jamaica's geographic footprint in comparison to first world superpowers like the United States but one that is nourished by the island's outsize cultural impact. In their 1979 single-verse winner, The Astronauts go even further to declare that "no matter where I roam," the "soil" where the "born Jamaican" is rooted will always pull the exile home.

In a striking parallel to the Festival sentiment, at a crucial moment in Colin Channer's *Waiting in Vain* (1998), the protagonist Fire tells his returning friend, "When the urge take me now, I jump on a plane and go where I feel like go. But this is my base, Ian. This is where I'm rooted. I'm a Jamaican, Ian. Yardie to de *bloodclaat* core" (213). This patriotic declaration comes as they are meeting again for the first time since the novel's opening pages six months before. On landing at Kingston's airport, Ian sees nothing but oppression and death: "a yucca plant . . . dying in a planter, slowly turning to ash like a piece of coal" (207). It is in response to Ian's utter disdain for his roots that Fire offers his patriotic boast, which is predicated on a particular articulation of what it means to be Jamaican at the turn of the twenty-first century. Like Fire, this idealized Jamaican is black, male, self-assured, and financially stable enough to travel and consume the goods and culture that mark him as cosmopolitan. However, his ability to retain his Jamaican "core" in diaspora stands in stark contrast to the insecurity and inauthenticity that define his exiled compatriots.

Waiting in Vain's depiction of rooted identity anticipates the contemporary obsession of Afro-descended peoples with genealogical and DNA research, largely inspired by Alex Haley's miniseries *Roots: The Next Generations*, in which he pieces together his African origins from a few linguistic clues transmitted over two hundred years. With this cultural compass, Haley traces his lineage to the contemporary branch of the Mande relatives of his enslaved forefather

Kunte Kinte. Haley's epic journey finally ends when he discovers "who I am" and is embraced as a member of the tribe by the female villagers, who sing, "Welcome to your village. . . . We are you and you are us" (episode 7, 1:35:00). More recently, *Motherland: A Genetic Journey* follows three black Britons as they use DNA testing to find their African roots. Beaula, born in England of Jamaican parents, reveals that a key part of her quest is to find "a small piece of land" in her ancestral home (30:55). After getting a mitochondrial (maternal) match to the Bubi peoples of Bioko, Equatorial Guinea, and traveling to meet her kin, she reflects that the villagers' welcome made her feel "like a daughter returning. It felt like blood touching blood. It wasn't just anybody, it was family" (32:30). These examples, with their language of kinship ("blood," "family") and territory ("land," "home"), reveal that African diaspora root-seekers envision heritage as physical territory. They imagine a return to the soil in which the blueprint of "who I am" is rooted and where they can reauthenticate identity when it has been diluted or "degraded" in foreign climes.

Despite scientific criticism of the advertising claims of sites like Ancestry.com,[1] for peoples of African descent, genealogical root-seeking—whether by family tree records research, DNA testing, or a combination thereof—remains a vital project. Such quests continue to rely on essentialist concepts of identity, the belief that traces of one's roots are hidden in the body and that discovering genomic roots will enable one to physically return to lost homelands (Nelson 3–4). This is the very idea that Louise Bennett critiqued decades earlier. In "Back to Africa" (1947; *Jamaica Labrish*), the Jamaican poet interrogates the repatriation narrative promulgated by Marcus Garvey's Universal Negro Improvement Association. Bennett's narrator satirizes her interlocutor's focus on the singular African root of her "great / great great / Granma" despite the creolized ancestries that would register in her DNA as traces of English, French, and Jewish blood. She concludes that the Caribbean subject's true homeland is found not "back" there in a romanticized Africa but "right here so" in Jamaica, the place where "oonoo all barn" (you were all born; Bennett 214). This radical reorientation of the homeland to Jamaica anticipates the postindependence reimagining of roots that, as I will show, reflects the cultural work of Jamaica's reggae music.

This chapter interrogates *Waiting in Vain*'s framing of cultural memory as a root-seeking repatriation project. As both Fire's claims of his rooting in Jamaica and Ian's self-image as a desiccated yucca plant suggest, the novel deploys numerous agricultural metaphors that depict Jamaicanness as an indelible trait that can be recovered and marshaled in the service of nation-building. Root identities are often forged in diaspora to negotiate the fact that, as McKay bemoans, native songs are "dim remembered." Channer's three main characters—"born Jamaicans" who have lived abroad for significant periods of their lives—pursue physical, psychological, or performative repatriation as a balm to the trauma of exile and the perceived loss of the fidelity of cultural memory.

The novel's primary strand tracks the summer love affair between A. J. "Fire" Heath and Sylvia Lucas. A well-to-do but down-to-earth artist and novelist, Fire traverses diasporic communities in New York and London on a quest for his one true love. But given that Sylvia has not returned to the island since migrating to New York at age nine, their relationship is primarily imperiled by her lack of markers of Jamaicanness. Although gesturing to mainstream Harlequin, Silhouette, and urban romances, this arc is an ostensible novelization of the Bob Marley song that gives the novel its title.[2] *Waiting* has been hailed as an early example of the reggae novel; in *Natural Mysticism*, published the same year, Kwame Dawes coins the term "the reggae aesthetic" to advocate for a postcolonial Jamaican literary poetics rooted in the local music and, on *Waiting*'s back cover, hails Channer as "Bob Marley with a pen." Although critics of the novel have focused almost exclusively on the Fire/reggae arc, I contend that the romance surface masks a more profound quest: Sylvia's developing romance with her native land. As I will show, Fire is not so much the romantic hero as the medium through which Sylvia recovers her repressed Jamaican memories. In its depiction of cultural memory as rooted, genetically encoded, and thus sexually transmissible, the novel borrows from a key characteristic of reggae: its relationship to a politics of repatriation to a black homeland.

The novel's second arc concerns Ian, a celebrated but troubled Indo-Jamaican sculptor whose misogyny and self-loathing make him unable to both commune with his one true love and feel at home in Jamaica. Despite its romance novel beginnings, the story devolves into the tragic account of Ian's insecurities about his ethnicity and class as he returns to a Jamaica he cannot love. This thread oscillates between erotic pulp fiction and traditional Caribbean literary narratives of identity, exile, and return. With graphic sex and "slackness" talk, it also tracks more closely with dancehall music, reggae's raunchier offshoot. These qualities, along with the novel's idealization of the mobile middle-class male hero and its flippant materialism and name-dropping, make the novel ripe for critique as pandering to problematic notions of gender, sexuality, and class, particularly given Jamaica's postcolonial angst over respectability. I would further argue that its formal modalities of reggae, dancehall, and romance cast it far outside the acceptable modes of elite postcolonial Caribbean literature.

While romances usually feature an antihero who contributes to the impediment between hero and heroine (P. Regis; Radway), Ian's story remains secondary to the courtship plot. He is simply the mutual friend who occasions their meet-cute and at whose funeral they reunite after the requisite separation. It is neither his actions nor his death that tear them apart; it is not even his death that reunites them. Read as a romance between Fire and Sylvia, many of the novel's generic elements seem illogical; read as a repatriation narrative, a love story between Sylvia and her country of origin and a *failed* love story between Ian and Jamaica, the novel takes on a radically different tenor. Focusing on this B side—the connection between Sylvia's and Ian's return narratives—I argue that Fire functions as a repository of Jamaican cultural memory, a "sound system" to amplify Jamaicanness in diaspora and to facilitate the "re-memorization" and repatriation of diasporic yardies (Hall, "Caribbean Culture" 30). I attend to the technologies that enable the circulation of Jamaicanness throughout and beyond the island's shores as well as characters like Fire who become mobile vectors of Jamaican culture. Moving among the three branches of reggae with which the primary characters are aligned, this chapter explores how each idiom circulates divergent notions of Jamaican cultural memory a-*yaad* (at home) and a-b*raad* (abroad). Roots reggae creates a romance of the nation bound up in biological memory and identity, which is in turn performed in diaspora via subgenres like lovers rock. In contrast, I read dancehall-coded consumption, sexual performativity, and violence as mechanisms of fugal avoidance of the kind of root memory work with which reggae is invested. In this way, the novel conceptualizes both remembering and forgetting as performative and informed by place.

Channer's deployment of the aesthetics of Jamaican popular music thus yields new insights into conceptions of sites of memory and illuminates the physical aspects of memory work. In this chapter, memory sites include both the body and the physical soil of the homeland. In an elaboration of the previous chapter's depiction of remembering as both a physical and a political project of piecing bodies, histories, and nations back together and of rehabilitating black female sexuality, here, cultural memory work necessarily involves the female body; Sylvia and Fire's sexual union leads to her reunion with the physical soil of Jamaica. As a contrast with this figuration of memory as a successful return, the final section of the chapter considers how, without a place in the nation, certain constituents negotiate displacement through performative forgetting. It therefore illuminates a third memory site: the nation or yaad, ideologically constructed as the location of culture.

Reggae Roots: The Romance of Yaad

Reggae articulates a New World black consciousness that is both global in scope and rooted in Jamaica—a rerouting of the Garveyist Back-to-Africa platform as a Back-to-Jamaica ideology. Although I will use it as the umbrella term for all postindependence Jamaican recorded music, *reggae* generally refers to the new "roots" music that emerged in the ghettos of West Kingston in the late 1960s. The development of a local modern music resulted from a confluence of technologies and cultural practices: an emerging recording and record-pressing industry, the euphoria of independence that fed the need for new patriotic songs in both the Festival Song Competition and ska, and sound system culture, which saw the erection of massive speaker systems for public music listening and broadcasting. The rivalry among sound system operators for the patronage of dance hall crowds ushered in a period of intense musical innovation as producers experimented with Afro-Jamaican and African American song forms to create a recognizably Jamaican music, one that was distinct in sound and structure from its sonic inspirations. Iterations of this local idiom grew to prominence as the nation came into being: first, the jubilant, fast-paced ska (1966), followed by the slower-paced rocksteady by the summer of 1966–1967, and then roots reggae by 1968.

An ensemble form with layered instrumental patterns, a circular song structure, and a call-and-response between instruments and between lead singer and backing vocals, reggae is characterized by its offbeat syncopation with a counterintuitive stress, a dominant "repetitive and melodic" bass that calls to the hips and pelvis, and Rastafarian drum patterns that echo West African cultural memory (Dawes, *Natural Mysticism* 111). As evident in Count Ossie's "Oh Carolina" (1959), cited as the first autochthonous Jamaican recording, the *burru* and *kette* drums paired with bass rhythms lend reggae its characteristic sound and its referential quality to African memory (Mack 82). Layered on top of those fundamental elements are various other instruments that contribute to its "hybrid but coherent whole" (Dawes, *Natural Mysticism* 114). When Rastafarians took shelter among the slum dwellers of West Kingston following their expulsion from their separatist camp Pinnacle in 1964, their doctrines connected with the "sufferahs" and gave them, and the music emerging from the space, an ideology and language with which to express their frustrations.

Reggae's instrumental structure evinces its unique relationship to memory: its rhythmic pattern creates a dynamic tension between sound and silence, foregrounding empty space as a metaphor for diasporic loss. Dawes has suggested that this pattern creates in the listener a hyperawareness of the missing rhythmic elements. He likens their impact to a "tangible absence" akin to "the sensation of feeling in the amputee's absent limb, and, correspondingly, the re-arrival of the rhythm section amounts to a moment of relief and a signal to throw oneself into the earth-centred throes of dancing" (*Natural Mysticism* 112–113). The missing referent that reggae's silences foreground is the black homeland. Stuart Hall has argued that for African diaspora peoples, Africa is only a trace that is "silenced beyond memory by the power of the experience of slavery" ("Cultural Identity" 230). Access to this sublimated memory is often accomplished through "mnemonic commodities"—objects and technologies that recall the missing referent (Nesbitt xiv).

To assert an aspirational, liberated blackness, the Rastafari movement draws on the revolutionary symbolism of Ethiopia's emperor Haile Selassie I as the black divine ruler and the UNIA's "Africa for Africans" platform. Garvey dreamed of securing the Black Star Line fleet to convey diasporic Africans in a reverse Middle Passage to reclaim their precolonial homelands; he argued that "Africa is the legitimate, moral and righteous home of all Negroes, and now that the time is coming for all to assemble under their own vine and fig tree, we feel it our duty to arouse every Negro to a consciousness of himself" (169). Garvey's deployment of the vine-and-fig-tree prophetic language of Micah 4:4 reveals that the biblical sources for the deification of Selassie often rest on the same messianic prophecies with which Jews articulate their genealogical birthright to the land of Israel, and it thus connects Jewish and African iterations of the term *diaspora*, or scattering. Here, *root* relates to genealogy—the prophecy that Messiah must come from the "root" and blood lineage of the Davidic dynasty (Rev 22:16). The diasporic African awaits the one who will return the scattered "seed" from the infertile lands to which they have been exiled by wicked Babylon (the Western capitalist and white supremacist system) and who will, in turn, root righteous Rastafarians in "Ethiopia the land of our fathers," the ancestral and divine right of diaspora blacks, as the lyrics of the UNIA anthem indicate (Isa 43:5–7; Heb 11:14).

During the two Rastafarian missions to Africa in the 1960s, the heads of state of five African nations welcomed the delegates as brothers and offered them land with language replete with biological essentialism. Ethiopia's emperor granted in perpetuity to all diaspora blacks a plot of land in Shashamane, where some Caribbean migrants, inspired by Garveyism, had already settled. Selassie decreed that "Ethiopia would always be open to those who wanted to return home" but framed kinship between diasporic blacks and Ethiopians literally, claiming that "slaves were sent to Jamaica from Ethiopia" (Mack 100). Although Nigeria's minister of state deeded land in the Bende region to "anyone who was able to trace his descent back to this tribe" and promised that "your land according to [your] parent's possession, would be restored to you," the official land grant extended the welcome to "any Jamaican of African descent whose desire was to return" (Mack 104). The invitation by Ghana's Nkrumah was equally contradictory: he told the delegates "we were blood brothers," which presupposes DNA evidence of kinship, but later added, "Look upon yourselves as Africans and land is here for the asking" (Mack 106). This latter statement defines birthright access to African lands by cultural identification rather than blood. These contradictory policies frame identity in terms that seem to enshrine notions antithetical to postmodern rhizomatic concepts. In fact, Hall considers root-seeking "the wrong way of going about diaspora" ("Caribbean Culture" 32).[3] In the same way that the rights of return to the Jewish homeland (*aliyah*) depend on blood lineage and DNA, black nationalism reclaims "Africa for Africans" based on biological but global Africanness—understandable perhaps given that it is presumed biology (one drop of black blood, African phenotype) that causes persecution in the unhomely West.

The 1961 Africa mission occurred in the context of decades of persecution of Rastas at the hands of the police and the very government that commissioned the trip; the "sufferation" delegates experienced in Jamaica increased their diasporic longing for a welcoming home elsewhere. But by the second mission (1963–1965) when they were met with some hostility and the dream of an African homeland came under threat, they began to consider the newly independent Jamaica "home" (Mack 142). As the Rastafari example illustrates, root-seeking and return quests have much to do with a diasporic crisis. Dispossession amplifies the desire to belong somewhere else than the present place of abjection, as movingly evoked in reggae artiste Buju Banton's ode to Selassie, who would "free the people": "It haad it haad it haad / make dem know me want go home a me yaad" ("Hills and Valleys"). Banton suggests that the response to hardships or "sufferation" is an obsession with a *yaad* or homeland elsewhere.

The Jamaican term *yaad* refers to the bounded plot of land that frames the dwelling house and distinguishes it from communal or neighboring spaces. In its various usages from slavery to the present, yaad has come to denote a physical and psychic space of black liberty, safety, and ownership in the face of the dispossession of the plantation. It took on new meaning with Kingston's urban explosion at the turn of the twentieth century, giving rise to tenement (tenant) and government yards. These communal compounds provided precarious housing for masses of low-income migrants from rural parishes while they sought employment, upward social mobility, and more respectable nuclear living situations (Brodber, *Study of Yards* 55). The root metaphor central to Jamaican cultural fashioning derives from the ritual in which the newborn's umbilical cord or "navel string" is buried in the soil and a tree planted over it to mark her belonging to that specific place (Mintz 246–247). Yaad thus refers to the site of identity formation, the locus that ensures the continuity of kinship and cultural memory (Chevannes 130–131).

Historically, the yaad is separate from *grung*, the land that provides sustenance, a dichotomy that distinguishes yaad from sites of labor like Kingston free zones and offices, and foreign countries (*a-braad*). As such, yaad extends to the nation itself, with national identity articulated as rooted and natural—where "me bawn an me grow" (Grant). Bennett's speaker advises Miss Mattie to "go a-foreign, seek your fortune" (214), which demonstrates both a key engine for emigration from the Caribbean and how the distinction between yaad and grung informs the way Jamaicans construct national and diasporic identities. For Rastafarians, yaad is necessarily Africa, the ancestral homeland for the diasporic black subject and the physical territory in which black identity is rooted. Jamaica and other New World spaces are collapsed under the rubric of Babylon, the site of exile and sufferation.

Despite reggae's thematic orientation to Africa, however, its diasporic memory work creates a romance of Jamaica. Hall calls this a deferral of the homeland that recreates—or, more accurately, performs—African memory in the New World ("Cultural Identity" 231). Although it would take a few decades for the establishment to embrace reggae as nation music, from its inception, reggae was articulated as the sound of Jamaican "authenticity," both in its coterminous rise with independence and in its characteristic elements and techniques of reconciling disparate and foreign influences into a "hybrid and coherent" sound that is uniquely referential to Jamaican reality (Dawes, *Natural Mysticism* 114). Since African return is not ordinarily possible, yaad is re-membered or reconstituted in the present on Jamaican soil, newly freed from British control. Even as Bob Marley sang about his hope of an "Exodus" back to "our father's land," his international fame and his moving odes to Trench Town meant that reggae would come to index Jamaican place. The most vivid imagery in his music evokes fond memories of "when we used to sit / inna govament yaad in Trench Town" ("No Woman"). His Trench Town songs are not dim remembered at all. Decades after his death, his music has created an outsize industry of tourism and pilgrimage not so much to Ethiopia as to Trench Town and his birthplace of St. Ann. Reggae's spiritual home might be Ethiopia, but its yaad is Jamaica. Yaad memory has also shifted from an imaginary to a physical and political project in line with governmental and institutional drives to integrate the diaspora and to inspire exiles to return.

In his assertion of an indelible "yardie" identity, Fire insists on the cultural purchase of an oppositional and sustaining Jamaican cultural memory in a globalized world. As a born-diasporic term, *yardie* represents an orientation not to the diasporic and "foreign" spaces in which the Jamaican-born person lives or works but to the country of her birth and site of her foundational memories.[4] Claiming the yardie moniker is a marker of difference from foreign-born or metropolitan blacks, those poor souls who have to suffer in racist spaces without an "elsewhere" to retreat to when life "here" becomes untenable; it is an assertion of identification with a locatable and accessible place of belonging to which one could return—regardless of whether that is actually true. Diasporic memory is thus memory created at a distance, to fill the gap created by the trauma of exile. This is especially true for African diaspora denizens of hostile majority white spaces. Whereas Ethiopia represents the aspirational yaad where Babylon-weary Rastafari can find rest, for Jamaican migrants in diasporic Jamaican communities in Brooklyn, Brixton, Toronto, or Tottenham, the romance of a yaad in Jamaica provides a psychological sanctuary amid racist violence and antiblack sentiment. Life in Babylon is presumed to degrade cultural authenticity and produce an obsession with roots. Like Haley and the *Motherland* root-seekers, recovering memory enables and precedes returning to the site of one's cultural memories, a physical place that will tell the root-seekers who they are, who they are related to, and where they belong.

Sound System: Disseminating Roots in Diaspora

Broadcasting and amplification are central to reggae's development and its diasporic work: since local radio stations would not play this raggy ghetto music, producers and promoters constructed their own broadcasting systems—the towering sound system speaker boxes that served as rallying points for whole communities—and ushered in an entire economy from creation to transmission that would include engineers, songwriters, singers, producers, selectors, deejays,[5] listeners, and dancers. Even before Bob Marley and the Wailers rose to international fame and embarked on the extensive tours of "Babylon by Bus" that put reggae, Rastafari, and Jamaica on the map, ska and rocksteady were already making inroads in the club scene in diasporic communities. Early reggae producers brought foreign technologies and sonic inspiration back to Jamaica to inflect their music and praxis, then circulated reggae and its ideologies in diaspora. In tandem with local pressing and distribution facilities, the industry's development depended on a system of local and international record stores and grocery stores, as well as traveling migrants and musicians who carried suitcases full of 45s and 33s beyond Jamaica's shores.[6] New music styles developed in Jamaica quickly made their way to diasporic communities through underground systems of circulation that fed their need for a sustained connection to the island. Indeed, *Exodus*, the album that launched Marley into superstardom, was recorded in exile in London after an attempt on his life.

Bob Marley and the Wailers saw reggae as the missionary arm of Rastafari, the sonic medium through which the band's evangelizing mission could be accomplished.[7] They envisioned themselves as griots, recollecting and transmitting cultural memory for the black nation. The purpose of recording and touring was therefore not to become pop stars but to disseminate the Rastafari message to the global company of black brethren and *sistren*. Accordingly, Marley rarely performed from his love song catalog on tour, focusing instead on his overtly political songs.[8] For Jamaicans abroad, the diasporic circulation of reggae music through live performances and broadcast technologies enables a "re-memorization . . . of all those parts of ourselves, aspects of our culture, of our people's experience, which were never told to us, which didn't form part of the dominant culture, which was excluded, rendered invisible"; Hall calls "that moment of recovery . . . the moment of roots" ("Caribbean Culture" 30). Given reggae's emergence in the era of recording technologies, capitalizing on these technologies allows for the narration of memories in a form that enables their wide circulation even without the body of the musician. In doing so, reggae and its broadcasting technologies create and sustain a diasporic community united by awakened collective memory. As the reggae musician travels on tour, he brings new versions of the memory "document" to audiences and newfound communities living throughout Babylon. Carol Bailey has referred to this as "performing yard . . . [by] transplanting it into foreign spaces" (149). Tuning in to yaad music in foreign spaces is an act of resistance and survival. Music becomes one mechanism of return and nostalgia, a way for exiles to remember childhoods and cultural touchstones and to shore up—if not establish—their cultural identity.

The context of Marley and reggae as a global amplification system for Jamaican cultural memory illuminates Fire's function in *Waiting in Vain*. In his travels throughout the Jamaican diaspora, he disseminates and ultimately inseminates essential Jamaicanness, tracing with his steps a Jamaican Atlantic and reorienting diasporic Jamaicans to yaad. At the heart of reggae and Rastafari is a mission to awaken racial memory; by "awaken," I want to suggest that roots reggae envisions memory as embedded in deep recesses, inaccessible until the advent of the prophet, whether in the guise of Garvey or the reggae griot who calls up that memory. Fire functions as both a prophet—he who disseminates cultural memory in diaspora in order to interpellate the exile—and a messiah—he whose rootedness enables him to gather the uprooted and settle them in their own land.

With a series of direct references and comparisons, the novel positions Fire as a stand-in for Marley and reggae: his face is described as "a new world hybrid" of many ethnic influences, much "like reggae" that resolves various sonic and ethnic influences into a single signifier of blackness (Channer, *WIV* 6). At their first meeting, Sylvia knows that he is "Jamaican, obviously" from his constant code-switching between Jamaican Patois ("Patwa") and English (37) and his natty Afro that triggers her recognition of his resemblance to Marley on early album covers (145). His introduction wearing an *Exodus* T-shirt signals early on that his diasporic circulation will inspire his compatriots to leave Babylon for their motherland. *Exodus* is, of course, the album that constellates the Rastafari desire for repatriation; the lettering of its title on the album cover evokes "Ethiopia" as written in Amharic script. Fire is not only hyperlegible to Sylvia and diasporic readers as Jamaican but also "loveable" and a romantic and racial ideal for both Sylvia and readers alike (Frederick 64).

Thanks to his international success as a painter and writer, Fire is as mobile as Garvey and McKay; he boasts, "When the urge take me now, I jump on a plane and go where I feel like go" (*WIV* 213), even hopping to Brooklyn from London for a weekend to seduce a girl he has just met. Unlike many real and fictional compatriots, his ability to live and travel throughout the diaspora is not a marker of the failure of Jamaica to provide adequate avenues for uplift. Instead, it indicates the opportunities provided by creative and commercial enterprise in the reggae and dancehall eras.[9] Fire does not *need* to migrate; secure in his roots, he has the grounding from which to be cosmopolitan. This self-assurance is framed through his possession of fertile lands in diaspora and in Jamaica and by the sustenance he is able to draw as "a black man" in "a black country" from the black soil (77). When his reggae musician uncle I-Nelik advises him to embark on a spiritual retreat to purge the impurities he imbibed on his most recent travels, Fire takes to Jamaica's hinterland and meditates on the lyrics of Burning Spear's "Slavery Days," a song notable for seeding in the minds of auditors the cultural memory of revolutionary blackness unrecorded in history books (*WIV* 281–284). The connection between song, soil, and Fire's recovery of a black consciousness supposedly unsullied by diasporic travel suggests that it is due to deep roots in this fertile black soil and the ancestral memory it holds that Fire can serve as a vector of cultural memory for his culturally degraded compatriots.

Lovers Rock: Sexually Transmitted Memory

In contrast to Fire's obvious and indelible Jamaicanness, Sylvia's cultural heritage and ethnicity are near indecipherable amid a kind of generic blackness and globalized blandness. As a key element of the romance formula (P. Regis 43), the primary barrier to Sylvia and Fire's relationship is her presumed cultural inauthenticity—because "she don't know herself" (*WIV* 279). As the novel progresses, both Fire and the reader discover that Sylvia's repressed Jamaican past is the root of her present struggles as a writer and lover. She spent more than half of her first eight years in a sanatorium for tuberculosis, then was shipped to New York upon becoming orphaned only a year later. She has submerged all memories of Jamaica, retaining only the smell of the ubiquitous antiseptic Dettol and the sounds of a butcher knife striking squealing animals, which gesture to her father's murder of her mother. As a result, although she is a "born Jamaican" like Fire, she has little memory of her parents and lacks a sustaining narrative of her origins, "how much she was like them . . . which of their traits were hers" (39). Sylvia's violent separation from her parents and her subsequent uprooting from the site of her cultural memories caused profound damage, her normative maturation further forestalled by incest. True to its romantic plot, the novel has Sylvia quite quickly overcoming her sexual trauma after one night of lovemaking with Fire, but Sylvia's "dragons" are bigger than achieving orgasm with a lover. Although highly educated, she has difficulties narrating her interiority: she rarely voices what she feels or thinks, she allows the men in her life to beat her down "beneath a cataract of words" (128), and she is unable to write creatively until she meets Fire and quickly composes and performs deeply felt slam poetry. Fire's uncle I-Nelik diagnoses Sylvia's problem thus: she "has been away from Jamaica too long" (280).

Sylvia's relationship with Lewis symptomizes her assimilation to African American culture; Lewis is the prototypical "wrong love" from whom the heroine must turn to find her one true love (Radway 133). However, the novel frames Sylvia's Lewis-Fire dilemma as really a vacillation between African American and Jamaican identity. It suggests that to be Lewis's match, Sylvia suppresses her Jamaican self, indicated by her subordinating her musical tastes to his (*WIV* 66). Bailey has interrogated Afro-Caribbean writers' tendency to privilege yaad values over African American ones, which she argues is rooted in the widely held belief that "performing another's culture constitutes a rejection, suppression or deferral of yard culture" (149). As both Faith Smith and Belinda Edmondson have argued, the novel's umbrage at the prospect of losing Jamaican specificity to international blackness is consonant with turn-of-the-millennium anxieties about "authenticity" ushered in by globalization.[10] I would go further to suggest that the novel's politics reflect a long-standing tension between Caribbean migrants and African Americans.[11]

Whatever the truth value of this notion of Caribbean exceptionality, *Waiting* depicts Sylvia's time in the United States as a process of cultural degradation, an echo of imperialist conceptions of race and identity. The British, for instance, imagined that living in the foreign climes of the colonies would cause "supposedly 'natural' features [to change] into their opposites, as nationality was transmuted into a degraded copy" (Wilson 14). As Ian's yucca plant metaphor implies, cultural degradation occurs because the subject attempts to thrive in the "wrong" climate and soil, one that cannot provide it the requisite sustenance. If, as Pamela Regis argues, the trajectory of the romance is to "put right" a "disordered society" (41), *Waiting* insists that migration and its subsequent degraded cultural memory are disorders that must be rectified. It suggests that Sylvia's dilemma will only be resolved when she rejects the false love and identity—African Americanness as represented by Lewis, jazz, and R & B—and finds her true love and identity—Jamaicanness as represented by Fire and reggae. Fire's first function, then, is to complete her socialization as a Jamaican, serving as a vehicle for Jamaican culture—gift-sized clichéd consumables like a bag of Blue Mountain coffee (*WIV* 67) or a catalog of reggae albums to strengthen her "kinda weak" reggae collection (146). Fire is and has the answer to the exile's many questions about Jamaica. The list of essential reggae albums and many such catalogs in the novel serve to tell diasporic Jamaican readers what songs and albums they have to know and own to be "authentically" Jamaican.

Beyond the list of must-have CDs, reggae functions throughout the novel as Sylvia's conduit back to her culture, to reclaim her from assimilation and degraded cultural memory. Significantly, their first date involves attending a Brooklyn reggae concert headlined by Jamaican lovers rock artiste Gregory Isaacs. Lovers rock (alternately lovers' rock) is a subgenre of reggae that emerged in Jamaican communities in Thatcherite Britain in the 1970s and 1980s. With no access to mainstream spaces for music and sociality, black Britons gathered at house and blues parties where selectors played dub plates sent from Jamaica. The diasporic circulation of these Jamaican records allowed British yardies to engage in a distinctly Jamaican subculture that connected them to the yaad that they might never have known and to negotiate their subaltern status within mainstream white British culture. Dennis Bovell, who coined the term, later sought to create a uniquely British reggae sound, featuring teenaged girls as young as fourteen singing about their loves and longing in a musical style that bridged reggae and African American soul, partly to counter the entrenched notions that any music not coming directly from Kingston was inauthentic.[12]

The presumed dichotomy between a male, militant roots reggae and a female apolitical lovers rock obscures much fluidity of style and content within the reggae genre and in Marley's oeuvre. Marley's romantic ballads are central to his politics and musical origins, and his discography suggests that romantic, erotic, national, and divine love exist on a continuum.[13] If divine love empowers the fight against Babylon system, romantic love is Jah Jah blessing, as marked by the providential "Jah moon" in "Turn Your Lights Down Low." Romance provides a sanctuary from the hardship of the world of sufferation outside, as expressed in the shared roof, bed, or bread in "Is This Love?" "Jamming," a staple of the Wailers' live set list, at first seems to be an invitation to party and/or have sex ("I wanna jam it with you"), yet it belies a covert political message. Togetherness, here articulated as the black couple dancing together and loving on each other, is central to the liberatory political project of repatriation and nation-making. The lyrics insist that, while jamming to reggae, "no bullet can stop us now." In other words, dancing and loving are defensive and offensive strategies in the fight against Babylon. Not only is the couple "jamming in the name of the Lawd," but in live performances the I-Threes also punctuate the lyrical break during the song's bridge—"Holy Mt. Zion / Jah seated in Mt. Zion"—by pointing to the backdrop featuring a banner of Selassie in his imperial garments. That this song about conjugal and corporate dancing devolves into a worship song underscores the connections between the spiritual and the sexual throughout Marley's work[14] and recalls the erotic roots of the Rastafari religion.[15]

Consonant with the erotics of politics in reggae and Rastafari, through the lovers rock mode, *Waiting* relocates politics in the rehabilitation of black female sexuality. Black feminist scholars have argued that centering black female sexuality and black romance is important political work.[16] The Gregory Isaacs concert and the reggae subgenre of lovers rock thus provide more than a backdrop for Fire and Sylvia's developing sexual attraction; rather, they telegraph the work that Fire will undertake to rehabilitate Sylvia's cultural memory through lovemaking. In so doing, Channer confronts assumptions about both lovers rock and romance as vehicles for radical politics. *Waiting in Vain* foregrounds Sylvia's embodied responses to both Fire and Jamaican music. During Isaacs's performance, she "began to feel a comfort with the music that she hadn't felt at first. And as she stood there, caught in a tidal draft of bass . . . she closed her eyes, hugged herself, and listened through her pores" (60). Demonstrating the attention, reception, and amplification inherent in Jamaican sound system culture (Henriques), Sylvia's embodied listening begins to resolve her initial lack of "comfort with the music," and soon "she became more aware of her body, of how much of it she couldn't feel, of how much of it she wanted to touch, to re-explore, to reassure herself that it was all there, all hers—all hers to give to whomever she pleased" (*WIV* 60). The music's initial effect is to reconnect Sylvia to her own body as a site of desire and ultimately the site of memory. The language here bridges the political and the sexual, linking her ownership of her body with Caliban's declaration that since "this island's mine," he can show "the scamels in the rock" to whomever he pleases (Shakespeare 1.2.396, 2.2.172). But her first act is to enjoy her own body through masturbation. Fire and Sylvia's eventual coupling centers *her* desire for *him*. In fact, he does not get release until the novel's closing pages, allowing Sylvia ample space to explore her own bodily pleasure. Although Fire's self-control and attention to his lover's pleasure coheres with Channer's avowed project to "rehabilitate black masculinity" ("Problem with Women" 114), it also displaces Fire to privilege female release and Sylvia's sexual and cultural rehabilitation.

Sylvia's response to Fire and reggae reflects how, as reggae disseminates cultural memory throughout Babylon, it interpellates yardies so identified by the bodily responses the music calls up. Broadcasting is inseparable from reception, evinced in the call-and-response pattern central to reggae's sonic and lyrical structure, as well as its technologies and performance. Reggae songs often feature a call-and-response between the male lead singer and the female chorus. In addition, Julian Henriques has noted that the sound system requires a medium—that which enables the propagation of sound waves. Such media include the speaker system, the broader culture, and the bodies of the audience members who receive and amplify the vibrations and the call of the bass (Henriques 39–41). Studio engineers and live DJs manipulate and monitor the system's controls to, as it were, control their effect on the live audience, and the sound system's microphones and amplifiers propagate the selector's carefully chosen message to the community who registers (dis)approval of the selections by gathering close to the speakers, dancing, singing along, walking away, or displaying other embodied signs of assent or dissent (Henriques 85, 131).

A key aspect of lovers rock is the rub-a-dub, a slow dance in which the couple anchors itself in a single spot on the dance floor and marks the rhythm of the music with sensual, circular motions of pelvis rubbing against pelvis. In an earlier scene, Fire and his "wrong love," Blanche, rub-a-dub to a Marley love song, and the language used to describe the "wine"—the simulated and stimulating pelvic-centric rub-a-dub motion—connects dancing and dialogue as Blanche "answer[s] his circumlocutions with her own" (Channer, *WIV* 9). The novel thus positions wining as both a way of knowing and a way of listening to music. The rub-a-dub is a call-and-response form, connecting music(ian) and audience and male and female dance partners. That Sylvia connects to the music by "listening through her pores" shows that, far from merely a receiver and potential sexual receptacle, she registers her attentiveness to the sound waves and the music's message by her embodied answer, amplifying them in her body in return (60). For Henriques, the body with its vast expanses of skin is a complete "haptic sensory" surface (53). Through the rub-a-dub wine, the body becomes a liminal site that connects the visual and the sonic regimes as the body makes visible the dancer's internalization of the music. But the novel suggests that Sylvia internalizes more than the Gregory Isaacs song. She also answers the call of Fire's body, mirrored here in her triggered memory of attending Marley's final show at Madison Square Garden: "Whenever [Marley] would call out, I'd cup my hands over my mouth and scream the loudest. Wo-yoy. *Wo-yoy*. Wo-yo-yo-yo-uh. *Wo-yo-yo-yo-uh*. There was a sensuality to him. . . . not plain sex appeal . . . but a spiritual magnetism . . . as if he were a shaman . . . as if he had the power to draw people out of themselves into this new space . . . his space" (145). Part of the significance of this reference is that this was Marley's penultimate show before his collapse and cancer diagnosis and the first (and only) show with a significant African American and diasporic Afro-Jamaican audience—it was here that black audiences had finally answered Marley's call (Steffens 375–378).

In connecting her vocal response to Marley's call with her embodied response to Fire's, Sylvia reveals both Fire's shamanic function in drawing her "into . . . his space" and that her reconnection to Jamaica will necessarily be through sound and music. Their only coupling before the novel's final pages is largely verbal, in line with the command mode of the dancehall—largely consisting of Fire's commands to Sylvia as he coaches her to overcome her sexual trauma and to "slay the dragon" (*WIV* 157). This sexual call-and-response foregrounds the role of music and sonority in calling to her buried identity markers and reconstituting cultural memory. Since the ability to "answer [Fire's] circumlocutions" presumes Jamaican rhythm, the body language to match her dub to his rub,[17] it is through embodied call-and-response that Fire equips her to respond to his more crucial appeal: the call to repatriate.

Like the bolero, the lovers rock mode imbricates romantic and national love and gestures to a larger project of cultural memory work and nation-building. Whereas in Hijuelos the lover was both clearly Cuban and located "back there" in Cuba, here Fire encounters his true love in diaspora and must renaturalize her as Jamaican before she can return to be his life partner. In her investigation of the relationship between romance and patriotism in Latin American novels that use the romance as "synecdoches of the marriage between Eros and Polis," Doris Sommer observes that "after the creation of new nations, the domestic romance is an exhortation to be fruitful and multiply" (6, 32). Correspondingly, the novel suggests that for Jamaica to be a thriving postindependence nation, the sons and daughters of her soil must return to participate in the nation-building project. Given that human genetic information is transmitted via reproduction, the novel's imbrication of the sexual and the patriotic reifies the heterosexual reproduction and nation-building that feminist critics call out in Harlequin-style romance novels.[18] Since patriotism thrives on sexual and ideological reproduction, the ultimate purpose of Fire's diasporic circulation is to co-opt denaturalized citizens back into the reproductive project through which the young postcolonial nation will thrive. This is not far from Garvey's own reasoning for opposing interracial relationships: the black nation he was building required the reproduction of authentic blackness (162). It is thus not far-fetched to read Lewis's closeted sexuality as the ultimate marker of his status as an unviable choice for Sylvia.

Sylvia's primal and mystical connection to Fire is constantly articulated as a connection to Jamaica. Rather than the generic soul mate connection—the sense that the heroine and hero are fated to love each other and therefore their meeting is really a recognition—Sylvia's attraction to Fire rests on her recognition of his essential Jamaicanness, something in him that resonates with something buried within her. Within minutes of flirting with him, she rediscovers Jamaican curse words and raucous laughter. This underscores that their mutual connection relies on their shared sense of hailing "from somewhere" else (*WIV* 18). Pamela Regis flags moments like this as the attraction stage that establishes "the reason that this couple must marry. . . . Attraction can be based on a combination of sexual chemistry, friendship, shared goals or feelings, society's expectations, and economic issues" (33). I contend that Fire and Sylvia's attraction relies on their shared heritage that distinguishes and bonds them within the American space in which they meet. As their sexual connection intensifies, she keeps returning to a thrilling feeling: "You make me think about [Jamaica] in a way that had never been as important to me. . . . I remember thinking . . . 'God, why do I feel this way about this man?' And I guess the answer has something to do with the fact that, along with all the really wonderful things about you, you remind me of that place" (*WIV* 131). In the impromptu poem she recites at an open mic, she confesses how he has sparked not a desire for his body as much as a desire for Jamaica. "Exile," she extemporizes:

> is wanting to hear the lisp
> of the sea, curled on the tongues of passersby
> [. . .] to taste beads of tamarind
> that drop from terraced hillsides.
> [. . .] to feel the pulp of star-apple,
> its dark flesh, moist between my hands.
> It is, it is wanting you. (142)[19]

As in McKay's nostalgic poems like "I Shall Return," Sylvia expresses the migrant's longing for rural Jamaican landscape, sounds, smells, and tastes—a desire particularly grounded on sensual and embodied memories. She suggests that Fire's body is the source of both sexual pleasure and cultural nourishment that she must consume in order to regain her essence.

Without her own direct ancestral ties to Jamaica, Sylvia seeks access through Fire's body. In the cab on the way back from the Gregory Isaacs concert, "she . . .

clenched [his nipples] between her teeth, lapping at him hungrily, wanting to *nourish* her spirit with his *essence*" (*WIV* 63; emphasis added). Although ostensibly demonstrating Fire's confidence in his sexuality to mother a woman, this moment reads less erotic than cultural. Having lost her mother, Fire's body becomes the conduit to a maternally transmitted identity, much like the mitochondrial DNA that usually points African diaspora root-seekers to maternal African origins. While women are traditionally nurturers, here Fire adopts the role of the black mammy figure, whose body serves not to nourish whiteness but to restore black womanhood. In addition to allowing her to suck the marrow of Jamaicanness from his body in lieu of the Jamaican fruits she is unable to access in diaspora, he also combs her hair and cooks for her in a series of gender reversals that mark their attraction stage.

The language of biological essence and DNA echoes throughout their relationship. Awakened by lovers rock and her nourishment through his body, "she realized that she'd been quietly missing her culture for years. She loved jazz. She loved classical. And the blues and R&B. But she didn't feel them in the same way she felt some Trenchtown bass bussin her head or some Lavantille [*sic*] steel pan racklin through her bones" (*WIV* 66). Despite the fact that Sylvia has lived more years of her life in the United States than in Jamaica, it is reggae and steel pan, not blues, jazz, or R&B, that leave traces in the deep bodily recesses of the bone and that can be reawakened by music. Dennis Scott's play "An Echo in the Bone" uses the same language to explore the deep cultural and ancestral echoes that have been recorded "in the bone" of Afro-Jamaicans and that will resound in moments of profound traumatic and historical replay—whether revisiting the site of the original trauma or reliving situations that replay the traumatic event. The play demonstrates how music functions as a memory-retrieval device to access traumatic ancestral memories. The "echo" of its title foregrounds the sonority of Caribbean memory—what Carolyn Cooper calls "noises in the blood"—while the "bone" metaphor conveys genetic and genealogical conceptions of memory. *Waiting* similarly locates identity in the blood, that "common substance [transmitted] through heterosexual relations and birth" (Liu 271). Here, reggae animates the noises in the blood of exiled Jamaicans in a process of re-memorization.

Waiting in Vain's reliance on genomic language to describe Sylvia's reawakened cultural memory connects the novel's project to that of genetic root-seekers like the *Motherland* subjects, who believe that genetic markers in their blood will point the way—not to generic or hybrid African roots but to the specific ethnic group from which they hail. This in turn will enable them to know who they are—an intellectual and psychological project—and to travel to a land that is theirs and be embraced as kin by people to whom they belong—a physical and political project. Genomic root-seeking imagines racial identity as singular—root rather than rhizome, uncomplicated, locatable, and traceable, as if identity were a geolocation chip installed in the deepest recesses of the human body. DNA is often likened to both a genetic blueprint and a map. In the former case, genes encode the biological instructions for each individual cell, while mitochondrial or maternally transmitted DNA is often believed to point to the route and location of the mother. As Alondra Nelson has argued in *The Social Life of DNA*, *bios*—the genetic document that provides a narration of both biological origins and biological identity—connects to *biography*—a narrative of one's ancestry (89). The novel likewise envisages Jamaicanness as an indelible trait located in the blood and bone that can be recovered to provide the exile with a map back to yaad even when the external markers of Jamaicanness have been lost or degraded. But reggae's memory work both relies on and subverts rooted identity since diasporic memory is created in and through performance. Although *Waiting* seems to privilege rooted identity and cultural authenticity, Sylvia's experience reveals that even where Jamaicanness is not biological, it can be disseminated or, perhaps more accurately, *in*seminated. But the relational sexual transmission of memory still serves to bolster biological root-seeking; the logic of the romance narrative presumes that Sylvia already has the genetic markers of Jamaicanness that provide the essential connection to Fire and make her a suitable soil in which to inseminate cultural identity. In contrast to the popular rhizomatic, "anti-anti-essentialist" models of diaspora and identity circulated by Hall, Paul Gilroy, and others, the novel insists on a figuration of cultural memory that is rooted and rhizomatic, biological and cultural, mobile even as it reorients one to fixed origins, and transnational even as it reorients one to nation.[20] The diasporic circulation of roots reggae surfaces the nourishing sap of global blackness from which, counterintuitively, a *national* consciousness is cultivated.

Channer frames cultural memory as an embodied ancestral language, echoing L'Antoinette Stines's assertion that there is "historical and cultural data imprinted upon and within" Caribbean bodies (39). Sylvia reflects that "her life to this point had been a matter of avoiding history. . . . So most of her involvements, both romantic and platonic, had been *rooted* in shallow earth. But with Fire she was feeling wet *ground* beneath her, layers of *silt* brought down from the hills of her fore-parents and laid down over thousands of years in a cycle of flooding and retreat, a pulling away that had left behind a treasure of minerals to *nourish* her like a tree" (*WIV* 133; emphases added). Since her previous relationships were "shallow" and lacking deep roots, Fire serves to root her in the ancestral data embedded in the rich soil of her foreparents. The above passage returns to the ideas of "root," "ground," and "nourishment" that the name of Bita Plant, McKay's returning yardie protagonist, evokes. In a reversal of the traditional gender binary, here the man is the fertile, nourishing ground from which the woman draws sustenance. Fire is both the traveled Bita Plant *and* the rooted Jubban, Bita's earthy husband. Sylvia's avoidance of history also belies a conscious repression of memory and suggests that only people with intact memories can engage in history.

Often a subliminal quest for social rooting—belonging to a nation or ethnic group—genealogical research is particularly prevalent among African diaspora peoples because the link to cultural memory, a continuous narrative and archive of African identity, has been ruptured. Without specific ties to people and places on the island, Sylvia's relationship with Fire serves as a type of genealogical root-seeking to resolve her cultural disorientation. In the same way that Fire's patriotic boast is framed as a hierarchy of preferences for Jamaican rather than foreign culture, he replaces Sylvia's American-oriented cultural markers with Jamaican ones. The types of (pseudo)genealogical ancestral data that Fire awakens in Sylvia cover a range of senses including gustatory—reorienting her from bran muffins to cornmeal porridge—and aural—from Toni Braxton, Gal Costa, and jazz to Laventille steel pan and Trench Town bass. His oiling her scalp and drying her hair with a towel even restores memories of an old woman who used to comb her hair (*WIV* 150).

More importantly, Fire reconstructs for her an alternate family lineage. He becomes mother and grandmother, and when she finally returns to Jamaica, she immediately feels at home. Even strangers instinctively claim her as kin. She realizes that she "can't think of calling any other place home, because people [she's] known for less than an hour have been calling [her] 'darling' and referring to [her] as 'friend' when they introduce [her] to other people who've been telling [her she's] the 'dead stamp' of so-and-so from over so" (*WIV* 344–345). Fire's genealogical reconstitution of Sylvia's memory begins to redress what Nelson calls the "injurious repercussions of the past" (21). But the memories Sylvia recovers are not her own but Fire's; with his body as medium, *he* becomes her kin. She is related to other Jamaicans because she is related to him. As Sylvia's experience illustrates, diasporic memory is not a retrieval so much as the performance of a romance of roots and yaad that produces the quest for physical return.

Although Sylvia is a "born Jamaican" and eligible for citizenship by birth according to Article 3(1) of the Jamaican Constitution, her lack of family and a yaad to which to retreat from diasporic dispossession made the prospect of repatriation daunting, even untenable. This contextualizes why her return to Jamaica is on a whim, precipitated by Ian's death, not as a resolution to the love plot. By reclaiming her as kin, Fire thus enables her to return home. Her repatriation arc suggests that genealogy is really geography, a quest for the place where one's ancestors were once located—*where* you come from—and while geographic ancestry is not necessarily fixed, given human wanderings, African-descended peoples hope that genealogical research will enable them to find a place, a land, to which they belong. With his land, money, multiple homes, and rooted blackness, Fire becomes Sylvia's portal to reclaiming Jamaican citizenship. Although Jamaican citizenship can be transferred by legal means of marriage and adoption, Sylvia reacquires hers by sexually transmitted memory. I read the novel's closing scenes of their coupling on Jamaican soil as marking the consummation of Sylvia's reunion with her native land and her physical access to the nourishing earth where her memories and ancestral data are rooted.

With parallelism, Sylvia makes clear that to love Fire is to love Jamaica, and she performs the requisite verbal allegiance by which, according to Article 4(1)b of the constitution, she can become naturalized by marriage. In place of the cathartic love confession that would resolve the romance's barrier, she declares, "There was a time when I couldn't relate to Jamaica. I didn't even want to relate to love. Now I do—again because of you" (*WIV* 332). Feminist critics of romance novels often express justified outrage at their heteronormative matrimony-oriented endings that seem to normalize marital enslavement and extinguish the heroine's spirit. However, Sylvia's commitment proposal, or what I read as her oath of national allegiance, consummates her quest, consolidates her belonging and citizenship, and enables her to take ful(ler) advantage of her newly revitalized Jamaicanness. If the heroine's "choice to marry the hero is just one manifestation of her freedom" (P. Regis 15), then Sylvia's consummation proposal arguably marks not her normalization into heteronormativity—to become the washer of Fire's clothes and bearer of his children (*WIV* 346)—but of her ultimate triumph: resolving her exile.

Dancehall: Performative Fugue

Sylvia's and Ian's divergent return experiences underscore the importance of physical sites of memory and ethnicity in the construction of the nation. Ian's failed return is anticipated by Michael Thelwell's novelization of the eponymous 1970 film *The Harder They Come*. Thelwell's novel mirrors the aesthetic and thematic concerns that fed reggae's birth and development and traces the rise and fall of legendary rude-bwoi Ivanhoe "Rhygin" Martin as he leaves the rural hills and communal folkways to pursue fame and fortune as a reggae singer in the brutal shanties of 1960s Kingston. Rhygin's fatal devolution into an urban cowboy occurs immediately after his return to his "bush" to find nothing but "desolation. . . . There was no evidence of the passage of his generations, the ancestors whose intelligence, industry and skill had created a self-sufficient homestead there. . . . '*Nutten* no deh yah now. . . . Me people dem. Me people dem! Lawd, Jesas, me *people*'" (Thelwell 320–321). This pathos-filled cry conveys Rhygin's trauma at the loss of a sense of place—the fate of the dispossessed from slavery to the present. For those eking out an existence in Kingston's shanty towns, the thought of a rustic, pristine home somewhere in the country sustained them. Like them, Rhygin had dreamed of going back to visit his birthplace, "to feel the presence of his generations. To . . . lose himself in the warm untroubled waters of his beginnings" (325). Instead, his discovery of destruction and the loss of his ancestral "evidence" leaves him feeling "rootless and adrift" (323) and deals him a severe blow from which he never recovers.

Like Rhygin, Channer's migrant characters feel "rootless and adrift" without access to the ancestral homestead that grounds identity and archives their belonging. Even further, Rhygin's fate anticipates Ian's own tragic end. Whereas "Jamaica is the place . . . where" both Fire and Sylvia are "rooted" (*WIV* 213), Jamaica is a place of sterility and suffocation for Ian. While Sylvia returns from exile from her presumed inauthentic self, *Waiting in Vain* culminates in Ian's meltdown and the spectacular failure of his return to his native land. If Sylvia reconnects to her memories as a result of sexual congress with Fire, Ian's shame over his roots prevents his reconciliation to his birth country and manifests in performative sexuality. Rhygin's fate demonstrates what happens when the return to roots is unfruitful—when there is no home place in view, when the evidence of one's ancestral belonging is covered over with entangled roots, or when one finds the soil untenable for survival—as the desiccated yucca plant suggests.

Music explicitly appears in Ian's arc twice, and it is dancehall music, one of reggae's offshoots. Ethnomusicologists situate dancehall's emergence in the political, economic, and cultural upheavals that marked the failure of Manley socialism and the dread violence of the 1970s. Donna P. Hope considers dancehall music a definitive break with roots reggae, particularly due to the impact of new media and recording technologies and the insecurities and instabilities ushered in by late-twentieth-century neoliberal policies (*Inna di Dancehall* 21). With the proliferation of digital technologies, sound systems, and studios, the deejay art, originally an improvisational pseudosinging style, soon migrated from the purview of the sound system selector to recording studios where aspiring ghetto youths would record entire tracks showcasing their lyrical skill and their ability to "ride the riddim." Late-twentieth-century technologies and global capitalism transformed the deejay's art from participatory ("live in the dance") to high-fidelity ("playing recorded music") to studio music (Stanley Niaah 4). For the immediate postindependence generation, ghetto sufferation produced the self-assured black pride of roots reggae, but in the decade following Marley's 1981 death, the same context produced dancehall with its attendant insecurity. Adherence to the imperatives of capitalism and consumption led to a clash of values, with the new role models emerging not from old money but from the upstart dancehall deejays and dancers, whose materialism and evidence of low culture rubbed the "respectable" classes the wrong way. Dancehall's appeal for Ian thus resides in its empowerment of a new generation of sufferahs to engage in and subvert modernity, late-twentieth-century capitalism, and their values.

Ian has renounced his Jamaican citizenship for French citizenship, and his constant travel symptomizes his desire to flee both home and memory. Upon

Ian's return to Jamaica, Fire realizes that "none of [Ian's] reminiscences . . . were centered in his own environment. Downtown. The ghetto. . . . And the stories themselves . . . sounded like adaptations from the secondhand account of someone else's life, someone distant, a stranger, about whom he didn't care. They didn't have the vividness of adolescent memory" (*WIV* 214). Ian's circulation of borrowed memories suggests that memory and forgetting can be performed and performative. As Alison Landsberg has argued, such "memories" are not personally experienced but implanted in the audience by their circulation in mediated images (14). Like Sylvia, whose acquisition of memories is mediated through Fire's body, Ian acquires memories by their circulation in popular culture, repressing his own memories to fit into a shared narrative of what it means to be an ideal Jamaican man. The absence of authentic memories can be attributed to Ian's shame about his origins or possibly a conscious repression; he perhaps "had . . . chosen to forget" (*WIV* 214). Fire's description of Ian's memories as "secondhand" and estranged suggests that Ian is in a state of fugue from his roots. Fugue is a temporary psychological condition marked by amnesiac wandering. Typically afflicting men rather than women, it manifests in an oscillation between remembering and forgetting who one is and where one comes from (Rudnicki 14). Notably, in comparison to the intertwined psychological and physical remembering I have discussed so far, fugue is both a psychological and a physical flight. Although Ian is also a "born Jamaican [and] a son of the soil" (The Astronauts), he uses roaming to negotiate his lack of rootedness in his native soil. His fugal wanderings echo Sonjah Stanley Niaah's description of the inherent nomadism of dancehall events as organizers and participants negotiate constant policing and the precariousness of inner-city geographies in a performed rememory of the itinerancy of emancipated slaves (55).

While Fire's diasporic travels, his ability to survive racism in Brixton and Brooklyn, rest entirely on his knowledge that he has a yaad to which he can return, Ian has no such ground(ing). Displaced, rootless, and multiply homeless, Ian has no buffer to the unbelonging he experiences both a-yaad and a-braad. Whereas Fire travels internationally because "the urge take" him (*WIV* 213), Ian's travels and conspicuous consumption allow him to assuage his uneasiness with self and country. Although in the early periods of his exile Ian acquired many possessions, their recent *re*possession only symbolizes his larger *dis*possession; his focus on acquiring brand-name belongings only masks his lack of belonging. Arguably, Fire's true "superiority" in the return section of the novel is not his belongings or their tastefulness but his self-possession, his security in his belonging to this place. When Ian does return to Jamaica, his fixation on the symbolism of the desiccated yucca plant reveals that his sentiments are not of love but of suffocation. Unlike the prototypical Caribbean fugue, however, his wandering is not because of amnesia but to *instigate* amnesia.

On the surface, Ian's insecurity despite his success as a "famous sculptor who made the cover of *Time* magazine" seems illogical (*WIV* 19), and early exchanges depict him as simply a "bad" person: not only is he crass, selfish, and impolite, he has not made good art in some time, his status-signaling possessions have all been repossessed, and he bums around on the sofas of his less-famous friends. However, when he returns to Jamaica for the first time since emigrating, having to stay as a guest in Fire's two homes in Jamaica unmans him; he "imagine[s] himself as a denatured sperm, a dot being carried in another man's stream. . . . *What kind of man needs so many people to prop him up? . . . A man who isn't a man*, said his demon" (237, 238). Ian's reference to semen as a container of masculinity connects to the broader agricultural metaphors in the novel. The word *semen* is etymologically related to "seed," both its Jamaican cognate and the substance planted in the soil to produce fruit "after its kind" (Gen 1:11). That Ian imagines this "denatured sperm . . . carried in another man's stream" suggests that beyond his own unnatural barrenness—his un(re)productive sexual arousal and release—he is not even able to nourish his own seminal potential. Indeed, the novel affirms that Fire is inherently fecund, able to both propagate on others' behalf and nourish the engendering of others. In contrast to Ian's "denatured sperm," Fire's "stream" contains the seeds of Jamaicanness, ready to be deposited in the "core" of his lover. In the novel's heteronormative economy, however, Fire can only serve as disseminator of Jamaicanness for women in general and Sylvia in particular.

If Sylvia's loss of cultural memory stemmed in part from the violent death of her mother, Ian's fugue results from his attempt to flee associations with *his* mother, Miss Gita. Much of his performative forgetting is compounded by shame about her perceived status as a "white liver coolie," a slur on Indo-Jamaican women's presumed insatiable sexual appetites (*WIV* 173), which amplifies the othering and ridicule associated with the derogatory "coolie" term. Originally the term for an ethnic group in India, the term *coolie* came to mean "unskilled laborer" and then a pejorative term for Caribbean peoples from the Indian subcontinent.[21] Ian's experience reveals how the romantic treatment of race, identity, and music further alienates Indo-Jamaicans from the national yaad. His alignment with the desiccated yucca plant reveals that his roots are neither fertile nor nourishing. Rather, his resentment of his ethnic identity poisons in the bud his relationships with women. Characters often register a lack of surprise at Ian's violent outbursts, since the young man "come from bad seed" (220); this is despite Ian's access to breeding and culture due to his early transplantation by Fire's father to the rich soil of the Kingston and St. Andrew elites on account of his artistic talent. The novel suggests that, in the same way that Ian's acculturation to uptown presumably fails, his attempt at forgetting will always be a failed project, hence why his arc is the story of a failed romance and a toxic love. His inability to love mother and motherland is a prophylactic to both self-love and viable romantic love.

Whereas Fire often displays a sensibility aligned with lovers rock, the more romantic, sensitive side of Jamaican masculinity, Ian's embrace of dancehall mores consolidates his exclusion from the aspirational postcolonial construction of the nation. Disdainful of his origins, Ian engages in a variety of behaviors often associated with dancehall music—rampant consumerism, constant travel and home-hopping, gun violence, and particularly the violent sex and graphic sexual boasting of the "slackness" movement spearheaded by Yellowman and Shabba Ranks.[22] "Slackness" has its roots in both class and race, the dual roots of Ian's insecurity. Winston "Yellowman" Foster, credited as the first dancehall deejay of the period, used his lyrics to subvert his outsider status as an albino, which inaugurated the dancehall practice of self-aggrandizement that Ian displays throughout the novel (Hope, *Inna di Dancehall* 10). To compensate for his literal lack of black pigmentation, Yellowman magnifies his sexual prowess in explicit sexual boasts, while Rexton "Shabba Ranks" Gordon uses graphic boasting to compensate for his perceived ugliness. Although there is much continuity between the idioms, reggae songs about sex, like the Fire-Sylvia arc, predominantly focus on romance, seduction, and mutual pleasure, while dancehall songs and the Ian arc typically celebrate prowess and sexual skill.

It is not without significance, then, that Fire and Ian play a Shabba Ranks selection while discussing Fire's desire to impregnate Sylvia as a sign of his prowess (*WIV* 251). Here, the song "Love Punnany Bad" signals Fire's and Ian's shared understanding of Jamaican masculinity; by listening to the song together and voicing the lyrics in unison, both men affirm their belonging to the community of "punnany" (vagina) lovers the deejay espouses. This participatory inculcation of cultural values is a key characteristic of Jamaican music culture. Before the proliferation of radio stations in the 1980s and privately owned cars at the turn of the century, the musical soundscape was largely monolithic and communal. Auditors were exposed to the same radio playlists, the same catalog of Festival songs, the same mixtapes and bootlegged CDs played in commuter bus and taxi stereos.[23] The repetitive, shared listening fosters communal memory and a social construction of identity, and these spaces and technologies form sonic subcultures that enforce their own behaviors and contest dominant ones.

This musically constructed sociality is further reinforced by the prevalence of command lyrics in dancehall music. A staple of the early juggling and sound clash segments of the dance, command and affirmation songs are among the principal modes of cultural identity formation.[24] The collective, public nature of music listening combines with boastful lyrics to produce cultural belonging or exclusion. In the same way that Fire's "yardie to de core" boast evinces a hierarchy of preferences of Jamaica over London, stout over wine, and Bob Marley over Beethoven (*WIV* 213), command lyrics affirm certain behaviors and values:

the ideal shape (Coca-Cola bottle), skin tone (browning), material things (car keys), or skill (ability to cook or perform a sexual feat). The sonic subculture thus normalizes women into heteronormative and often misogynistic behaviors centered on pleasing men and warding off "mateys" (rivals) and, for male listeners, encodes and rewards heteronormative masculinity. The latter extends to songs like Buju Banton's "Boom Bye Bye" and T. O. K.'s "Chi-Chi Man," which invite actual or symbolic violence against homosexuals, effeminate men, and those who perform fellatio on their women. By enforcing performative conformity to heteronormativity, the island's sound culture marginalizes or punishes men who do not adhere to the status quo.

Fire and Ian's momentary bonding over "Love Punnany Bad" thus has much to do with the circulation of Shabba's slackness songs in the informal bootleg tape economy in a way that contributed to the formation of young Jamaican men's sexual identities. The collective identity constructed and sustained by the public, performative music culture contextualizes Ian's pressure to perform codes of black masculinity. Even as he flees the associations of Indianness and promiscuity, his sense of inferiority to black masculinity compels him to affirm his belonging to the class of real Jamaican men by any means necessary. Since heteronormative masculinity is always already performative, Ian's belonging remains precarious and his performance the more vital and urgent. Slackness dancehall appeals to him for its aggrandizing lyrics, its public proclamation of sexual prowess, and its often detailed instructions on how to achieve and recognize this reclamation. In a macabre subversion of the romance arc where sex reconciles Sylvia to her cultural memories, Ian's arc centers on his use of sexual performativity to forget his roots and to numb the pain of witnessing and participating in the gang rape of his one true love, Margaret. Deploying sexual brutality as a mask for his insecurity, he uses what Cooper calls a "lyrical gun" (*Sound Clash* 154) in an attempt to destroy Margaret: he denigrates her as a "mattress," an object for men's sexual comfort and subordination, and refers to her as "beef" who he will "slap every now and then" (*WIV* 53). Prophetically enough, the sexual euphemism "slap" takes on its etymological connotations when he later "take out him stiff-up cocky and baton [Margaret's] face. Buss up her lip. Blood up her mout'" (184). His relationship with Margaret is thus marked by self-hatred turned outward in violent language, violent sex, and violent behaviors more broadly as he converts the white Southern virgin into a "coolie" stereotype to justify his performed hatred of her.

Flipping the restorative call-and-response that Fire and Sylvia share, Ian stage-manages a sexual relationship between Margaret and a mutual friend Phil, whom he instructs in the art of sexual prowess—in almost unreadably macabre and vulgar language—to construct himself as a sexual "master" and to sustain a perverse tether on Margaret's sexuality (*WIV* 175, 121). In a parallel scene, a group of African American musicians teach Phil how to play jazz with soul and feeling (193). While these musicians play from their racial experience, Phil eventually masters jazz, despite being white, by also playing from his root memories. Whereas Phil fails as a lover when he tries to imitate a racial stereotype, he succeeds as a jazz musician by playing from his cultural memories rather than mimicking black musicians. This sexual/musical tutelage subplot suggests that cultural markers can be learned and performed if transmitted by someone who is coded authentic, in the same way that Sylvia acquires secondhand cultural memory from the presumed authentic Fire. With the popularity of Jamaican contemporary music in far-flung places like Germany, Japan, and Ghana, itinerant Jamaicans can easily reconnect with the island, but this circulation also subverts notions of cultural authenticity as non-Jamaican artists like the Torontonian Drake and the Barbadian Rihanna become more mainstream vectors for the amplification of Jamaican culture than "born Jamaicans." Jacob Dorman calls this a peer-to-peer transmission, a meme rather than a memory, in which cultural markers "jump" from practitioner to practitioner (6–7).[25] In the case of Drake and Rihanna, the musical dissemination of Jamaicanness to the island's diasporic communities interpellates other black subjects, forming what Cooper calls a "dancehall transnation" that exceeds biology (*Sound Clash* 297–300).[26] Despite *Waiting*'s investment in roots, its depiction of cultural and memory transmission prefigures the kind of contemporary memetic musical appropriations that make cultural gatekeepers nervous in the era of globalization. In this way, the novel's musical phonotopes and the richness of literary representation remain in tension as characters' experiences resist the tendency to flatten culture into singular root and markers of racial and cultural authenticity.

But if Fire is a vector for the transmission of cultural memory to diasporic Jamaicans, it is a function that he can never serve for Ian. In contrast to the twisted tutelage relationship that Ian has with Phil as he schools his white friend on how to be black—be a good lover; play jazz well—and to the underlying shared Afro-Jamaican identity that connects Fire and Sylvia, Ian and Fire's interactions remain largely in competition mode. Instead of honesty and vulnerability, they police their bodily closeness and remain behind walls of hardness enshrined in the proverbial dancehall refrain "man a wall." There is no place here for mutual engagement and sharing, not even the uneven and sexist tutelage where Fire subjects Sylvia to the "cataract of words" and ideas that constitutes her weekend internship in Jamaicanness (*WIV* 128). Fire's heroic perfection causes Ian to retreat into silence, brooding, and jealousy. In fact, the only time they see eye to eye is when listening together to the Shabba Ranks song. Stuck in male camaraderie and competition, and thus unable to access the sexual relationship that reconnects Sylvia to her roots, Ian attempts to undermine Fire the only way he knows how: by publicly assailing his masculinity. In another reversal of the romance arc, where attending a public performance of reggae awakens Sylvia's cultural memory, it is at a dancehall session that Ian and Fire's relationship finally erupts into verbal and physical violence. Ian's outburst telegraphs his sense that constructing himself in the crowd's psyche as the better lover will grant him ascendancy over Fire, since public acknowledgment of sexual prowess is the key marker of masculinity in dancehall culture. Contrary to the expectations of its romance plot, the novel's crisis is not the dustup between the lovers but the fistfight between the friends. Ian's subsequent suicide results not from a characterological flaw or a "bad seed" but from Fire's public and definitive rejection of Ian within the dancehall space.

Ian's migration from lyrical to physical gun reveals performative masculinity and "badness" as not only a defensive mechanism against insecurity but a kind of self-defense against *himself*. This illuminates the link between contemporary dancehall and the rude-bwoi cultures of the early rocksteady era chronicled in *The Harder They Come*. Like the dispossessed Rhygin, who turns to the gun to shore up his metaphoric impotence, Ian's self-loathing ends in self-annihilation; indeed, he takes the term *shotta* to its ambiguous lengths, capturing what Hope terms "the hard, phallic power that resides in the image of a gun—a symbolic and perpetually erect penis" (*Inna di Dancehall* 119). Rather than consolidating his belonging, as it does for Sylvia, Ian's return to Jamaica resurrects his suppressed memories of his placelessness and shatters his performative forgetting. With the failure of physical return, Ian has no viable space to retreat from the trauma of exile. If Rhygin becomes "rootless and adrift" when he loses his ancestral yaad, Ian is doubly exiled—both a-braad and a-yaad. His Indian roots exclude him from the return to the native land that Sylvia enjoys, and his failed return confirms what Sylvia feared: that not all returnees will find a place in Jamaica. Unable to go back or forward, he literally ends his narrative.

Dancehall songs often return to the trope of failed travel, often in the image of the deportee—emigrants ejected from first world countries due to either criminal behavior or immigration irregularities, who are returned to Jamaica in shame with little but a checkered plastic bag with a few belongings at best or only the clothes on their backs at worst. In comic songs like Buju Banton's "Deportee," the narrators invite the nation to deride these problematic compatriots for betraying their citizenship by leaving paradise only to discover that "foreign" is often a hostile space devoid of the natural blessings of bountiful fruit trees or sustaining kinship ties that patriotic Jamaicans enjoy on the rock.[27] The failed-travel narrative polices the well-established practice of fleeing the island for betterment instead of remaining to build the nation. According to failed-travel songs, patriotism even extends to rejecting foreign travel and "foreign mind" completely, even as this rejection presumes having the opportunity to travel in the first place. But Ian's narrative reveals that some yardies might have to leave home in order to thrive, even as *he* ultimately perishes.

Although failed-travel songs suggest that it is better to perish a-yaad than a-braad, in an essay in the *New York Times Magazine*, Marlon James, the Booker Prize–winning author of a more recent spin on the reggae novel, *A Brief*

History of Seven Killings (2014), recounts his epiphany that due to its ingrained homophobia and normalized antigay violence, Jamaica was not a place where he could thrive. He describes a lifetime of performing heteronormative masculinity through media consumption and affect, training his body to not betray its nonconformity and eventually performing a kind of code-switching that more accurately approximates self-erasure and masquerade. After years of suicidal ideation, he realized that he would have "to leave [his] home country—whether in a coffin or on plane" ("From Jamaica"). McKay also had to leave Jamaica to thrive as an artist, possibly also due to his (unconfirmed) homosexuality. Except in his poetry and fiction, McKay never physically returned to his birthplace. His dream in "I Shall Return" and *Banana Bottom* is possible for Fire and Sylvia, not for citizens who do not fit into the heteronormative or Afro-centric romance of the nation. As M. Jacqui Alexander has argued, "Not just (any)body can be a citizen." In the wake of the HIV/AIDS crisis, Caribbean governments enacted legislation to exclude birthright citizens whose sexual identities are considered nonnormative and nonproductive; Jamaica's former prime minister Bruce Golding even famously declared on BBC's *Hard Talk* that there could never be any homosexuals "in [his] cabinet" (Golding).

The trope of the nation as lover forecloses both homosexual and homosocial community formation. Jamaican music invites and inspires a return to the native land to reunite with the lover and Jamaica the "land we love," as the national anthem declares. Notice, for example, that near the end of the novel, the only reason Sylvia stops in Jamaica en route to St. Lucia is because of the prospect of a lover there. For Ian, however, there is no mechanism to enjoy this kind of successful return. Derek Walcott has theorized that "the traveller cannot love, since love is stasis and travel is motion. If he returns to what he loved in a landscape and stays there, he is no longer a traveller but [. . .] a native. So many people say they 'love the Caribbean,' meaning that someday they plan to return for a visit but could never live there, the usual benign insult of the traveller, the tourist" (*Twilight* 77). Walcott here intimates that fugue is antithetical not only to roots and return but perhaps also to the project of rehabilitated black love in which Channer is invested. *Waiting in Vain* insists that to heal black families and black nations, what is needed is rooting and memory. However, existing only as a foil—one of the novel's many "bad men"—to underscore Fire's uniqueness and perfection, Ian is doomed to performative fugue and problematic loving and his narrative place will always be circumscribed. True, his increasingly violent story dominates and sidelines the main narrative for entire stretches, but the romantic plot needs to excise him to get on with the business of reproducing the black nation through the consummation of Fire's and Sylvia's relationship and their establishing a home together in Jamaica. Ian is disqualified from the requisite "happily ever after" ending and thus from the national project in the same way that dancehall artistes continue to be marginalized from the acceptable construction of contemporary Jamaica.

From Yaad to Dis/Place

In his introduction to *Iron Balloons*, a collection of reggae-inspired short fiction, Channer reminds readers of the foundations of reggae "inna govament yaad in Trench Town" (ix), as Marley would sing in "No Woman No Cry." But if the yaad was central to reggae's development, where is dancehall's space? Stanley Niaah argues that dancehall emerges from both social and physical marginalization and has evolved its values and techniques in relation to spatial constraints, primarily occupying "marginal lanes, river banks and gully (ravine) banks, not only for housing and subsistence, but for performance as well" (18). She adds that dancehall's geographies recall the constrained spaces of the slave ship as remembered in the black body through the limbo dance that is frequently resurrected in popular dance moves as an embodied rememory (20). In the early 2000s, the phrase "me deh paa gully side" (I'm standing precariously on the sides of a ravine) resonated through dancehall music and popular parlance as a profound expression of precariousness, both literal—those who have had to erect makeshift homes in riverbeds—and figurative—those living hand to mouth. A recent *Vice Magazine* video, "Jamaica's Gully Queens," also brought to widespread attention that a number of LGBTQ Jamaicans have taken up residence in the "gully sides" of Kingston and St. Andrew to evade persecution and physical violence from homophobic compatriots. While reggae emerged from the displacement of Rastafarians to ghetto communes like "Back O' Wall" and Dungle, the municipal garbage dump, after their uprooting from Pinnacle and other fertile spaces of ownership and resistance, dancehall is today the site of the continued negotiation of marginalization within the national yaad.

In *Inna di Dancehall*, Hope condenses dancehall's social, political, and spatial marginalization in her term *dis/place*, which evinces the displacement, disorientation, and disrespect by the mainstream society that feeds the music culture. The term also captures the radical disruption that dancehall practitioners employ to disturb the peace, disregard respectability and social mores, and insist on their rights to personhood and human dignity (21–26). This concept of sonic disturbance already featured in early reggae. In "Bad Card," Marley fantasizes about using his loud, irreverent, and countercultural black music to "disturb my neighbor," in effect, to create what Erna Brodber calls a "black space" within the soundscape of the nation ("Reggae as Blackspace"). For Marley, black music was a sonic disturbance, located in the sound system's massive speakers, distorting reverb effects, and the lyrics' radical recentering of blackness that would "blow them to full watts tonight." But although roots reggae was the privileged locus of social and political disturbance, with reggae's ascendancy as the sound of the nation and Marley's oeuvre defanged into a "One Love" message despite that very song's radical political lyrics, it is dancehall music that today most often disturbs the Jamaican status quo.[28] Eternally irreverent, especially in its slackness mode, dancehall continues to disturb respectable Jamaicans. Its privileged mode, Jamaican Patwa, as opposed to the Patwa-inflected English of much of Marley's oeuvre, is still considered uncouth and disrespectful although it is Jamaica's mother tongue and nation language. Ian's "disturbing" behaviors throughout the novel, including his insistence on speaking Patwa even to non-Jamaicans, register his displeasure at cultural marginalization in the same way that dancehall practitioners contest their political and social marginalization with bright lights, loudness, lewdness, and carnivalesque, bottom-centered performances. Although Fire and Sylvia command the narrative spotlight, Ian uses dancehall tactics to divert attention to himself, insisting on his personhood even as the narrative and national discourses work to snuff out his presence and attenuate his disturbance.

As metaphors for civil rights, the novel's dancehall phonotopes depict the effects of erasure from national narratives. Ian's negotiation of marginal narrative space mirrors his attempt to counteract social marginalization. With little space for him in the national yaad and the national romance, his body—the only territory he possesses—becomes the site of his contestation of liminality and erasure. Stanley Niaah suggests that dancehall's violence is a rememory of colonial violence "learned well" and that risky behaviors in the music culture echo the desperate methods of self-harm on the slave ship and plantation: "In the midst of the violence that marginal existences offer, death, even suicide, becomes a choice" (46). Ian's "self-negation" is thus an inversion of and resignation to the failure of the quest for personhood and has analogs in other dancehall practices like skin bleaching. *Waiting in Vain* demonstrates how the repression or disavowal of aspects of memory and identity that do not fit orthodox narratives can cause psychic as well as sociopolitical harm. It depicts personal and cultural memory as an unstable and precarious document; its selective and performed retrievals can be as damaging as not remembering at all. But repressed, censored, or disallowed memories will interrupt and rupture the narrative. If forgetting is itself a form of psychic violence, its ultimate outcome for Ian in self-harm shows the psychic and physical ramifications of both cultural forgetting and certain kinds of cultural memory making.

Ian's violent expulsion from the novel illuminates the limits of musical ethnonationalism in an age of global citizenship and raises questions about whose cultural memories must be forgotten and erased to sustain national fictions. The very roots of nationalism, black liberty, and belonging are in slave revolts that marked the black reclamation of the plantation exile space as yaad; indeed, the Calibanesque reclamation of physical territory—"this island's mine"—is itself a violent statement. Although the Jamaican national crest and motto "Out of Many, One People" seems on the surface to celebrate ethnic diversity, Edmondson has argued that it collapses other ethnicities into a romanticized blackness even as the crest retains the memory of the violently erased and forgotten pre-Columbian peoples (*Caribbean Middlebrow* 117). Indeed, for former prime minister Edward Seaga, the visual memory of the Aruacs is an affront to his idealized image of a black nation and how it should be represented in its national symbols. "Out of Many, One" telegraphs an attitude to identity that flattens multiplicity—ethnicities in the nation, sonic influences in the music, genetic origins in the individual subject—into a single strand. It also demonstrates a kind of selective censorship where memories are evaluated then edited to forget those that trouble the project of self-making that precipitates remembering to begin with (Connerton; Slotnick 96).

Ian's marginalization from both the successful romantic arc and a successful return arc thus enables an interrogation of the ways that nation music can become an unsound record for subaltern citizens. Dawes has argued that the postcolonial power of reggae music stems from its recording of experiences absent from the literature of the same period (*Natural Mysticism* 24). But *Waiting* reminds us that even the most liberatory New World music idioms have more often than not privileged the black demographic even as they incorporate the sounds and contributions of musicians from a variety of ethnic groups: the story of jazz is told as black sonic resistance, reggae as the record of urban black suffering and quest for an African homeland, calypso as the perseverance of West African griot traditions and memory in the New World. In a truly Caribbean irony, blackness can and has become—at least discursively—its own hegemony. Where is the record of Indo-Caribbean experience, and how might Caribbean nation music include Indians not as objects of derision but as complete and complex subjects? As I explore in the final chapter, Indo-Caribbean subjects like Ian, seeking to rectify this exclusion, will need to interrupt the record of the nation and insert their voices and subjectivities into the narrative. If exclusion is a kind of violence, reinsertion has to be violent as well: the master narrative has to be disassembled and its fragments reassembled to create a more inclusive record.

CHAPTER 5

Memory as Mixtape

THE DUB AESTHETIC IN RAMABAI ESPINET'S *THE SWINGING BRIDGE*

Those of us Indians who moved towards greater integration were oddities whose task was to cut and paste and achieve some kind of fit into a Caribbean rapidly defining itself after Independence out of a colonial reality into something else.

—Ramabai Espinet, *Talk Yuh Talk*

If we take the extant depiction of the Indo-Caribbean woman in music until the mid-1990s, it would perhaps largely consist of her silence, the humming "mmm-mmm-mmm-mmm" that comprises the entirety of her audible presence in the Massala Stone folk song, her story told by a (presumed Afro-Creole) passerby who notes her demureness and her never-ending domestic labor ("grinding massala" "every time"). But her hum is not silence; it gestures to the undertones of music(ality) and an interiority to which passersby have no access. What is the unsung song being hummed? What is the Massala Stone woman thinking through song?[1] And where can we hear her sing, full-throated, all the repressed and unheard stories to which we have no access in the Creole nation space? As Merle Collins suggests by her poem, "Shame Bush," if subaltern communities keep silent, it is not always due to an absence of rich lives but a collective "curl[ing] inside itself . . . to defend itself" (52). But by hiding the shameful secrets of Indo-Caribbean women's experience, the community disallows negative representations from becoming visible and audible in the Creole nation sphere and leaves single stories in circulation; it also means there is little public access to sites of female resistance and subjectivity.

Trinidadian Canadian poet and novelist Ramabai Espinet has often voiced her concerns with the representations of Indo-Caribbean women in the region's literature, framing their invisibility and silencing as an "absent voice." Multiply subaltern, these women are rarely seen and even more rarely heard, poignantly encapsulated by the Massala Stone folk song. Espinet's poetry, fiction, and activism all serve to give voice to previously elided or caricatured aspects of the Indo-Caribbean experience.[2] Her 2003 debut novel *The Swinging Bridge* seeks to recover the "untold story" of female indentured workers and to break the silence around sexual violence within the Indo-Trinidadian household. Perhaps because of this, scholars have taken an almost exclusive interest in the novel's depiction of gender, sexuality, and ethnicity, focusing in particular on the exile experience of the narrator, Mona Singh, and the indenture experience of her great-grandmother, Gainder, a widowed chutney singer who arrived in Trinidad in 1879.[3] Gainder's voice is thrice-suppressed: her raunchy singing is forbidden by her husband, and both she and her songs are edited out of the family history by her son-in-law. But aside from brief references to Gainder's chutney music and Mona's invented Caroni dub, scholars have paid scant attention to the relationship between music and Mona's developing subjectivity.

In this chapter, I extend the feminist attention to voice to contend that Indo-Trinidadian women are further rendered inaudible within musical constructions of the nation.[4] Indeed, the novel's musicality is inseparable from its project of writing the subaltern self into visibility and voice. In the same way that, in the previous chapter, Channer's Ian discovers that postcolonial Jamaican identity as articulated through reggae's Afro-nationalism prevents his full integration into society, Mona realizes that the music idioms that comprise the soundtrack of her life encode problematic ideologies. Because of the relationship between music and national identity, Mona, like Ian, often feels excluded from popular music cultures even when music provides enjoyment and recovers memory. Whereas in previous chapters characters imagine an idyllic Caribbean homeland filled with the sounds of belonging, here music only exacerbates and documents Mona's unbelonging. As previous chapters have shown, musical nationalism and national romance often combine to fetishize notions of cultural authenticity, bound up in analog and embodied music media like the vinyl record and live instrumentation and predicated on notions of memory as the return to a prior state. This chapter therefore distinguishes Caribbean women's writing from that of male authors who are often invested in the romance of home and return. *The Swinging Bridge* affirms Donette Francis's contention that Caribbean women writing is often antiromance, even the romance of the nation (*Fictions* 4–5). It is also continuous with the predominant orientation of Indo-Caribbean scholarship in considering the community's continued experience of exile both within the Caribbean and upon migration to North America. Since Mona experiences "home" as a space of ethnic marginalization and sexual threat, she cannot become invested in normative notions of home and belonging, including romance and relationships.

To rectify unbelonging, Espinet suggests, Indo-Caribbean remembering will need to be creative and subversive; it will have to interrupt and disrupt the master narratives and master tapes that encode the community's erasure. In tracing the novel's critique of the ways that jazz, Presbyterian hymns, and calypso create exclusive sonic communities, this chapter considers how gender and ethnicity interrogate popular music hegemonies. Rather than a single nation music as in previous chapters, Mona remembers her Trinidadian identity through what I call a "memory mixtape"—a collection of remembered songs from a variety of genres that soundtrack both the novel and her memories. The novel's primary phonotope of the cassette tape also calls attention to features of Caribbean sonority and memory as well as to compositional practices most valuable for subaltern subjects. Even as I focus on the tension between sound and unsound practices and the types of music listening that enable the Indo-Trinidadian woman to negotiate her marginalization within collective music forms, I theorize paradigms of memory work that mimic cassette-era technologies and practices—from mobile and isolated listening to the creative editing of original recordings. The latter section of this chapter traces Mona's discovery of the performance and authorship practices that her foremothers have used to challenge orthodoxies and articulate subaltern subjectivities. These women deploy the aesthetics of Indo-Trinidadian chutney music and techniques similar to Jamaican dub music to insert their own voices and stories into unsound religious, patriarchal, or national master records. As I will show, these cassette-era tropes invest memory work with both mutability and fidelity even in the face of trauma and exile, particularly as memory can be shared, collected, and composed in order to bypass any unreliability of autobiographical memory. In this way, cassette-era memory work offers up multiple versions of memory to fill in archival gaps.

In terms that evoke the studio technique of dub, Espinet has described her artistic project to take "those [fragments] cast out of the community's 'official story' [and] fit [them] all together . . . to begin to fill out the picture—a more complex picture than we have at present" (Dawes, "Ramabai Espinet" 113). That process of reinserting jettisoned fragments into official records holds true for broader Indian representation in the narratives of the nation. She continues, "Those of us Indians who moved towards greater integration were oddities whose task was to cut and paste and achieve some kind of fit into a Caribbean rapidly defining itself after Independence out of a colonial reality into something else" ("Ramabai Espinet" 109). Modeling an ethical historiography and ethical memory work, editing existing records by "cut and paste" enables the would-be archivist to register Indo-Trinidadian women's voices within extant audile technologies. Consequently, Espinet's deployment of cassette-era musical tropes also intervenes in debates about Caribbean identity and the places of various ethnic groups within constructions of the nation. If, as I argued in the previous chapter, music is used to demarcate space and belonging both in foreign locales and at home, Espinet's Indo-Trinidadian characters create space for themselves: private spaces such as the home protect the community from view but also allow men to hide their abuse of women from critique or justice. Private spaces for the Indian woman such as *matikor* and journal-keeping, which—like the interiority alluded to in the Massala Stone song—allow for free expression of unorthodox desires but only become a prelude to her embedding into abusive heteronormativity. Since these spaces can be violated and these analog expressions erased by men, in the end, the novel points to dub's engineering techniques and technologies to both create and interrogate the allotment of space. Not only does dub allow previously erased voices to be heard in the mix; it also holds key implications for ethical listening and remembering.

The Memory Mixtape

Previous chapters have focused on public and communal technologies and forms of music listening. Technologies like the radio, the vinyl record, and sound system speakers and practices like Festival, Carnival, live performances, and tours enable the formation of national identity and collective memory. The original "horn" shape of the phonograph speaker visualized the activity of broadcasting audio from a single source to multiple persons that later speaker technologies only amplified. But by the 1950s and 1960s, a new recording and playback format had arrived that would change the sociality of listening and the nature of recorded composition. Magnetic tape had been in use in recording studios since the late 1950s and became a mass-market commodity in the late 1960s with the introduction of home cassette decks. The cassette's compact size and dual function as both recorder and player gave it advantages over LP-based systems. This new technology increased the layperson's enthusiasm for making her own recordings; as blank cassettes and dual tape decks grew popular, auditors could create and carry their own recordings on their person for private and portable consumption. The arrival of Sony's portable Walkman in 1979 further enabled auditors to create personal "aural environments" or "private auditory soundscape[s]" even while moving in public spaces (Morton 168; Bull 83). The miniaturization and portability of music increased with the advent of compact disc technology in the 1990s and culminated in the launch of Apple's iPod and the MP3 format in the early 2000s.

The Swinging Bridge is published in 1995, but the only music technologies it explicitly references are the radio and the cassette. Instead of a mechanical listening device, Mona listens to the songs that she carries within her own memory, music recorded and replayed in her mind wherever she may be. While in the past Mona clung to the "nowarian" identity she adopted from an invented childhood game, in the present she retreats into memory to evade unbelonging, an unviable relationship with her Scottish boyfriend, and the implications of her brother's AIDS diagnosis. Although she is moving forward on the train ride between Montreal and Toronto, where her family now lives, her mental journey takes her further backward in both time and space to the Trinidad of her childhood as she searches for clues to her present malaise and to reconstruct her fractured identity.

Mona's first-person narrative bears the hallmarks of trauma: her interiority is often masked under the stories of others and, even when remembering intense personal experiences, she narrates them using video recording imagery, passive voice, and a third-person filmic point of view. The novel ultimately attributes Mona's psychic disconnect to suppressed sexual trauma as well as exile. Early in *The Swinging Bridge*, Mona reflects that Indo-Trinidadian families have to live within "close and thick and sheltering . . . family walls . . . and once you leave [home,] you have no shelter and no ready skills for finding a different one" (*TSB* 15). As its epigraph from Gabriela Mistral's "Doors" attests, the novel chronicles Mona's quest not for temporary shelter but a home. In the face of repeated rejection that "deadens / the songs we sing inside," Mona's emotional coldness or "mean rind" has grown to match her cold reception. Part of the irony and pathos of the poem is that the door of the house at which the speaker stands without hope of access is "my house," not a stranger's (Mistral 314–315). Like the speaker of "Doors" and Channer's Ian, Mona's response is psychic and physical fugue, or internal and external exile, the continual urge to "go away" whether by migration or memory. Mona's family fled an exclusionary nationalism in 1970s postcolonial Trinidad. But although Canada had opened up its borders to middle-class Indo-Caribbean migrants, the new arrivants were coldly received by their neighbors, as indexed by the "Keep Canada White" graffiti Mona's father encountered upon migration (*TSB* 243). Already "set adrift" from the Trinidad of her childhood, Mona continues to feel rootless and isolated in her new "home" country, even now in her forties. Unlike fellow immigrant Carene, whose apartment, like her speech, broadcasts her Haitian roots, Mona's apartment still reflects the unsettled uncertainty of college living, and her Caribbeanness has been scrubbed to a bland indefinability that matches her "nowarian" identity.

Her present exclusion from mainstream Canadian society is encapsulated in an exchange with a fellow train passenger that begins with a musical violation of Mona's personal space. Her reminiscing is "abruptly . . . interrupted by the sound of a radio two seats down," which drags her back to the present (*TSB* 46). When she deigns to upbraid the white Canadian passenger, she is invited to "go back to where [she] came from." Mona is profoundly "shaken, suddenly close to tears at . . . the racism of this place that was always ready to crack you across your back when you least expected it" (47). This early scene thus establishes the train as a microcosm of society and music as a marker of both belonging and exclusion. Far from a democratizing space, the train reinforces the anti-immigrant sentiment that reigns in the rest of society.

Despite not having a physical musical player, Mona turns the train into her own personal mobile listening and remembering space that allows her to tune out the racist sounds of the Canadian train and tune in to her memories instead. As Michael Bull has suggested, personal listening devices grant auditors a sense of control over their experiences as they use "auditory nostalgia" to transport themselves elsewhere in place and time and away from the encroachment of collective sonorities (83). Likewise, Heike Weber found that some midcentury West German tourists brought along portable audio devices that transmitted sounds from home to enable them to negotiate foreign culture through the creation "of a personally controlled auditory space" that "reassured mobile listeners of their autonomy and identity anytime, anywhere" (70). Similarly, even without a prosthetic device, Mona's sonic memories of her childhood make Trinidad portable and present while she traverses the exilic Canadian space. Remembering insulates her from the public social space of the unwelcoming hegemonic culture represented by the train, where mainstream sounds can seep in but private sounds barely seep out—or seep out enough to register one's difference.

Audition of portable music, and thus the insularity it fosters, is facilitated by the use of headphones. Popularized in the Walkman era, headphones enable auditors to construct private sonic worlds by enveloping them in a wall of sound that simultaneously dampens unwanted sounds from without. Later, noise-canceling headphones would further enable mobile listeners to determine the extent to which they allow outside sounds in—useful for commuters and pedestrians to hear vital sounds including car horns and approaching trains. Mona's annoyance at the passenger, whose "loud and unappetizing" radio-listening jolts her back to the present, registers how, by listening without "wear[ing] earphones," he imposes his tastes on other passengers (*TSB* 46). The use of headphones for individual and insular mobile listening enables the construction of subjectivity and privacy. Particularly in the early days of large metal cans, headphone-wearing also signals to the surrounding world the auditor's desire to be left alone. With this visible and sometimes audible "do not disturb" sign about their heads, mobile listeners can retreat not just into private sounds but also into private memories.

If the move from phonograph and radio to cassette technologies evinced a shift from collective to private listening, it also shifted nostalgia from collective to private. Private mobile listening renders recollection *consciously* individual and insular.[5] In Mona's case, remembering creates an invisible headphone that isolates her from the present in a personal bubble, even as, without the visible sign of unavailability, she is liable to be interrupted by fellow passengers. While radio culture presumes collective listening and lack of control over the music one hears, portable audio technologies move control and composition into the hands of the lay listener. Even before the advent of technologies—Apple's iPod, the iTunes store, file-sharing sites like Napster and Limewire, and more recently, streaming music sites like Spotify—that allowed listeners to create playlists suited to different moods or reflecting the listening tastes of a particular moment of one's life, the mass-market commoditization of the blank cassette and the double tape deck allowed consumers to create mixtapes. Consumer mixtapes are end-user-created recordings containing a "mix" of various songs that issue from multiple sources (Jansen).[6] Later in the chapter, I discuss the manipulation of tape in the recording studio to create dub plates, but here I want to distinguish two types of personal mixtapes.

In radio-centric societies like the Caribbean, the most common kind of mixtape was the composite cassette recording that a listener would make by recording favorite songs from the radio. This setup required a stereo equipped with at least a single cassette deck. Radio listening connotes passive remembering. Ben Anderson has called this "involuntary remembering" when a song or lyric suddenly comes to mind, interrupting the present and jolting the subject back to the past (9–10); Bob Snyder categorizes this under unconscious recognition, when something in current perception triggers a neural link to information stored in long-term memory (10). Mixtapes move music listening from public and passive to private and agented. As Mona's conscious replay and involuntary remembering illustrate, she was not in control of creating the tape reel of memories that burst through the novel's present nor the order of replay of the associated memories. Instead, intense emotion—trauma and happiness both—engraved songs and memories on her mind in random order.

Whereas the typical radio station in 1970s Trinidad played a heterogeneous mix of songs and genres interspersed with commercials, news, weather, and announcer talk, the personal mixtape would hold only those tunes that the listener liked and wanted to own and listen to at will (Balliger; Ramcharitar). Radio mixtapes might be single- or multigenre, but the selection and song order are relatively ad hoc—one might not know when the desired song will be replayed—and the ability to record the entire song without losing bits at the end or the beginning became a skillful practice. Because of the nature of radio play and the role of radio and communal singing as the dominant sources of music transmission, Mona's childhood soundscape and subsequent memory mixtape consist of a variety of individual songs and music forms—jazz, calypso, hymns, South Asian *bhajans* and chutney music, and even Jamaican dub—not all of which are immediately associated with Indo-Trinidadian identity.[7] The novel's sonority thus mimics the ad hoc characteristic of mixtapes and the interruptive nature of memory.

The frustration of not having complete control over song selections and recording quality lends itself to the popularity of the second type of mixtape: the personal playlist culled from owned or borrowed cassettes. Nick Hornby's popular novel *High Fidelity* is one of many depictions of mixtape practice: the careful planning and selection of songs and the order of their appearance on the tape for maximum emotional or narrative impact (88–89). The creation of such mixtapes required a stereo with either a dual cassette deck or, later, a combination CD-player and cassette deck, with the music listener moving from audience to creator in the guise of the radio DJ, themselves also famous for their expert mixes. It also presumes ownership of recorded music, whereas in the Caribbean, outside of collectors and aficionados, private mixtapes more likely included bootlegged or borrowed sources. The curated mixtape usually served one of two purposes: to narrate a musical message to a loved one—the confession or seduction mixtape being the most popular—or to create a personal playlist of songs to suit a mood or purpose. In this way, the latter type of mixtape more closely resembles contemporary streaming music playlists. But whereas a Spotify playlist can be constantly edited and updated with microchanges, a cassette mixtape has to be destroyed to be edited; a single accidental tape-over would destabilize the entire flow. Such mixtapes lend themselves to what Ben Anderson calls "intentional remembering" at both the composition and the listening stages; listening to remember is a curatorial act that includes selecting, evaluating, and storing music in anticipation of a future remembering, and it presupposes that this music is already meaningful to the listener (15).

The mixtape trope demonstrates the inherent sonority and musicality of Caribbean memory in general and Mona's memory in particular. Many of her memories are not just musical but sonic, comprising overheard conversations and sounds that she has recorded in her memory with a kind of technological fidelity—the phonographic memory that characters throughout this book have displayed. Although Mona's memory operates much like a tape recorder, in contrast to the presumptive accuracy of recorded music, Mona constantly questions the fidelity of her remembering and whether the absence of mechanical technology lessens the fidelity of capture and the possibility of later retrieval: a "melody [that] stays [while] those missing words of the song remain beyond reach" (*TSB* 69) or once-treasured "tales [that] fad[ed] from my memory" (80). Despite the requisite repetition and embedding in social contexts that once enabled their memorization, time and distance have broken the neural links that would allow her to call up the missing tales and song lyrics. Tina Ramnarine reports an account by a Trinidadian chutney singer who describes the challenge of documenting old-time songs: "I went to old people in the village who knew the songs. It took me about a year to compile these songs because, you know, the old people sometimes they tell you 'I remember a verse and I forget the next verse' . . . They used to sing and I wrote. Sometimes when they're singing they'll give you the first verse last and the last verse first. You have to think about it after you've written it down and put it in order'" (23).

Can remembered experience suffice as a faithful record, or might an archivist concerned with ethical historiography need a combination of remembering and recording, where the latter allows the archivist to rewind the tape, evaluate the recording, and "put [things] in order"? As I have argued throughout this book, the repetitive nature of Caribbean music culture enables a pseudotechnological memory capacity that is even further enhanced by trauma and other high-intensity experiences. Although short-term memory only holds information for a few seconds before it decays, repetition (rehearsal), intensity, or unexpectedness can allow data to persist and ultimately move into long-term memory storage. *The Swinging Bridge* seems to support the early record-keeping theory, which envisages memory as "a tape recorder or digital video camera, preserving all or most of our experiences accurately, and with near perfect fidelity" (Levitin 135). If both the emotional significance of an experience and its association with music increase its long-term encoding, trauma and music replay function in similar ways to engrave experiences in memory. Oliver Sacks has described the experience of people, who, following some trauma, develop an unusual musicality where their minds replay music with incredible fidelity. Given the repetitive nature of sexual violence and Mona's witnessing of it, her memories of music are cued with "the repeated stimuli" of intense, traumatic memories that become associated with particular sounds and music (Snyder 69–70). Exile separates the auditor from the memory cues that cultural immersion creates and reinforces; as Snyder explains, "When a particularly long-term memory is no longer actively used, its connections with other more active memories become much weaker, and there are fewer associative pathways through which to cue its recall" (71).

But counterintuitive as it may seem, trauma in some ways counteracts the rupturing of neural links caused by exile. Mona's deployment of a mental tape recorder suggests that her memory can replay traumatic experiences as if she had mechanical technology. She invokes a pair of field glasses as a model for her role as the archivist of the sexual victimization of Indo-Trinidadian women; although they are "not a camera" and are thus devoid of the capacity to record experience, she "continued to look through [them], and kept them all through [her] moves and uprooting" (*TSB* 33–34). While on the surface the trope of the field glasses seems to decry the inability of memory alone to record and reproduce events with fidelity, Mona in fact illuminates how memory stands in for the lack of a technological apparatus to record a stable document even while recognizing that memory is itself unstable. It is with her memory alone—and later, a few words scribbled in her journal—that she has recorded most of the memories she now recalls. The efficacy of retrieval, she suggests, depends on determining how to balance memory's one "loose and unfocused" lens with "the other tight as a drum" (33–34).

In her account of witnessing Uncle Baddall's assault on her mother, Mona reveals the origins of her adult narrative perspective as an invisible watcher. As with the broken field glasses, Mona simply watched the action with one good eye, recording traumatic events with her memory. This and other acts of intimate violence against women consequently have no written record, only the witness of a young girl. The mental snapshot also resonates with her reference to "the eye of the world" that looks on without intervening when a stranger tried to drag her off and rape her in a cane field (*TSB* 44). These tropes allow Mona to interrogate who sees, records, and remembers scenes of sexual violence. Memory records are not panoramic, omniscient views of time and experience but subjective, partial, perspectival renderings. This is the inherent "flaw" in even the most mimetic recording, and the novel repeatedly asks what happens when vital records are incomplete and marginalizing. Remembered testimonies of trauma survivors often turn out to be historically "inaccurate," which poses a quandary for researchers; such testimonies serve not to document history in objective terms but to evidence the experience of trauma and to enable the survivor to recollect her past and self (LaCapra 188–189). Although testimonies about traumatic experience are often marshaled in the service of justice, Mona's experience suggests that our minds are not recording events to service juridical testimony. Even as she remembers her near-rape with remarkable fidelity, she does not remember the entire license plate of the taxi that passed by without intervening—only because it "swooshed past" (*TSB* 43). But her memory remains faithful to details that had time to make a memory impression—for instance, the man's smell, "stale saffron powder and stinking ram-goat sweat," that still makes her nauseous (44).

That Mona conceives of these scenes as "permanent memory" suggests that if it could be brought into evidence, memory might serve as an alternate recording to the historical documents that bear no record of Indo-Trinidadian women's experiences. The novel itself becomes a music and memory player, with remembered music functioning as a kind of aural diary, enabling Mona to rifle through the story of her life and to call up a vivid replay of experiences associated with certain songs. Key memories of her Trinidadian childhood come preloaded with a soundtrack of the songs that constructed her identity beyond her control and curation. Now, as an adult, she must reevaluate and edit this sonic catalog into a cohesive record of her present and future self. As I show later in the chapter, the fact that cassette technology allows the editing of recorded memory and the remembered self will become crucial to Mona's historiographic practice.

Interrogating Master Records

The Swinging Bridge demonstrates that music can be *unsound* if it does not articulate the voices of the silenced or if it silences certain constituents in its turn. I extend *unsoundness* to not just musical records but written documents as well—not just male-authored texts like history books but even documents created by women. In her work as a film researcher, Mona uncovers the pivotal role played in the Haitian revolution by a *vodou* priestess named Cecile Fatiman, whereas the history books only focused on male heroes like "Toussaint L'Ouverture, Dessalines, and Henri Christophe" (*TSB* 10). The novel's foregrounding of this moment reveals history as a male-authored, male-centered record, or what Myriam Chancy calls a "faulty collective memory" that elides the contributions of women; these undocumented histories are only recovered through stories orally transmitted to Mona by migrant women, evincing a new kind of collective memory "that is rooted in women's personal interaction with each other" (Chancy, *Framing Silence* 21). However, in what Mona sees as an act of textual and historical violence, the filmmaker Carene edits out Fatiman's role (*TSB* 61). Carene's documentary becomes an unsound record in its own right: it leaves some women on the cutting room floor of history even as it recuperates others from erasure, and it depicts memory as selective and enmeshed in power relations.

The music of Mona's childhood also creates an unsound record of the Indo-Trinidadian experience; the various idioms she recalls in Canada all create collective sonorities that register her exclusion. Indeed, despite their hybrid origins, their cultural valence has been flattened to convey monolithic and exclusionary identities and experiences. Heard only in the background as the soundtrack to Canadian coldness and whiteness, the novel's jazz phonotopes mirror the relationship between the Caribbean migrant and the new home space, an alienation bound up in race—Roddy, Mona's Scottish boyfriend with whom she often listens to jazz, has no problems fitting in—which is even more ironic given this foreign musical form's ready acceptance into the Canadian soundscape. But Mona's present internal exile in Canada has its roots in the role of that country's Presbyterian missions in Trinidad in forming an Indian middle class estranged from its indentured background and culture. These memories are encoded alongside the hymns of her happy childhood, with lyrics that create a false consciousness for Indo-Trinidadian converts who internalize the racial economy of white Presbyterianism while accepting their marginalization—only able to attain "the edge of that circling sphere" (*TSB* 30). The hymns soundtrack Mona's memories of the wide-ranging deleterious effects of Presbyterian education and religious values on the Indo-Trinidadian psyche and traditional culture, including the dissolution of ethnic marriages, the erasure of Hindu names for Christian ones, and the repression of women's sexual identities.

Remembered music further reveals that even before migration, Mona's sense of home was already tenuous. Inspired by prime minister Eric Williams's promise to build a Trinidad in which "all o' we is one," as goes the unofficial motto romanticizing the nation's cultural and racial unity,[8] Mona's father uprooted the family from the yard where they buried their umbilical cords, a symbol of anchoring and belonging. Mona bemoans her traumatic uprooting from this memory site as the reason she is unable, at forty-odd years old, to find her place in the world: "I never put down roots again after Manahambre Road. . . . A settled life we had never had. How to begin to compare that precariousness with the settled lives of people we encounter in North American or Europe? What must it be like to take for granted a place for everything and everything in its place?" (*TSB* 204–205). Mona's father expressed his desire to move to the modern city of San Fernando as a desire for musical modernity: having access to electricity to play the radio, in contrast to their "backward" village where music was premodern and analog, experienced only through singing. More importantly, moving to San Fernando brought the family access to calypso (*kaiso*) music, the sound of the emergent independent Afro-Creole nation-state.

Having fermented for centuries in the plantation system as a counterhegemonic form of black performance and resistance, calypso is historically associated with Afro-Trinidadian culture. While not exclusionary by virtue of this, several factors led Indo-Trinidadians to feel excluded from calypso and Carnival, the rowdy subversive annual rituals during which and for which calypso songs are created and performed. The rising Afro-Trinidadian elite led by Williams imbricated black culture with Trinidadian culture and promoted calypso and Carnival as symbols of the nation (Morgan). The association of calypso and Carnival with bawdy lyrics and public licentiousness, which was anathema to conservative Indo-Trinidadians, kept them out of the calypso tents, but the matter was exacerbated by the lyrics of some popular calypsos that portrayed Indo-Trinidadians as comical, derisive outsiders to the Afro-Creole nation (Niranjana 131; Rohlehr 494). Like many Afro-Caribbean music forms, calypso problematically signals a romanticized national essence through performances that caricature or render nearly half of the population invisible.

Written two decades before *The Swinging Bridge*, Earl Lovelace's 1979 calypso novel *The Dragon Can't Dance* offers a meditation on the place of Indo-Trinidadians in the musical and social construction of the nation. With the Indo-Trinidadian character Pariag (perhaps a play on *pariah*) tagged as "the Spectator" in music culture as well as the nation-building process of the independence era, Lovelace uses music to register how Afro-Trinidadian neighbors continually rebuff Pariag's attempts at simple human recognition, showing very forcefully that there is no place for "the Indian" even in the yard, this symbol of communal living. As its own calypso phonotopes attest, *The Swinging Bridge* echoes concerns about the invisibility of the Indo-Trinidadian in the same historical period in which the earlier novel is set. Told from Mona's own "spectator" perspective, the novel chronicles Mona and her father's growing unease with the portrayal of Indo-Trinidadians in calypso. At first, the seven-year-old Mona and her father are enamored of calypso and consider it "our poetry." Like Pariag, who starts life on the Hill drawn to calypso and Carnival, Mona fondly remembers that "falling into sleep hearing the minor key dipping and falling and making music out of our daily lives, I was a happy child" (*TSB* 98). But this idyll is ruptured with a series of unsettling incidents. In one instance, calypso's trademark social commentary is turned on Indo-Trinidadians when the winning calypso road march song records a murder committed by two Indo-Trinidadian men: "Da-Da came home sickened by the revelry. The dancing crowds were urging the hanging of the two men because they were Indians, of that he was convinced. . . . 'It ain't have no place here for Indians. . . . I have to get out a here'" (100–101). Evidently, while on the surface Mona initially attributes her psychic disconnect to the destruction of her childhood home, calypso lyrics trigger the memory that Indo-Trinidadians were not even at home in their own nation.

Although the music and lyrics Mona remembers evoke happy memories of her premigratory self with the enhanced fidelity that music lends to memory, replaying her memory mixtape allows her to hear valences encoded in the music that she missed as a child. Young Mona happily sang along to Presbyterian hymns and calypso music because she was co-opted into collective belonging by the radio diffusion of these songs. But like her father had decades before, she now realizes that she is the object rather than the subject of calypso songs; that she can only approach "the edge" of hegemonic music cultures (*TSB* 30). She is neither the blue-eyed, white-as-snow subject of hymns who will enter into heaven nor the black subject who will find belonging in jazz. In effect, these idioms are sonic doors that invite her partway into audile communities but are "only half-open / turning their . . . backs" in a reminder that she is only a stranger and temporary dweller in the house to which they grant access (Mistral 314). Echoing Ian's fugue in the previous chapter, these scenes suggest that Caribbean exile might not be the *origin* but the *outcome* of performative memory and forgetting. Buffeted on one side by a self-denigrating Presbyterian respectability and on the other by a discursive and effective erasure in national discourse, Mona's family has no recourse but to "pitch . . . about from place to place" (*TSB* 204).

With both written and musical records complicit in the erasure of Indo-Trinidadian subjectivities, Espinet's solution is not to demand a place within the jazz, Presbyterian hymns, and calypso canons—although as the purported sound of the postcolonial Trinidadian nation, calypso has a greater burden of including the Indo-Trinidadian voice than the other "foreign" idioms. Instead, the novel proposes empowering women to unearth their own testimonies, construct their own archives, and write themselves into master records. As the second and most vital stage of Mona's remembering, then, she returns to Trinidad and turns to the insular space of the *matikor* to discover where and how Indo-Caribbean women sound (*TSB* 227).

Chutney: Sounding Indo-Trinidadian Woman Memory

As a counter to unsound master records, the novel's turn to Indo-Trinidadian music underscores the importance of oral modes of memory transmission through which, as Chancy notes in *Framing Silence*, "history . . . can be displaced in order to make room for an alternative remembrance of the erosion of time, of the formation of previously invisible cultures" (12). Helen Myers, Tina Ramnarine, and others distinguish two main categories of "Indian" music in the postindentureship Caroni region of southern Trinidad, Mona's birthplace.

Classical songs called *bhajans* are derived from religious texts such as the *Ramayana* and the *Mahabharata*, often learned by heart from radio, records, and temple singing (Myers 105). In contrast, composed songs include Afro-Trinidadian calypso music and wedding songs such as *lachari* and chutney—the latter referring to spicy or "hot" songs full of sexual suggestiveness drawn from the same epic source as *bhajans* (Myers 108). Wedding songs like chutney are performed in a ceremony called the *matikor*, a performance of unorthodox female sexuality that takes place in an exclusive female space where women are both performers and audience. Over the course of several days and nights, Hindu women prepare the bride for her wedding night by enacting sexual relations, parodying and satirizing men by forming phallic shapes with their clothes, and dancing to the sexually suggestive *lachari* songs. In the *matikor* space, woman memory is transmitted from generation to generation in a safe, private environment away from both the male and Western gaze, and Indian women's voices sound in song, laughter, and storytelling.

Beyond its significance as a female performance mode, chutney is also a key marker of Indo-Trinidadian specificity. After indentureship, Indo-Caribbean musicians maintained cultural links to India through transplanted and "half-remembered musical elements" (Manuel et al. 254). However, Patricia Mohammed notes that Indian cultural memory continued to be renewed during the 1930s when imported Indian films conveyed lively images of epics, classical music, and twentieth-century subcontinental culture (78–79). Ramnarine also contends that although chutney retains elements from Bhojpuri musical traditions, the *dhantal, dholak*, and harmonium have become synonymous with, if not sonic markers of, Caribbean Indian identity; they mark chutney as the sound of Indo-Trinidadian culture within Carnival and, later, as chutney-soca, within national popular music culture (68).[9]

Subaltern women in the novel recompose *bhajans*—which often celebrate monogamy and Ram's authority—into subversive chutney songs that bear witness to female experience, including the sexual violence of men visited on women and women's sexual or romantic longings. Subaltern sexuality is first revealed to Mona in the memory of Baboonie—a woman so downtrodden that her very name, Hindi for "little girl," is reductive. The entirety of Baboonie's experience is summed up in the male-authored tale of a loose and battered woman: "Everybody around here does beat that'" (*TSB* 111), with "beat" here doubling as physical violence and sexual subjection. Reconstructing Baboonie's tale from eavesdropped fragments of memory and song, Mona imagines that the woman "fought off intruders upon her body with curses and threats and words sung from the holy books" (112). Baboonie was "singing *Ramayana*"—indeed, voicing the very patriarchal narrative that empowered the men who abused her with impunity, who rose in the morning coddled by their wives and "walk[ed] upright, wielding their cutlasses" on their way to work (112). But if the *Ramayana* is the unassailable record of Indian gender norms, then Baboonie's "broken chords" and discordant voice interrupted this master record with her "curses and threats." She fragmented "the classical words of the *Ramayana* with her own tale" and "with broken chords and unexpected riffs" forced it to sound out her victimization. In so doing, she inserted herself in the grooves of the rigid epic of "purity" and chastity (114). Singing her feminist version of *Ramayana* was her antidote to sexual violence, her transmutation of pain into "music and a story," song and narrative (113).

For their part, the three recovered chutney songs of Mona's great-grandmother Gainder echo traditional chutney themes of marriage and courtship and Indian arrival and indenture. The one that became a popular song speaks of fidelity in the classic tradition of *Ramayana*: "Faithful like Sita / Virtuous like Lakshmi / . . . I will kiss your feet, offer water" (*TSB* 296). The lyric's tantalizing duality lies in the fact that it is sung in the subversive *matikor* space where young women are nevertheless prepared for marriage and domesticity. Even further—and likely why Gainder's husband prohibits her from walking through the village singing it—it expresses her desire for and fidelity to not Joshua, whom she is forced to marry, but the kind shipmate on the crossing from India who saved her from being raped and who paid for his insubordination by being abandoned off the coast of Africa. Having recorded on cassette tape a village *rand* pronouncing the Hindi words and singing the song, Mona remarks that the faithfully remembered and tape-recorded song evinces "the triumph of fidelity" (293). Here, marital fidelity is undercut by musical fidelity and the fidelity of woman memory. Gainder's songs simultaneously sound out subversive secret longings and desires that hide mask-like under their surface themes. They romanticize Ram's mobility and masculine prowess while idealizing Sita's demure fidelity as she waits for Ram to rescue her from the threat of sexual victimization. Indeed, the epic source of chutney means that the songs must negotiate the romanticization of marital rape in religious texts even as the same tales are used to promote female chastity and virtue (Mohammed 73–74).

If her remembered music registers the social exclusion and silencing of Indian subjectivity by Afro-Caribbean and North American music cultures, Mona's research into her family's history reveals censorship *within* the Indo-Caribbean community, where men rip certain stories out of official historical documents and the archives of collective memory. Suspecting her of looseness because she earned a living from singing unorthodox chutney music, which was anathema to Presbyterian respectability, Joshua forbade Gainder to sing and dance, and subsequent generations of men banned her daughters from singing and transmitting her songs, even from transmitting her memory (*TSB* 262). Even as the women of the family secretly record and transmit Gainder's memory, all that remains of Gainder in the family history is "a three-sentence history" on the last page and "the telltale marks of pages torn out. . . . This copy was the only one that I could find and [Grandpa Jamesie] had ripped out the songs" (271).

These unsound records reveal that such stories are internally censored partly due to the unspeakable nature of the Indo-Trinidadian woman's experience: the internal and domestic violence she must silently bear to not bring shame on the community in the eyes of majority culture and to protect their men from further disparagement by their Afro-Creole compatriots. The untold stories that Mona uncovers and replays from her own memory record all hinge on sexual and textual violence in the wake of women's sexual and romantic freedoms that are read as a threat to Indian masculinity. Like written records, the popular music these women enjoy does not tell that story. Espinet has bemoaned the "tacit communal guerilla" secret keeping that has enabled the community's survival but left Indian women locked in systems of complicity and voicelessness (Dawes, "Ramabai Espinet" 112). Instead, illiterate, battered women transmit this memory. Indeed, the next section of the novel opens with Mona waking up in Trinidad to the voice of another battered woman—whose name, Girlie, is the Creole version of Baboonie—singing a chutney song:

> If you love me
> Do not rough me
> Sweet soap and powder
> You must gi'e me. (*TSB* 282)

With this brash challenge to normalized domestic violence and a demand for sweetness and gentleness, chutney songs allow women like Girlie to move from the muted hum of the Massala song, remembered a few pages later, to an open-voiced articulation of women's concerns.

Although Mona seems to advocate censorship and repression when she argues that "some events should disappear entirely, banished forever from one's mind" (*TSB* 166), not only do those repressed events resurge in dreams and in the waves of nausea with which her body reminds her of the presence of sexual threat, but the novel also foregrounds the importance of remembering and documenting domestic abuse; indeed, censorship only allows victimization to continue in silent complicity. Even as Uncle Baddall accused his wife of premarital infidelity when in fact she was raped (169), he himself was carrying on a years-long incestuous interference with both Mona and her mother. Mona has secreted the memory of her initial assault into the name of the place where this first transgression occurred; the name "Jerningham Junction" functions as an audible trigger and physical memory palace that holds and hides the memory until it is cued (235–236). Mona's alternate memory record reveals that while calypso songs and the cultural narrative decry Indian girls' wantonness and the threat of Afro-Creole sexual "contamination" (Reddock 191), the real threat was behind closed doors: in family kitchens and bathrooms, places of privacy that should be safe spaces for women. The real threats to Indian girls' full development were their fathers and uncles and brothers, and this continued into adulthood (*TSB* 236–237). That her aunt Vannie, Baddall's wife, witnesses Mona's final struggle to avoid being raped by her uncle at age fifteen but keeps the secret unspoken attests to the insidiousness of intimate partner violence and the collusion of silence to protect the illusion of Indian respectability.

For Indo-Caribbean feminist scholars, chutney's "movement to the national stage is a transgressive one that creates the potential for hybridity without losing the reference of the female-centered *matikor*, thus opening up a space for a new inclusive form that transforms both the *matikor* songs and the calypso" (Mahabir and Pirbhai 8). This is what makes chutney singers like Drupatee Ramgoonai, who take spicy Indo-Trinidadian sexuality into the Afro-Creole and male-dominated calypso tent, so subversive and a frequent subject of Indo-Caribbean feminist inquiry. However, for all their counterhegemonic power, chutney songs do not necessarily dismantle the gender dynamics that oppress and silence the women in *The Swinging Bridge*. Gainder's female descendants from Lil to Mona do not enjoy the freedom Gainder dreams of in song. That Gainder herself loses that freedom once she marries Joshua suggests that the freedoms afforded by chutney and the *matikor* space are only performed and provisional. Once married, the empowered woman is tamed into submission and forced to jettison the freewill love offering that Gainder gives to her kind shipmate for lives of loveless respectability or emotional repression.

The novel also reveals that there still remains little space in the mainstream for a radical revision of the dominant narratives of Indian womanhood. In her preliminary gesture to restore indentured women's place in Trinidadian history, Mona edits Lil's written record to "replace the pages torn out from the family history" (*TSB* 294–295). She then mounts the song for her cousin Bess's Diwali display commemorating the 150th anniversary of the arrival of the first indentures. Mona's choices are curious: rather than a sonic record—a cassette tape or CD of the *rand* singing the song (this is 1995, after all)—she mounts a *written* and ultimately silent display. Bess's editorial decisions further silence the full history of the *rands*: "'You see, Mona, the grand picture is still what everybody wants. The righteous Indian family, intact, coming across the *kala pani* together. Like the way the migration is presented today. Not this story'" (297). The historical record is still censored to fit the unsound revisionist narrative created by indentures on their arrival in Trinidad and deployed as their myth of origins. For the story of Indian womanhood to enter the narrative and museums of Trinidadian history, it must conform to the same priorities of orthodoxy that silenced her in the first place. In the service of ethnonationalism, Indo-Trinidadian women's songs and stories continue to be excised from sonic and written records. If not in 1995, if not at Diwali, if not in a museum of Indo-Trinidadian history, then when and where can this story be told? It might seem that the novel leaves this question unanswered, ending as it does with both the premiere of Carene's Haitian film, which has space for a pig but not Cecile Fatiman, and the Diwali museum, which will allow a *visual* display of once-popular chutney songs but will *hear* neither the songs nor the experiences of the women who sung them. The fate of the Diwali display suggests that these recovered records remain silent until transmuted from silent writing back to sound. They must be *sounded* so that they can challenge orthodoxies, since written records can be erased, overwritten, or ripped out of official versions.

With authorship, recording, and history traditionally male-centered,[10] the novel tracks Mona's attempt to find a form to articulate female victimization at the hands of men and male-authored records. This form must carry the double weight of sounding out sexual and narrative trauma. This is consonant with Francis's contention in *Fictions of Feminine Citizenship* that since "regulation[s] of Caribbean intimacy are often violently enacted upon the bodies of Caribbean women and girls . . . writing such violence—both in terms of social practices as well as physical acts of sexual violence—has become the grounds for an emergent Caribbean feminist poetics" (2–3). In contrast to analog media that rely on aura and authenticity as defined by proximity to the body of the performer (Benjamin 220–223) and whose single master copies are originals that if destroyed are lost forever, modernity enabled sound to become technologized and commoditized—replicable, repeatable, and transportable in exact copies that decentralize the importance of the master. Mona's recuperative historiography thus has to convert purely oral testimonies into records that can survive, and even resist, destruction. Silenced both as pure song and as pure writing, the story of Indo-Trinidadian women's experiences requires a form that allows both songs and untold stories to be played and heard with fidelity—in other words, a new *technique* of recording memory.

The Dub Aesthetic: Ethical Remembering

Even though Mona returns to her Caribbean birthplace to reclaim the land where her navel string is buried, this return this does not reroot her in her native soil; instead, it allows her to draw enough sustenance from her roots to nourish her continued exile. Her experience affirms that the high-fidelity engraving of music on the mind results from frequent and repeated listening, each repetition deepening the grooves of the memory record and moving the sound event from short-term to long-term memory. Refreshing the gaps in her own memories and recollecting the memories of others deepen the neural links between self, music, and culture that will ensure more faithful replay in the future. Indeed, Mona avers on her return to Montreal that her "memory [is] intact" (*TSB* 305).

The sonic marker of her newly found anchoring to this "place" in Montreal is what Mona calls "Caroni dub" (*TSB* 305), which, although it only appears at the end of the novel, retroactively describes the novel's broader aesthetic. In labeling this "new beat" a "dub rhythm," she signals her appropriation of the music production technique that emerged out of Jamaica in the 1960s. Studio engineers like Lee "Scratch" Perry and King Tubby used the equalizer to manipulate already popular recorded tracks to create new sonic texts called dub versions (Hebdige 83). These B-side versions were then pressed onto dub plates, fragile acetate discs originally created as temporary pressings to test transcription or as exclusive cuts of new music made explicitly for sound system operators. But the technology soon became a medium for experimentation, with both the record and the sound mixing board developing into instruments in their own right. Both a technology and a compositional technique, dub is coterminous with cassette technology. Unlike earlier phonograph recordings, one of the advantages of magnetic tape as a recording medium is its predisposition for editing, which afforded both the quick correction of recording errors and the creation of new "versions" by erasing, stacking, or splicing extant recordings. It is significant, then, that the only novel in this study written by a woman focuses on cassette tape rather than vinyl: cassette tape allows the negotiation and rectification of erasure by and through recording technology. The technology thus enables the interrogation of sonic marginalization.

Mona's Caroni dub has implications for both Caribbean aesthetics and memory. *The Swinging Bridge* constructs memory as a recorded tape reel marred by violence and trauma; this results not in mere scratches, as one would find on a phonograph record, but in entire gaps. In contrast to the phonograph record—symbol of unassailable orthodoxy—which, once recorded, cannot be altered except by the introduction of flaws and manipulating how it plays, creation of a dub version requires the simultaneous destruction and recreation of the cassette tape even as dub plates are delicate, fragile, and short-lived. The language of scratching phonograph records already hews to notions of remembering as the retrieval of the unvarnished original. Cassette technology and dub techniques, in contrast, depict a process that is simultaneously destructive and creative. In dub practice, perversion and degradation are not the issue—in fact, the tape might necessarily become degraded in order to create the record.

Instead, what I am calling the dub aesthetic frames Caribbean memory as manipulable, whether for erasure or inclusion. Like a mixtape or a dub plate, memory can be composed, deconstructed, and recomposed. That the technology allows engineers to manipulate rather than simply record sound exposes the artificiality of the technology.[11] Dub enables new versions to be created even as each becomes an "original" and "authentic" document in its own right. While vinyl aficionados romanticize the technology for its supposed warmth and authenticity—its presumed ability to replay the original sound event as it was experienced—tape recording upends the very concept of recording as authentic replay. The continued pursuit of fidelity in recording technology also deconstructs the romanticizing of vinyl; vinyl recordings simply could not pick up with complete accuracy all the information available in the original sound event, and as such, the recorded product is always only partial and lossy even before further loss of data in the file compression process. Not only that, but in the dub and cassette era, this manipulation was done on tape, then sent to wax or vinyl as the final product, further subverting popular notions of the LP as authenticity on wax. Cassette practices like mixtape and dub tape creation analogize the ability to edit and recompose recorded memory and the remembered self, thus revealing remembering to be a kind of postproduction work to negotiate a present-tense crisis.

With Mona's Caroni dub, Espinet suggests that Mona has blurred the borders between documentary and creation, between memory as recovery and memory as invention. The dub aesthetic thus reveals the constructedness of memory work. It suggests that neither Mona's memory mixtape nor her ethnographic document is a playback reel of an experience exactly as it happened but a construction and deconstruction, a continual editing and remixing process, sometimes conscious and sometimes subconscious. The "original" recording becomes only one ingredient in continual reinvention. While the sounds emanating from recorded music are fixed, the memories they evoke are mutable, not just revisiting but rewriting the associations each time they are replayed. As previous chapters have shown, remembering is often more synonymous with creation or reconstruction than retrieval. Neither the dub version nor the remembered narrative is a diminished or inferior copy but an original document in its own right. As Dick Hebdige has argued, dub, like jazz, models an endlessly inventive form of memory work built on reconstructing new documents from preexisting material (84).

Dub engineers modify a known song by various methods to create a new song composition from an old one, and the advent of tape recording opened up new compositional possibilities such as multitrack recording and overdubbing, which entails recording several discrete recordings on top of the other (Morton 142; Hebdige 83). In the documentary *The Upsetter*, Perry recounts how in the 1950s he would construct his arrangements layer by layer: "People want to know how I get so much track on a four-track [cassette]. A me make the cassette live while nobody not there, and when the session start, that cassette is playing . . . So we put them two [copies] together and put them through the equalizer" (28:00–30:00). In so doing, Perry expanded the capacity of the technology in order to create multiple tracks and copies.[12] These "sound collages" might eventually stack "several generations of fragmented text" in an "aesthetic of accumulation" (Veal 87, 89). Dub versions are consequently haunted by the ghosts of intertextual sonic fragments that disrupt audience expectations and increase listeners' attention.

Creating a dub version includes adding echo and delay effects, changing the tape's playing speed, or including rewind sounds that disrupt the listener's sense of time and continually reorient her to the past—the past of familiar songs or that of recently played song fragments. Dub's echo effects are intimately bound up with memory and cognition, with a sound heard a moment ago lingering in the present. Dub versions therefore manipulate sonic expectations and memory: creating sonic pleasure in the dancehall relies on the listener's familiarity with the original iteration of the song, which then creates connections and synaptic links as various elements are backgrounded, foregrounded, faded out, or even spliced elsewhere. *The Swinging Bridge* depicts Caribbean memory interrupting and busting up the logic of the Canada-based narrative in the same way that lyrics and sounds interrupt the prose narrative, and Caribbean sounds echo in the exile's present time and place—the Caroni chutney beat that echoes in Montreal—in a way that stacks different memories, identities, and temporalities like a dub track. For Louis Chude-Sokei, dub's echo effects destabilize temporality as past sounds leave audible traces in the sonic present and future; for her part, Isis Semaj-Hall calls on dub's use of echo and reverb to argue for a diasporic conception of home and identity that articulates the echoic spatiality of being situated here and elsewhere.[13] Mona's B-side dub version of the national record registers how India echoes in the Caribbean and how the Caribbean echoes in secondary diasporas; diaspora thus involves multiple echoes reverberating at different time delays and with different amplitude. Espinet consequently opens up the Atlantic for us to hear other echoes as well: the Atlantic is not "black" only because of the Middle Passage and the circulation of enslaved black peoples; it is also the "black water," or the *kala pani*, that continues to take Indian, Chinese, Jewish, and Syro-Lebanese Caribbean migrants to new ports, new exiles, and new homes.

Earlier in the novel, primed by her train memories and having reminisced together with her parents, just before returning to Trinidad for the first time since her migration, Mona awakens to a sound that was out of place and that hearkens back to a memory of "sleeping in borrowed time . . . on a borrowed bed, in a borrowed village. The village itself was strung along a roadway between somewhere and somewhere" (*TSB* 108). Espinet constructs "borrowed time" as a temporal swinging bridge, a liminal space between past and present that allows for the displacement of the ocular for the aural. Situated in the last chapter of the "Borrowed Time" section, this memory also connects the Canadian present with the Trinidadian past. In a literalization of the bridge motif, Mona is suspended between past and present, unable to discern which of the two temporalities she is inhabiting. Instead of going backward in her memory, the sounds of the past erupt forward into the time and space of present-day Canada (112). Like Channer's Sylvia, Mona's central role here is attention; in both cases, diasporic attention precedes and produces return to the Caribbean past to find and recompose root memories.

But Mona's attentiveness is also in the service of a broader ethical and ethnographic project in which she tunes in to untold stories and songs in order to resituate them into the historical account of Trinidad and eventually to find her own belonging in Canada. "Scratch" Perry often incorporated found sounds into his compositions, capitalizing on the mobility of the cassette tape to leave the studio space and create field recordings as if he were an anthropologist (*Upsetter* 28:00–32:00). Indeed, cassette tape has been central to anthropological fieldwork, as Mona illustrates when she uses a tape recorder to record a *rand* singing remembered chutney songs. Ramnarine notes that "given that one cannot turn to a large body of literature or to sound recordings from the more distant past (before about 1939), finding people who not only remember but are also able to relate their musical memories provides the researcher with source materials. These oral testimonies are invaluable in attempting to record and reconstruct past Indian-Caribbean musical practices" (22). This anthropological function is dramatized and extended into an even deeper memory retrieval and historiography in Erna Brodber's 1994 novel *Louisiana*, which stages the challenge of the recovery and transcription of memory through technology. At the heart of the novel is an anthropologist Ella's transcription of the tale of two women connected by psychic memory and the names of their birthplaces, one in the Caribbean, the other in the United States. Herself a recording and playback device for voices and sounds that are not ordinarily audible, Ella's memory retrieves and records an impossible yet vital transcription. In showing how Ella "listened, back-tracked [rewound], listened and wrote . . . until the words were clear" (51), *Louisiana* demonstrates how cassette technology facilitates the repetition and replay of sound recordings to better hear, memorize, and transcribe the data.

Mona likewise evokes the ethnographic function of tape recording to reconstitute previously unrecorded memories. Her grandmother Lil is remembered for her ability to "work backwards and piece together the real story" (*TSB* 259). Lil displays an ability akin to Ella's memory and tape recorder that can be "back-tracked and back-tracked" so as to reconstruct the truth of narrative. Mona coopts similar techniques to perform a dub version of her family history. Although Audre Lorde famously contended that the master's tools can never dismantle the master's house (110–113), Mona uses recording techniques that are typically "man-made" (Lanser 8) in order to assert and insert Indo-Trinidadian women's subjectivity and voice. Since her remembering is analog—there are few records of Indian music—the novel models the ethnographic move from memory to speech to tape recording to transcript. Although tape technology displaces the living singer, it nevertheless preserves her voice for posterity even as its preservation is always under threat of erasure. Technologized music thus offers new modalities for the Indo-Trinidadian woman to come to voice beyond merely singing or writing. Indeed, Evelyn O'Callaghan has read anglophone Caribbean women's writing "as a kind of remix or dub version, which utilizes elements from the 'master tape' of Caribbean literary discourse (combining, stretching, modifying them in new ways) . . . to create a *unique* literary entity" (11). In so doing, they create a "woman version" that "like the dub version, makes a political point of incorporating the marginal, the peripheral, the apparently irrelevant" (13).

One of dub engineer's editing techniques is to omit or fragment song lyrics by manipulating the mute switch or fader controls, causing sonic elements of the "original" sound recording to drop out. Beyond its valence as a trope for memory, then, the dub aesthetic offers Mona a provocative musical model for the sounding of silenced voices. On the one hand, the technique of muting tracks within the composition reveals how musical records, rather than *creating* a high-fidelity documentation of experience, can be manipulated to *erase* sonic evidence. Prior to this moment, Mona has rifled through numerous technologies of subaltern recording that she realizes are all lossy media: the field glasses see but do not record, her diary only contains fragmented sentences that reflect the traumatized psyche of the young self who wrote them, and documentary is a selective recording and driven by the agenda of the producer. The dub aesthetic reorients what is background and foreground, what is text and subtext, what is marginal and centered. As Mona learned working on Carene's documentary, inclusivity depends on who gets to see and the ways of seeing their perspectives and technologies afford. Already, by focusing on ordinary Haitian women rather than male heroes, Carene refocuses the narrative of Haitian revolutionary struggles. Yet even as she does so, she relegates other figures to the background. Mona's gift is her attunement to what makes a good dub mix: which voices to amplify and how to equalize them into a sonic composition that gives each sound fragment its proper due. However, she cannot accomplish this on someone else's document. When women are not in control of their own stories, their testimonies are subject to erasure and silencing.

For Indo-Trinidadian women whose voices and subjectivities have been muted within the mix of national culture and erased from the record of Trinidadian history, the dub aesthetic models how they might insert themselves back into audibility. Whereas chutney is an embodied, private, woman-centered mode of community and resistance, Caroni dub moves song from the insular woman's space into contact with non-Indian idioms and with music technologies from home and abroad, thus widening the spaces and modalities where the Indian woman sounds. Since much of Caribbean memory work focuses on Afro-Caribbean peoples at the expense of other minority groups, Espinet interrogates how the recording of memory can become an ethical project that does not reproduce silence and erasure in its own turn. Musical creolization has often meant the erasure of the Indian presence even within recorded music; in addition to the paucity of prechutney Indian records amid the vast archives of Trinidadian recordings, even in chutney-soca "the *dholak*, which is difficult to amplify, has tended to drop out, so that there is often little chutney in the chutney-soca"

(Manuel et al. 256). Just as dub articulates Mona's hybrid identity, dub's multitrack form also connotes an artistic practice that allows for the hearing and sounding of multiple voices, of keeping even ghosts of voices present in the mix. Even further, it allows marginalized groups to challenge musical and cultural orthodoxies by reinserting their voices and songs where previously erased. Espinet inserts the Indo-Trinidadian experience into the unsound narratives of the music idioms both to challenge elision and to assert that voices like Mona's, Baboonie's, and Gainder's were always present even when rendered inaudible.

If *Louisiana* depicts improvising women who use singing as editorializing and historiography and who with their voices "fill out gaps" built into songs by songwriters (9), *The Swinging Bridge* features women like Baboonie and Lil, who provide Mona a compositional model for inserting unrepresented voices into the narrative. While Lil reinserts Gainder's songs into the unsound family history, Baboonie dubs her own story into the unsound record of the *Ramayana*. Baboonie's fragmenting of the *Ramayana* is reminiscent of what Veal calls the "interruptive performance logic" of Jamaican deejays (2). With their atonal toasting over popular songs and rhythms, deejays not only fragment the sonic wholeness of the song but also force their voices, lyrics, and subjectivity onto the auditor. Like Jamaican dancehall patrons who respond to the shock of the muting of sounds they anticipate hearing in the mix by singing out loud (Veal 52), Gainder's and Baboonie's response to silencing within master records is also to sing out the missing sounds. Baboonie inserts her singing voice and subjectivity in place of what was removed, revealing dub as an ideal form and practice for rectifying erasure and marginalization even as it is itself a form that erases. While Baboonie and Gainder do not succeed in creating a permanent and public record of their dub versions of the *Ramayana*, armed only with the technology of the voice, they dismantle and disrupt the unsound master narratives that silence and victimize them.

Reverb, one of dub's primary effects that adds the illusion of space within the mix, aptly analogizes Mona's quest for a space for Indo-Trinidadians and women within national sonorities. Using the language of cassette-era dub techniques, Espinet has argued that creating a space for Indianness to thrive within national culture has required them "to cut and paste and achieve some kind of fit" within the postcolonial Caribbean nation (Dawes, "Ramabai Espinet" 109). Espinet shows that recording Indo-Caribbean women's experience will require fragmenting established master documents, finding a space to "cut and paste" their voices and make their silencing audible like the voices and sounds that haunt the mix. Whereas public and collective records alike have been complicit in the erasure of Indo-Caribbean women's stories, Lil's shopkeeping ledger masks a private journal and a record of Gainder's forbidden songs behind shopkeeping minutiae. Lil transformed her journal into an alternate type of recorded music. Rather than the needle-centric vinyl record, these are *written* recordings of sung songs, tucked away in her shopkeeping ledger. The private journal and personal recording therefore recover female voice and history in ways that the other music forms that constitute Mona's soundscape do not.

Like the *matikor*, the autobiographical mode and the private journal function as spaces for recording, narrating, and even "engineering" women's experiences censored from public knowledge (O'Callaghan 49). Susan Lanser has referred to the use of "private voice" in women's narratives as "an enabling strategy for writing what is manifestly forbidden as 'public' narrative" (14–15). These texts are often double-voiced with a surface text and an "undertext" in a sort of public/private split (13). Using the form of the journal as a private space of female agency and interiority, Lil secreted "rough sentences, obviously made for her own private consumption. *Went by Alice to spend the day. Nice time. . . . Sweetie is so wild. . . . He was owing money again and I had to give him 20 dollars. I can't tell Jamesie*" (*TSB* 272). Like Baboonie's insertion of her narrative in the grooves of the *Ramayana*, Lil has both inserted her subjectivity into a record of public interactions and recuperated and inserted unorthodox woman memory back into family and ethnic history, which in turn enables Mona's own recovery of memory and history. It is women like Lil, the housekeeper Nani, and the outcaste *dougla* cousin, Bess, who archive woman memory so that others in the future can consult and complete these untold stories, "an entire history that we had never been taught at school" (133).

The role of Lil's journal in Mona's memory work reframes autobiographical memory to incorporate the memories of others. As Rodolphe Solbiac has argued, much of Mona's reconstruction depends on comparing her own memories to the remembered and documented archives of family members (232–233); her numerous dreams also reconstruct the memories of others from and within her own consciousness. In this way, Espinet continues the shared and collaborative memory work throughout this book. Mona relies on the collective memories of both male and female family members to bypass the limits of autobiographical memory and to create a collective genealogy of Indo-Trinidadian experience. This kind of allied memory, echoing the linkages formed between shipmates such as Gainder and the unnamed man on the *Fatel Rozack*, does not necessarily make the recomposed narrative any more reliable or mimetic, but it offers up multiple versions as a way to fill in archive gaps. Lil leaves behind a powerful record and a historiographic technique that defy the stereotypes of Indian women's silence while eschewing traditional male-dominated avenues of musical recording; she has also created a memory document that anchors Mona in a community and begins to alleviate her initial sense of isolation and alienation. With the echoic collective memory created by dub's versioning techniques, characters like Baboonie, Lil, and Mona recreate selves that have been damaged by migration or by the colonialism, patriarchy, and ethnocentric nationalism sounded by the music idioms I have discussed throughout this book.

"Caroni Dub": Multitracked Sonorities

The presence of a Caroni dub rhythm in Montreal testifies to Mona's success at remembering and retrieving the essential components of herself by sampling the various unsound musical records of her youth and recomposing them into an idiom that more accurately expresses her experience. This dub form is oriented toward secondary diaspora spaces like Toronto where Caribbean migrants from different islands meet, share space, and consume a broad spectrum of Caribbean music as markers of difference. Caroni dub revises the Caribbean exile experience—a loss-oriented identity—into a diaspora experience—an accretive and celebratory identity.[14] Mona's resituating Trinidad in Canada echoes Derek Walcott's figuration of a Caribbean performative memory that transforms and displaces rather than mourns (*Twilight* 68). Using the example of cultural retentions in the same Caroni region where *The Swinging Bridge* is set, in his Nobel lecture, he conceives of Caribbean memory as a "remaking" and "conjugation" of fragments of memory—fragments that represent not ruptures but detours, "branches," and "dialects." In fact, he argues that preindentureship cultural memory survived and continues in the present-day Caribbean as "partially remembered customs . . . [that] are not decayed but strong" (*Twilight* 70). The transformation of subcontinental "Indian" culture into something both distinctly Caribbean and distinctly Indian, able to travel to new locales as such, posits a new understanding of Caribbeanness that depends not on whether cultural markers remain "true" to the "original" but on how exiles construct and circulate mobile and malleable cultural markers as sources of sustenance. Mona's Caroni dub thus signals her reimagining of musical belonging as a way to hear and hold all these fragments of memory and identity in the same mix.

That the most successful articulation of Mona's newfound Indo-Trinidadian subjectivity is mediated through Afro-Caribbean music reflects a cultural rather than ethnic conception of identity. Shalini Puri sees Mona's Caroni dub as evidence of a *dougla* aesthetic, a discursive embracing of the forbidden intercourse between Indian and black cultures.[15] However, in contrast to the dougla nation articulated in Drupatee Ramgoonai's "Indian Soca," where "rhythm from Africa and India / blend together [in] a perfect mixture" (Ramnarine 84), Espinet forgoes a black/Indian or "Laventille/Caroni" coalition for an interisland connection. Dub identity is thus distinct from *créolité*, defined by its proponents as "neither European, nor African, nor Asian" but a "nonharmonious mix" that results from plantation and postplantation cultural encounters (Bernabé et al. 75, 92). Tellingly, Espinet critiques fellow Indo-Trinidadian Samuel Selvon for abandoning his exploration of Indian subjectivity for "the simplistic falsehood of the all ah we is one agenda" and for "position[ing] himself within the 'progressive' agenda of mixing and merging and inventing a true-true Caribbean *creolized* self" (Dawes, "Ramabai Espinet" 114–115).

A brief return to Lovelace's *The Dragon Can't Dance* illustrates the contrast between extant identitarian models and Mona's Caroni dub. Unlike his former colleague Balliram, who boasts about his Creole girlfriends and participation in calypso, Pariag concludes that to be fully integrated into Trinidadian society, he needed to have approached the city differently, to "walk with a flute or a sitar, and walk in right there in the middle of the steelband yard where they was making new drums, new sounds, a new music" and offer his own instruments, sound, and ethnic experience to the cultural mix as one track within a compositional wholeness that retains the distinct parts as "me" and "my own self" (224). Lovelace constructs music as a potential site of true harmony, with each instrument sounding its own unique note and encoding entire narratives of the communities that play them. In her introduction to the novel, Carolyn Cooper agrees that "it is to Pariag that Lovelace gives the vision of a fundamentally transformed society in which the fusion of the music of steelband, sitar and flute is an epiphanic expression of cultural pluralism; the antithesis of assimilation" (*Dragon* 14). With Pariag's insistence that "no. We didn't have to melt into one. I woulda be me for my own self. . . . A self to go in the world with" (224), Lovelace offers the urbanized but not creolized Indo-Trinidadian as one answer to the exclusionary or assimilationist ethnic visions of nation and identity that characterize Indo-Trinidadian politics and culture. Rather than retreat into the insularity of the purely Indian chutney space, Pariag and Mona both insist on a space within the so-called national music and capitalize on the characteristics of creolized music forms such as Afro-Trinidadian calypso and Afro-Jamaican dub, respectively, to be heard.

Likewise, the Caroni dub phonotope imagines a construction of the nation that allows for cultural mixing without losing individual, cultural, and ethnic specificity, since the various tracks that comprise the mix remain identifiable and discretely audible. In the same way that the aesthetics of the dub involve the juxtaposition of "historically and formally (supposedly) disparate artifacts and methodological approaches to yield new meanings, intensities, and textures" (Weheliye 8), *The Swinging Bridge* likewise stacks and multitracks different and seemingly irreconcilable musical idioms and song fragments in its bid to find the most "sound" articulation of Indo-Trinidadian female subjectivity. By inflecting Afro-Jamaican dub with the chutney valences of the Caroni region, Espinet reimagines cultural appropriation as a key tool for subaltern constituents without their own sonic place; it sees the careful curation of diasporic or regional cultures to create new expressive forms that model valuable practices and political moves. Espinet has previously elaborated this concept through cuisine, particularly "privilege," a Barbadian one-pot dish and the subject of a short story culled from *The Swinging Bridge*, where Mona shows her cosmopolitanism in Canada by preparing a feast comprising various dishes from across the Caribbean ("Indian Cuisine"). Whether as the selector of perfect ingredients and dishes or of meaningful and pleasurable sounds, Mona positions herself in the guise of the dub engineer, who expertly joins "separate parts [so that they] merge seamlessly" (*TSB* 305).

Mona's Caroni dub thus figures Caribbean memory as continual post hoc editing and narration in an ongoing bid to negotiate structural forgetting. It is ultimately reflective of a conception of Caribbean creolization defined by using found fragments to improvise a provisional wholeness—in Mona's case, the fragments of unsound records are dubbed into a "seamless whole." Caroni dub reflects the polyphony of the region's musical idioms, allowing difference and discord to remain audible so that all constituents hear themselves even as the whole coheres. That Mona includes in her Caroni dub all the unsound records that caused her psychic suffering and continue to impact her as an adult suggests that these musical and memory fragments are vital in her subject formation. In this way, Espinet underscores the ethical imperative to keep all kinds of memories available to conscious contemplation.

Alexander G. Weheliye has described the moment of creating a dub mix as a kind of "schizophonia" or "a sonorous double consciousness" in which the turntable selector exists on the border between the private sonic space enabled by his headphones and the social space he is creating for his audience (91). This dub/double consciousness illuminates not only the textured sense of self that Mona embodies as she walks the streets of Montreal with her chutney-inflected dub beat but also how the dub engineer equalizes disparate sound fragments by careful atemporal listening—listening to past, present, and future simultaneously. Mona's present resembles the moment of dubbing; by listening through a pair of headphones that is simultaneously one object and two channels of listening, the subject holds both past and present sounds and selves in one moment before synchronizing them in the mix. The intermediary present, the moment of remembering, involves anticipation: in a few seconds, I will hear the result of the mix. As Weheliye phrases it, it is the recognition and resolution of the "I am" with the "I will be" (154). Mona's "I am" is constructed from the sonic and mnemic fragments she accrues through her psychic and physical return to the land where her umbilical cord and even her primal scent are buried (*TSB* 270) and that archives the told and untold family histories. That she hears the echoes of these rediscovered roots in Montreal affirms that she has brought all of these collated fragments with her, back over the second *kala pani* to the space of "I will be."

"Out of Nothing"

Near the end of the novel, Mona meditates on what her cousin Bess has accomplished. Previously edited out of the family records because of her extramarital parentage, Bess, who has constructed a familial and Indian historical archive at home, is nevertheless "balanced," and "this order was [necessary] to her and how much she had invented herself, out of virtually nothing" (*TSB* 292). It is the illegitimate cousin who ironically has created a solid foothold in the new Trinidad, framed here in the language of the dub engineer listening and balancing otherwise irreconcilable tracks on his equalizer. The repetition of "out of nothing" in these pages proffers a corrective to Naipaul's infamous remark that "nothing was created in the Caribbean" (19). But as Mona and Bess have shown, "nothing" is the fodder from which to invent the Caribbean. Walcott has spent a career demonstrating how this creation of new realities of fragments and found objects that wash up on its shores to be reinvented and repurposed, Crusoe-like, is the very essence of Caribbeanness.[16] Similarly, Mona notes that Baboonie's music is "beaten out of nothing but pain" (*TSB* 297). The "nothing but" construction reminds us what colonialist and patriarchal eyes refuse to see, partly because of their complicity in the violence and erasure that created both the nothing and the pain. The novel thus culminates in a celebration of the subaltern, overlooked, and silenced predecessors who created new spaces of belonging and subjectivity in places of primary and secondary exile: "That nothing was us, flung by one turn of the wheel of fortune into a place entirely unknown, where we built our lives not out of nothing, but out of the back-breaking work of reinvention" (303). This is the heart of the dub aesthetic: engineering sound "out of nothing but" fragments, with the heightened reinvention skills and techniques Caribbean peoples have had to master in this space.

In her insistence on centering music and sonority within the mute world of the written text, Espinet makes audible the silencing of entire memory archives in the production of orthodox national narratives and respectability politics—the subaltern voices of women, South Asian citizens, and nonmainstream music and cultural practices. Espinet thus shares the view of Scott, Hijuelos, Maximin, and Channer that the work of the musician can also migrate to other artistic forms, with the writer, the documentarian, or the artist transducing the griot function into other media. Espinet's deployment of a dub aesthetic transforms the novel into a sound record of Caribbean memory as she inserts into the mix silenced and unspeakable histories. In this way, as Lil's journal demonstrates, writing surrogates for recording technology; the novel itself archives the present-tense reconstruction of reappropriated music fragments that elicit memories of their original sonic texts even while enabling the reader-listener to construct new meanings. The dub aesthetic as literary poetics ultimately models how to keep visible and audible the violence done to Caribbean peoples and cultures while offering new possibilities of negotiating those fragmentary pasts in order to (re)constitute future identities.

Coda

[. . .] On your favourite CD
the overwhelming moment is in the space
between tracks, full of the last song's echo and full
of what is to come.

—Kei Miller, *There Is an Anger That Moves*

In his poem "The Broken/VI," Jamaican poet Kei Miller meditates on the anticipatory effects of playing a "favourite CD" (29). That the CD is beloved presumes that both the songs and their order are firmly encoded in memory; it is this familiarity, the mind of the listener functioning as a recording in its own right, that forges a link between the end of the "last song" and "what is to come." Borrowing Miller's evocation of echoes filling the temporal gap between the past and future, I want to close by teasing out some threads that echo from the last chapter's turn to dub music and that preview "what is to come" in Caribbean musical fictions and musical remembering beyond the examples I have examined in the preceding pages.

Phonographic Memories has explored moments of music listening, musical remembering, and compositional techniques facilitated by and modeled on postcolonial, twentieth-century Caribbean popular music. Even when written in the twenty-first century, however, musical fictions still often belie an affinity for older technologies, nostalgic memory work, and physical returns to the Caribbean. They also privilege calypso rather than soca, sung chutney rather than recorded chutney-soca, reggae rather than dancehall, traditional gwoka rather than gwoka *modènn*, mambo and bolero rather than salsa, and so on. The foregoing discussion suggests that curation, cultural nationalism, and phonographic memories have in common a certain conservatism. Contemporary musical fictions often deploy essentialist notions of culture and memory even as they depict them traveling far beyond roots and origins (Gilroy, *Black Atlantic* 35). Remembering music is couched in authenticity because its purpose is to help those in the present survive the "crisis" that precipitates memory work, and auditors turn to the past because they imagine something worth revisiting, consulting, or preserving there or they want to protect the present from further depredations. But by the end of the previous chapter, I suggested that a return to a past space, time, or music might enable the exile, now a diasporic citizen, to move to new spaces and to imagine new futures filled with the sounds of belonging. Indeed, in their introduction to *Sound Souvenirs*, José Van Dijck and Karin Bijsterveld argued that even more than a "desired return to an ideal past in response to a troubled present," technostalgia—the obsession with old music formats and technologies—is rooted in the pleasures of "sound—the sounds of the past and the sounds of the future" (20).

While these five musical fictions often depict memory work as a present-tense hiatus during which unsettled characters turn to the past to evade a problematic present, in each chapter, I have shown how remembering and return serve to rehabilitate Caribbean listeners for an anticipated future as well. Whether the traumatic amnesia and aphasia I discussed in chapter 1, the obsessive nostalgia of chapter 2, the cultural and physical devastation of chapter 3, the unbelonging and fugue of chapter 4, or the marginalization and silencing of chapter 5, present-tense realities inhibit unsettled characters from fully engaging with the here and now, which extends into the future as the present passes her by. Whereas Hijuelos could not imagine a life for his characters without physical return to the past and island, other authors envision the possibility of finding in the past the tools that will equip characters for and clarify both the present and the future paths. Recovering roots enables new plants and the possibility of new fruit to emerge; discovering *who I was* helps me construct *who I am* and *who I will be*.

From Analog to Digital

The privileging of technostalgia and return in the previous examples leaves open the question of how increased digital access and the shift to digital music technologies might lead to further innovations of the contemporary Caribbean novel that are not yet fully in evidence. The explosion of personal computing and internet access at the turn of the twentieth century ushered in an ever-changing mediascape that reshaped music, memory, and literature as well as societies at large. The digital era has introduced new technologies for communication and creation that have new features that reflect both the globalization and democratization of culture. The interfaces feature screens that demand user interaction and input and styles of information presentation that privilege the modular and graphical (Manovich 69). These technologies have enabled collaborative and networked production and consumption of content (Paul 626). Both Ken Bilby and Curwen Best have underscored that Caribbean music combines both old and new technologies and ways of knowing. As a result, even as Caribbean musicians quickly took to digital technologies[1] and engineers adopted digital music production in Caribbean studios in the 1990s, producers and performers often brought new technologies such as the drum machine, synthesizer, MIDI, Cubase, and Pro Tools to bear on "traditional" music idioms (Best 219). In fact, although digital audio workstations quickly replaced early analog tape systems, Best notes that "some studios maintained both analogue and digital capability" (202). This dual conservatism and innovation makes sense in light of the examples I have shown throughout this book, where globalization and the diasporic circulation of Caribbean peoples and music only increase the desire to distinguish Caribbean nation music within the international soundscape. Still, the advent of digital technologies changed the sound, scope, and even composition of Caribbean music, including who gets to create and perform. Home computing and YouTube opened up beat-making, recording, and distribution to those who would not have access to studios, instruments, and professional development in the early music industry.

While music formats centered on physical media for most of the twentieth century, the twenty-first century has seen numerous advancements in digital formats. Although high fidelity is still possible with lossless formats such as FLAC (Free Lossless Audio Codec), this era is marked by increased anxiety over lossiness and compression. The digital era privileges small file sizes over high fidelity. To facilitate transmission over the internet even with slow data speeds, formats like the MP3 saw the stripping out of much of the dynamic range of the "original" recording in order to reduce the file size, a process called "compression" (Sterne, *MP3* 2). For the ordinary listener, compression has no discernible effect on sound quality, but audiophiles insist that with the right technology, one can hear the difference between a lossless CD-quality file and a lossy compressed one. Digitization privileges the extraction of individual songs from their original contexts for insertion into playlists and mixes, and digital-era music and memory can be stripped from cultural contexts or roots—as is evident in the "tropical" wave in 2010s pop music that has drawn from dancehall sounds without attribution and generated great chart and popular success for North American acts like Drake and Justin Bieber. Whereas cultural memory traveled in the latter decades of the twentieth century as bootleg tapes and rare LPs in the luggage of migrants (who would become hip-hop heads and sow the cultural seeds of Jamaican sound system culture in new spaces and cultural contexts), in the contemporary digital moment, culture travels in downloads, streams, and feeds. Even as new generations negotiate cultural loss, assimilation, and the fear of not having enough of their own cultural memories to sustain them, in the digital era, memory commodities become even more accessible not "with a flick of your wrist on your phonograph switch," as for Hijuelos's characters, but with a click of the mouse on YouTube or iTunes. Musical nostalgia does not abate with digital playlists. In fact, digital playlists have become alternate sites of memory, a virtual place to curate and archive our listening—which songs we want to keep versus which ones get cycled out as newer hits rise to the top of the charts. With the advent of Spotify, Apple Music, and other music streaming platforms, cosmopolitan auditors reckon that they no longer have to worry about where to store all these hits. Since they are stored in the cloud (in reality on a corporation's massive physical servers), they can always turn to the cloud or an app to take a trip down memory lane and find songs they loved in their youth.

Digital music and the internet go hand in hand and involve vast networks of connected computers, gadgets, servers, internet service providers, and end users. It is not incidental that global-era identity models favor rhizomes or networked roots over singular roots. The association of digital culture with memes in contrast to memory, rhizomes rather than roots, implies that the kind of phonographic memory displayed by auditors in this book will be harder to develop. Distinct from Mneme, the Greek muse of memory, a contemporary meme is a decontextualized unit of culture, chosen for its ability to generate reactions in new contexts.[2] Disconnected from its "source" as it circulates, it can pop up in new spaces and times. The meme obviously inspires comparison to the ephemerality and lack of historicity of digital culture, but might the recurrence of a meme allegorize an alternate form of long-term memory? Indeed, a meme is what remains, is archived, and is brought back to consciousness long after the "moment" has moved on. The rise of meme culture and digital playlists underscores the new forms of mobility in this era and the ways digitization problematizes earlier notions of memory and identity. Arun Appadurai has theorized the connections between the mass migrations of the global era with the mobility of electronic cultural products as a key factor in the reshaping of modern subjectivities. As *Waiting in Vain* and *The Swinging Bridge* portray, the ability of culture to travel far beyond its site of production or referent both tropes and enables the forms of enterprising self-making undertaken by migrants, refugees, and diasporic citizens in the twenty-first century. The interlocking circuits of peoples and cultural commodities thus simultaneously destabilize conceptions of the nation even while redrawing its contours as imagined community (Appadurai 3–8). Tzarina Prater illustrates these ideas by tracing how "digital Caribbean subjects" take advantage of YouTube videos, comments, and blogs to challenge North American narratives about the Caribbean (in this case, how American judges on the singing competition *The Voice* misread and misheard Chinese Jamaican contestant Tessanne Chin) and to create virtual spaces within which to assert and enact their diasporic identities.

I want to suggest that memes, like digital music files, convey salient Caribbean epistemologies. The region's peoples and music have always been mobile, evincing what Édouard Glissant called a plague of "elsewhereness" (*Caribbean*

Discourse 35). But this mobility is not limited to the recent migrations ushered in by globalization; rather, it is the very foundation of the region populated by people wrenched from their roots and who have had to reformulate cultures and identities in new contexts as they interact with others. While contemporary musical fictions foreground phonographic memory as localized in individual auditors or rooted in the specificity of the Caribbean space, the emphasis in the digital era turns to networks of memory reconfigured in new spaces and times. Developing earlier gestures to networked, shared, or rhizomatic memory, digital-era musical fictions problematize the spatial and temporal orientations of technostalgic musical fictions. Their continued recourse to old tech suggests that rather than reflecting the influence of new media, contemporary authors are in fact exploring a more expansive view of Caribbean memory and identity predicated on long-standing conceptions of tidalectic and archipelagic memory.[3]

Digital-Era Musical Fictions

In the same way that digital technologies impact the form(ats) of music, they also reshape the form and content of narratives. Jarrel De Matas has argued that a "writers' digital sensibility informs the content [of literature] as much as it organizes the recollection of memory," with specific reference to Kamau Brathwaite's work (15). If changes in media restructure consciousness as Walter Ong has theorized and this in turn informs both literary form and memory, how might digital music inform and transform the Caribbean novel and remembering practices? Digital music and technologies rarely appear in contemporary Caribbean musical novels except as CDs, computers, and dub music. As Annie Paul argues in "Log On," Caribbean writers have remained torn between two seeming polarities: the aficionados of the printed book format, like Derek Walcott, express disdain for new media, while others, like Kamau Brathwaite, readily embrace new media not only as integral to their composition but also as ways of thinking and narrating Caribbeanness (Paul 627). As the brief overview below of digital-era musical fictions will illustrate, new media only shifts earlier issues at the heart of Caribbean literary and memory studies into new domains. Music-playing technologies have increased in portability—first, the portability of the formats, and second, the content: one can carry more music in a smaller package than the most dedicated collectors in the past could acquire over a lifetime. The same is true for fiction as well; even as publishing and academia continue to privilege the print book and physical libraries and collections (deliberately stanching the e-book industry by pricing and release strategies), electronic books and readers continue to appeal to those desiring greater portability to match an increasingly mobile lifestyle. Likewise, as Caribbean peoples gain new avenues for moving about the world, the portability of memory and memory media becomes more desirable. Digitization, compression, and memes therefore offer generative metaphors for twenty-first-century memory in general and Caribbean memory in particular.

Consonant with its influence on numerous contemporary digital and global music forms and trends, Jamaican dub enjoys increasing popularity in new Caribbean speculative and science fiction due to its innovative qualities and perhaps because it is associated with newer technologies. In the past two decades, authors such as Marcia Douglas, Nalo Hopkinson, and Anthony Joseph have constructed highly experimental works that continue to interrogate ways to render in novel form the temporal and mnemic ruptures of the Caribbean experience. Their musical novels remain very much concerned with the Caribbean place and in extending the borders of the nation into new diasporas. Afrofuturist novels like Hopkinson's *Midnight Robber* (2000) and Joseph's *The African Origins of UFOs* (2006) displace the Caribbean past and present to alternate spaces and times, including spaceships and the future. Memories, music, and people travel beyond their temporal and spatial origins, evincing both the violent and the volitional displacements that mark Caribbean history and present. Even as these authors build alternate spaces on recognizable Caribbean islands, their soundscapes reflect the Caribbean as a musical region and are less interested in the national specificity of music than in evoking Caribbeanness more broadly.

In *Midnight Robber*, Hopkinson updates Jamaican dub and Trinidadian calypso—reflecting her tidalectic Caribbean roots—in ways that evoke digital-era and even future technologies; dub creates alternate spaces, with the dub side figured as an underside or alternate dimension to the real (2). Calypso is reimagined as a programming language to reengineer the known world into a space of black liberty—freedom from labor—but even in this space women and children are not free from sexual violence. Hopkinson revises calypso's rhetorical devices like robber talk to empower her protagonist, the young Tan Tan, to remember and narrate childhood sexual trauma. But she also updates calypso as a futuristic computer code that can biohack and reengineer bodies and realities. It is the basis for an advanced version of the World Wide Web that alludes to both the folk figure Anansi the spider and the maroon heroine Nanny. As a supercomputer, a God-like knowledge and information system, and a nanotechnology, Granny Nanny is not merely a metaphor for the internet but a thoroughly Caribbean epistemology rooted in the region's music, history, and folklore. Hopkinson's deployment of calypso and dub as the foundation of her Afrofuturistic world-building suggests that older and newer Caribbean music idioms alike remain key tropes, both for memory as archival work and for engineering new futures. Further transducing music into novelistic form in innovative ways beyond the traditional musical aesthetic model that this book has examined, Hopkinson renders calypso and dub as potent and generative languages.

Digital music media often become appendages to the body and appendices to embodied memory, creating a kind of cyborg (De Matas 11). The interface/cyborg trope holds true for Erna Brodber's Ella in *Louisiana*, who, as I argued in the introduction, becomes a tape recorder that replays submerged collective memory. It is also the case for Hopkinson's Tubman, who becomes fused with the listening and communication technology that ultimately connects her to Nanny/nano-tech, the Akashic record of Afro-Caribbean historical memory, which shares features of a computer interface and a Web search engine or database (Manovich 69). De Matas connects this cyborg effect with reading e-books or hyperlinked texts that invite or require the reader to interact with the text as part of the reading process (11).[4] Similarly, reading these musical fictions invites a call-and-response with the reader, who must supply additional information either from her own memory or through media technologies—searching for the referenced lyric or song on YouTube or Spotify, for instance.

For her part, Douglas's primary tools to awaken the memory of legacies of colonial violence, localized around the site of the Halfway Tree clock tower in Kingston, Jamaica, are structural metaphors drawn from postindependence Jamaican music—primarily dub but also roots reggae and dancehall. These include the motifs of remix, versioning, dub sides, and tracks, or even graphics showing a record from which vibrations visibly emanate. Surprisingly, her phonotopes are all analog, with the lone exception of a young Kingstonian's mobile phone that plays dancehall music, presumably in MP3 format. Even as the young girl's "ringtune" lends one section its title, the subsequent pages identify the tune not as a digital-era song but as an old ring game tune, "Brown Girl in the Ring." In this digital age, a mobile phone becomes a "sound system" (Douglas 139), and dancehall music provides the metronome that keeps time even as the revenant Bob Marley "steps into a different year, a new era" and an ancestor "steps forward" in space and time to deliver "hindsight" and "foresight" to the living (184–186). Reflecting a digital-era sensibility, anxieties around loss become productive and generative, with copies—and "copies of copies"—of memories and peoples circulating in the same space but across dimensions, since "according to the law of conservation of mass"—and, I argue, the laws of dub and file-sharing—"matter can neither be created nor destroyed; however, it can be rearranged in space" (263). This provocative assertion opens up the possibilities for figuring digital-era identity and memory not as "destroyed" in transit and in dislocations but as "rearranged" into new configurations.

The musical fictions I have discussed throughout this book employ the antiphonal features of Caribbean music to depict memory work as a relational, transmitted, and collaborative project as musicians create and convey rememoried texts to their audiences. Hopkinson and Douglas update that tradition for the digital era with characters hooked into central networks, or connected to each other as "I&I," the dual singular and collective first-person Rastafari subject. In its insistence that people can travel through time and space via webs, threads, and c(h)ords (both textile and musical), Douglas's *The Marvellous Equations of the Dread* highlights the dimension-shifting capability of digital technology and digital music (Hamilton, "Rastaman Vibrations"). It deploys webbed and networked metaphors as a way of forging connections not only between peoples and cultures but also between memories. Even when privileging networks, rhizomes, and quantum entanglements of times, spaces, and peoples, these novels remain as invested in remembering and technostalgia as earlier fictions, but the influence of new media and new music allows authors to craft further innovations on both musical fictions and the Caribbean novel form.

A Format for Musical Memory

In *Caribbean Discourse*, Édouard Glissant wondered if a speakerly, musical, and communal Caribbean novel, born from natural rather than forced poetics, could ever exist: "Will we ever invent those forms of expression that will leave the book behind, will transform it, will adapt it" to the poetics of Creole? (224). The musical fictions I have discussed throughout this book demonstrate that the novelist must invent a form to "speak . . . down in the book" what cannot be heard in text, including "bass groove[s]" and other musical sounds (Douglas 34, 274). This form does not jettison the book but transforms it with musical technologies and techniques of memory and storytelling. In contrast to Channer's characters, who fetishize early-twentieth-century typewriters, rotary telephones, and handwritten love letters even in the late 1990s when computer technologies and mobile phone use were on the rise, Brathwaite has long embraced the computer and digital composition in addition to sound recordings to "unmute" his poetry.[5] Douglas and Joseph both incorporate typographic font changes, photographs, drawings, and graphic design to make legible subaltern vibes, destabilize the traditional novel form, and mimic the multimodality of Caribbean consciousness. But as a visual and linguistic medium, a novel can only transduce sound in the reader's inner ear or invent novelistic metaphors for music. Novelized music remains textual and or thematic, requiring an extratextual supplement (De Matas 11; Bolter 122). One might imagine a future where digital publishing offers new ways of composing and publishing novels, with embedded hyperlinks and sound or video clips. New online formats and magazines might begin to open this portal to the future of musical fictions, with short fiction formats such as *Small Axe*'s *SX Salon*, *CaribbeanInTransit*, and the newly launched *Pree* magazine.

If, as this book has demonstrated, the musical novel is a new format of memory, it is a format that remains both limited and advantageous. In the introduction, I showed how Brodber's *Louisiana* exposed the limitations of the tape recorder in capturing the fullness of human memory, particularly as memory changes and expands each time it is recalled. Even when supplementing tape recording with both Ella's consciousness and the novel itself, Brodber suggests that "the full has never been told," as reggae artist Buju Banton would phrase it ("Untold Stories"). Similarly, in the same way that Hijuelos's *Mambo Kings* LP sprouts a third side to show that the Castillo brothers' memories exceed the capacity of dual-sided records, in *Marvellous Equations*, Douglas's structuring trope of the vinyl record is continually disrupted and expanded to register the limits of extant recording media as a format for Caribbean memory. Chapter titles announce increasingly unrealistic track numbers, disrupting the album-length concept as the book goes on—for instance, "track 33.0" or "track 13.5" (Douglas 127, 179). By structuring the novel with more tracks than a single album can hold, Douglas suggests that the novel format might enable types of memory work that the album format cannot; the reverse is true as well. But in their shared project of attempting to archive and dimension-shift Caribbean sonorities and memories into new media, times, and spaces, they might find ways to complement each other.

The metafictional plots or subplots of Caribbean musical fictions suggest that the art of the musician inspires the art of the writer or filmmaker through the shared project of recuperating memory and redressing historical lacunae; as such, *Phonographic Memories* contends that musical fictions extend the range of Caribbean music into the revered format of the postcolonial novel. As long-playing records of Caribbean music and memory, musical fictions lose some of the sonority of music even as they enable an in-depth exploration of themes or alternate perspectives only limned in a song or album. And whereas a novel is a form that presumes concentration, immersion, and engaged private reading, even with attention-grabbing videos, contemporary popular music can still only hope to hold attention for a few minutes. It is not surprising, then, that authors of musical fictions often privilege the LP format and modes of memory that presume concentration and leisure. While Caribbean novelists writing in the digital music era still display technostalgia, some of the key attributes of the digital era share features with with the long-standing features of Caribbean memory.

Memory in Glissant's hands becomes a way of preserving the past as well as a tool for approaching the future. He frames the region's aesthetics as "a search for temporal duration" that "is opposed in particular to European poetics, which are characterized by the inspiration or the sudden burst of a single moment." Consequently, he argues, our "writers are prey to a kind of future remembering. By that I mean that it is almost certain that we are writers in an embryonic phase and our public is yet to come. . . . We must struggle against time in order to reconstitute the past, even when it concerns those parts of the Americas where historical memory has not been obliterated" (*Caribbean Discourse* 145). I have suggested throughout this book that remembering is not only the reimagining of the past but the construction of viable futures for Caribbean peoples and nations. Whether through past- or future-oriented memory work, the project of the Caribbean musical writer remains one of inventing (re)memoried texts for the consumption of Caribbean readers at home and abroad, works that draw on Caribbean pasts to create memories that we might remember together in the future, with authors standing in as contemporary griots who seed the memories that we share and that create a template for future sociality and for future remembering.

Acknowledgments

I want to express my deep gratitude to everyone who had a hand in my transformation from student to scholar and this document from dissertation to monograph: at the University of the West Indies, Nadi Edwards, my first inspiration, critic, and mentor; Elizabeth "Betty" Wilson, who inspired me to walk in the rich legacy of Caribbean women who were both novelists and scholars; David Williams, who made me believe I was smart; Michael Bucknor, who challenged me to deeper critical thinking; and J. Michael Dash (NYU) and Marie-Jose N'Zengou-Tayo, who opened to me the rich world of francophone Caribbean literature. My time at Brandeis University was all the more rewarding for the generous mentorship of Sue Lanser, Ulka Anjaria, and Aliyyah Abdur-Rahman. I had the good fortune of having Faith Smith as my advisor and dissertation chair. I am grateful that she took Colin Channer's *Waiting in Vain* seriously enough to put it on a syllabus and that she always listened attentively to my ideas—inchoate as they were—with a genuine interest that made me grow in confidence.

My colleagues at the University of Virginia have made this the best place for a young scholar to grow her mind. Many thanks to my Carter G. Woodson Institute colleagues, including Marlene Daut, Claudrena Harold, Deborah MacDowell, and Maurice Wallace; my English colleagues, including Mrinalini Chakrabarty, Emily Ogden, Brad Pasanek, Jahan Ramazani, Caroline Rody, Marlon Ross, and Lisa Woolfork; my writing partners, Jennifer Tsein and Kwame Otu; and my colleagues in Media Studies and Music, Jack Hamilton and Karl Miller, who provided key music resources and insights along the way. Many thanks go to UVA's College of Arts and Sciences for various research grants to complete this project. I would be remiss if I didn't also thank Sarah Winstein-Hibbs and Anastasia Curley for their research assistance and the students in my Musical Fictions, Narrating Trauma, Routes/Writing/Reggae, and Caribbean Poetics courses over the years who were the guinea pigs for many of the ideas herein.

Caribbeanist and sound studies peers have provided invaluable feedback on parts of this project over the years. Thanks to the Caribbean Studies Association; the editors and reviewers of *Anthurium*; Joy Mahabir and Miriam Pirbhai, editors of *Critical Perspectives in Indo-Caribbean Women Literature*; Rhonda Frederick and the participants of Boston College's African Diaspora Works in Progress Series; my dear friend Jason Allen-Paisant of Leeds University; and Carolyn Cooper at the University of the West Indies, who cut the road and is an all-around amazing soul. My heartfelt gratitude to Carter Mathes at Rutgers University for convening the "Theorizing Literary Sound" symposium and to Jennifer Stoever and Julie Huntington for the stimulating conversations that pushed this project to new heights. Mad love to Kaiama Glover for founding the Greater Caribbean Studies Network and to Petal Samuel, Anne-Garland Mahler, and others for their invaluable critiques and recommendations for the book's introduction. Sincere thanks to Donette Francis, Rafe Dalleo, and Junot Díaz for going beyond themselves to offer pointed professional mentorship. Nuff respeck to Kwame Dawes for inspiring this project and for all his advice and encouragement at various stages of my academic career. Special thanks to my editor Kimberly Guinta, Jasper Chang, and the entire Rutgers University Press team for stewarding this book into existence.

I am grateful for the authors and musicians, especially Colin Channer, Lawrence Scott, and Jacques Schwarz-Bart, whose generosity with their work, time, and memories have made my research so fun and rewarding. Mad love to Ishion Hutchinson, who sent my seminar paper to Colin and made the introduction. Shout-out to the musicians who sustained my spirit so I could finish this book: Chronixx, a living legend, extraordinary griot, and all-round good soul; and Solange Knowles, whose album *A Seat at the Table* and her soul-affirming performance at AFROPUNK Brooklyn in Summer 2017 revived and nourished my spirit in the dark days of Nazi marches in Charlottesville.

Warmest gratitude to the friends who remind me to live, laugh, and love: Lydia Fash, Alix Fitzpatrick, Keisha John, Nitya Kallivayalil, Lesmalene Morris-Cummings, Sophie Osotimehin, Charlotte Rogers, Heather Rose-Smith, and Metasebia Woldemariam. The friends with whom I share fond musical memories: José Lambour (Ricky Martin's "La Copa de Vida," Marseille 1998), Rachid Abdelali (Slaï's "Flamme," Marseille 2000), Géraldine Finot (Ricky Martin, *Life*, Paris 2005), Amirh Venner (*Le Roi Soleil* comédie musicale, Paris 2005), Alexandra Herzog (Gotye, *Making Mirrors*, Boston 2008), and LaTasha Levy (Maxwell, *BlackSummersNight*, Norfolk 2016).

I send my overflowing gratitude to my family, who has put up with my incessant writing all my life: Mommy, Esther Hamilton, who raised me in a bookstore and is to blame for all of it; my big sister Avarine Bradshaw, who is my hero and inspiration; and my brother-in-law and me bredren Devon Bradshaw, bass guitarist extraordinaire, with whom I've spent hours listening and discussing

"Scratch" Perry's dub lyrics and rifling through old *Burning Spear* tour photographs. Haunting this book, of course, is the memory of Daddy, dear Daddy, who inspired my love for music and sound technology.

I am grateful for the permission to republish the following:

An early version of chapter 1 was previously published as "'From Silent Wounds to Narrated Words': Calypso Storytelling in Lawrence Scott's *Night Calypso*." *Anthurium: A Caribbean Studies Journal*, vol. 10, no. 1, 2013, article 3, https://scholarlyrepository.miami.edu/anthurium/vol10/iss1/3.

An early version of chapter 5 appears as "'Music and a Story': Sound Writing in Ramabai Espinet's *The Swinging Bridge*." *Critical Perspectives on Indo-Caribbean Women's Literature*, edited by Joy Mahabir and Mariam Pirbhai, Routledge, 2013, pp. 70–92.

Notes

INTRODUCTION

1. See Sterne's elaboration of format theory and the implications of changing music technologies and formats in *MP3* (237–240).

2. Music and recording cultures fetishize authenticity in their pursuit of high fidelity, defined by the technology's presumed approximation of live or "original" sound performances. This echoes Walter Benjamin's privileging of the aura or the proximity of the "real" or embodied performer over the constructed and cold—mediated—technological copy (*Illuminations* 220–223).

3. Originally, these terms referred to the recording mechanism. Later, they came to refer to the record player and the recorded disc as well. While the other terms fell out of usage, the word *gramophone* is used in England and British-influenced countries to refer to the turntable-and-speaker-horn record players, while *phonograph* was the preferred American term. The recorded medium itself was known in the United States as the phonograph record until the mid-1900s when the terms *record*, *vinyl*, and *LP* became successively more popular as the technology developed.

4. Whereas "to recall" refers to the process of retrieving information from memory storage in response to a cue or trigger (and thus applies to the brain's response to a cue), "to remember" is the subjective experience of recall, how the present self makes meaning of previously encountered information (episodes, knowledge; Slotnick 3–5; Trouillot 15).

5. See, for example, Nicola King's theorization of autobiographical memory as the post-hoc reconstruction of the past in order to make sense of the self in the present; she argues that we construct selfhood through memory and construct memory through narrative (*Memory, Narrative, Identity* 5–9).

6. It is often in the work of women writers and female scholars that autobiographical memory is brought into central focus. See, for instance, Anim-Addo, *Centre of Remembrance: Memory and Caribbean Women's Literature*.

7. Stuart Hall, for instance, questions the diasporic obsession with roots, which, as I show in chapter 4, inhere notions of singular origin and a spatial economy that mirrors archaeological concepts of memory. Both archaeology and rootwork presume that

memories can be retraced to their singular source and the process of remembering is one of coming into contact again with the information or identity one seeks. But Hall argues that memory cannot be recovered as it was; we cannot go back in time, and even when returns to a particular space is in view, both the returnee and the place have been transformed by time ("Cultural Identity").

8. The contemporary backlash against nationalism in Europe and North America rightly stems from the very real damage that expansive and violent nationalisms inflicted on ethnic groups and entire regions in the early twentieth century. But nationalism for Caribbean and other postcolonial states emerged in midcentury in response to empire; in other words, nationalist movements in the Caribbean were oriented toward the establishment of sovereignty after centuries of colonial rule. Since that sovereignty is always under threat from neocolonial powers like the United States, it must always be defended and reified. While this book does not argue for a romantic nationalism, I want to highlight here the fact that despite the creolized and diasporic nature of Caribbean identity and culture, seemingly outdated notions of authenticity, origins, roots, and romantic nationality remain entrenched in the music and its musical fictions.

9. See, for instance, Sylvia Wynter's *The Hills of Hebron* (1962) and Roger Mais's *Brother Man* (1954).

10. I am borrowing the concept of a musical transnation from Carolyn Cooper, who coined the term "dancehall transnation" to theorize the global circulation of contemporary Jamaican music (*Sound Clash* 279). More recently, Ifeona Fulani's edited collection *Archipelagos of Sound* has constellated essays that think through the continued tidalectic flows of Caribbean music alongside the movements of the region's peoples.

11. Major Caribbean memory theorists, even when they mention other arrivants, often base their conceptions on the Afro-Caribbean experience, the Middle Passage, and plantation slavery. But Chinese migrants often brought entire families to the Caribbean and did not always need to relinquish language and customs; Indian indentured servants also experienced deleterious colonization but over a shorter period, and key customs remained intact by fiercely conservative traditions and were renewed in the twentieth century by the arrival of Bollywood films and broadcasts in the Caribbean in the 1930s (see Patricia Mohammed, "From Myth").

12. Other recent studies on contemporary Caribbean migrations include Donette A. Francis, *Fictions of Feminine Citizenship*; Myriam J. A. Chancy, *Searching for Safe Spaces*; and Kezia Page, *Transnational Negotiations*.

13. In *From Nation to Diaspora*, Forbes defines diasporic consciousness as "a celebratory attitude to diaspora, which is opposed to an attitude of mourning and loss. 'Diasporic' in this sense is the antithesis of 'exile' or 'exilic consciousness'" (230).

14. *The Pleasures of Exile* is the title of Lamming's 1960 collection of essays, in which he romanticizes the unique circumstance of "a small group of men" who willingly "exchange life" in their islands of birth for foreign climes (23). Rather than the broad migrations of ordinary folk and women in this and later decades, Lamming suggests that one of the pleasures of exile for the Caribbean male writer is to find a literate and literary-leaning audience.

15. This is not always the case, of course. Large numbers of Caribbean peoples have had to flee their homelands without much luggage due to hurricanes, volcanoes, dictatorship, local or state violence, and so on.

16. Recorded media has a quality of mimesis in its ability to repeat sound just as it was recorded. It therefore hides the constructedness of recorded sound and its associated

memories and obscures how we have changed between each memory occasion, how our memories change each time we rehearse them.

17. The proliferation of publications by ethnomusicologists and cultural theorists who have given serious sustained attention to Caribbean music forms provides both a rich tradition for a newer generation of writers and the tools that enable literary critics to use music with integrity to read novels for which such criticism is warranted. For studies on region-wide musicality, see Kenneth Bilby and Peter Manuel et al.; on calypso, Gordon Rohlehr and Louis Regis; on Latin music, Ed Morales and Ned Sublette; on reggae, Lloyd Bradley and O'Brien and Chang; on dancehall, Donna Hope and Sonjah Stanley Niaah; on chutney-soca, Helen Myers and Tina Ramnarine; on zouk and gwoka, Jocelyne Guilbault and Brenda Berrian; and on dub, Michael Veal and Dick Hebdige.

18. Edited collections that think music and literature together include Sandra Pouchet Paquet et al., *Music, Memory, Resistance*; Timothy J. Reiss, *Music, Writing, and Cultural Unity in the Caribbean*; and Ifeona Fulani, *Archipelagos of Sound*.

19. In *Phonographies: Grooves in Sonic Afro-Modernity*, Weheliye is primarily concerned with asserting the centrality of music and sound in black figurations of and participation in modernity. His theorization of "sonic Afro-modernity" hinges on analyses of filmic and fictional characters' conceptualization of subjectivity through audio technologies and rests on the historical sound/writing binary in Western conceptions of modernity.

20. In *Nationalists, Cosmopolitans, and Popular Music in Zimbabwe*, Michael Turino describes "four very different modes of musical activity" that might overlap even as they describe a progression in forms of music-making: participatory, presentational, high-fidelity, and studio music (46–47). In the Caribbean, participatory and presentational calypso, experienced most often during Carnival season, coexist with studio calypso meant for radio play and private collections. In Jamaican dancehalls, the night's proceedings might involve performance and participation through the deejay's call-and-response over studio recordings, whose high-fidelity status has already been undercut by dubbing in-studio, and the entire live performance is often recorded on cassette for later isolated replay by patrons or enthusiasts.

21. See, for instance, Brathwaite's elaboration of a jazz aesthetic in Roger Mais's *Brother Man* (*Roots* 103–106), Funso Aiyejina's theorization and application of a calypso aesthetic to Trinidadian fiction ("Novelypso"), or the more recent porting of a calypso aesthetic to the work of Barbadian George Lamming (Margaret Diana Gill, "Calypso Aesthetic") and to decidedly reggae-inspired novels (Curdella Forbes, "Fracturing Subjectivities").

22. Some ways of writing sound are hyperlegible to us a readers more so than others. This is made clear in the conundrum faced by readers as they encounter the musical notations that head each of the chapters in Du Bois's *The Souls of Black Folk* (Weheliye 82–105); Leon Scott's phonautograms, the etchings in black soot meant to represent recorded sound (Sterne, *Audible* 35); or instances like Adorno's attempt to read the grooves of a recorded vinyl (Adorno 56; Gitelman 3). While some texted sound can be understood and imagined, some novelized music might remain opaque; when rendered as lyric fragments, for instance, full understanding might require knowledge of the key, tempo, melody, and accompanying instrumentals, not to mention the idiom and its cultural context. For some readers, the lyric fragment can be sounded in the mind's ear as text but not music. Some readers might take the time to Google and listen to the referenced songs, but not all musical allusions are marked in the novel text as lyric or song (e.g., in Marlon James's *A Brief History*, many of the lyric fragments are rendered in Roman type indistinguishable from the rest of the prose).

CHAPTER 1 — PHONOGRAPHIC MEMORY

1. Margaret Diana Gill extends this "calypso aesthetic" even to novels beyond the twin island republic that replicate the narrative strategies of the chantwell.

2. In an interview with the author, Scott explained how his inspiration as a novelist came from reading aloud to British students the vernacular fictions of Selvon and others and has noted the impact of Lovelace's calypso aesthetics on the development of his own Caribbean poetics (Hamilton, "On Memory"). He has also recounted how, listening to Caribbean music and discussing literary form with Lovelace and C. L R. James in Trinidad, he got his "first lessons in what has come to be called the 'bacchanal aesthetics,' the writing of the 'novelypso'" ("Matura Days" 155, 157).

3. For this overview of calypso's development during the war years, I am indebted to Cowley; Neptune Jr; Rohlehr; L. Regis; Spottswood; Warner; and *West Indian Rhythm*. On calypso's roots in the West African griot tradition, see Warner-Lewis, *Guinea's Other Suns* (141–158).

4. For example, on receiving the news of King George's death on January 10, 1935, Raymond "Atilla" Quevedo immediately extemporized a eulogy at the Crystal Palace tent: "I am sorry to sing this in Calypso / But we just got it over the radio / That His Majesty died near 12 o'clock" (Cowley, "Calypso" 26). Patrons erupted in shock and distress at the breaking news.

5. In the novel's fictional version of the 1937 Fyzabad labor riots, during which a policeman is burned alive, characters also remember the historical event they have just reenacted (127–128). This moment in Trinidadian history is immortalized in Radio's calypso "Murder in Fyzabad," part of which is reproduced in the novel. A sidebar in the exhaustive collection *West Indian Rhythm* reveals that this is the original censored version of the calypso "The Strike in Trinidad." As the new title attests, "The version sent for censorship de-emphasized the idea of murder at Fyzabad" (109).

6. For discussions of comparable treatment of postcolonial Caribbean wounds, see Jahan Ramazani, "Wound of History"; and Patricia Krus, "Ethic of Postcolonial Healing."

7. Hanétha Vété-Congolo argues that *Pawòl* bears the marks of the colonial violence and silencing and the struggle to produce speech in the face of it (33).

8. See Hilar, *Sonar*; Shiga, "Sonar: Empire, Media"; and D'Amico and Pittenger, "A Brief History of Active Sonar."

9. Caribbean remembering is often figured as a form of marine archaeology. Writers like Glissant and Walcott have imagined the Caribbean Sea as a kind of Akashic record of absent cultural memory and have suggested that imaginative recuperation of historical memory requires diving into the otherwise unfathomable depths of the collective unconscious to trawl for and salvage submerged mnemonic traces. Walcott, for instance, posits the sea as the repository of history, replete with submerged mnemonic markers. See, for example, his claim in *Twilight* that "the illimitable sea . . . remembers" (82) and his poem "The Schooner Flight," which depicts the fugal Shabine trawling the Atlantic to "dredge" memory "from the deep" (*Collected Poems* 353).

10. Since traumatic memory is by nature antinarrative, Arthur Frank argues that "the wounded storyteller" must eventually rise above chaos through temporal distance in order to successfully accomplish narration; by reordering events, the narrator grafts agency that she would not have had in the living of it (98).

11. For an overview of the use of "I and I" in Rasta speech, see Pollard, *Dread Talk*.

12. In his use of the term *demasking*, Gerard Aching notes that removing the mask might not reveal identity but make a previously hidden reality more visible (6).

13. Hale transmits one example of a contemporary Hausa griotte who inherits the tradition from her father (176). Only some go on to earn the distinction of excellence as a "master griot" (184).

14. Caribbean feminist scholars like Shalini Puri ("Race, Rape, and Representation") and Tejaswini Niranjana have contested the exclusion of women from the calypso tent while women's half-naked bodies are paraded on the Carnival streets. See also the accounts of pseudoromantic calypsos in *West Indian Rhythm*: male-female relationships are rendered with the male calypsonian's suspicion of his female partner, distancing himself from his feelings either by anticipating his male peers' derision or by highlighting the woman's deception. "Love" songs are merely a pretext for trenchant critiques of male-female relationships and gender politics.

15. See Susan Harewood's discussion of the relationship between masquerade, gender, and sexuality in "Masquerade Performance."

16. Beliso-De Jesús argues that "copresences are Santería ontologies—they are the sensing of a multiplicity of being (and beings joined together) that are felt on the body. . . . Copresences are not simply dead or missing persons but rather are social figures of a past still present, proof that hauntings have taken place" (9).

17. For a discussion of French Creoles within the hierarchy of preindependence Trinidad, see Bridget Brereton, 116–117.

18. For instance, Scott's story "King Sailor One J'Ouvert Morning" depicts a white French Creole character finding belonging in the Carnival masquerade and steel pan.

19. Lovelace's *The Dragon Can't Dance*, although taken as a model novelypso, critiques the facile "all o' we is one" rhetoric of calypso and Carnival that is not borne out in lived experience outside of Carnival time. But Lovelace continues to draw on the potent cultural and political function of the calypsonian in his novels, most recently in *Is Just a Movie* (2011). His continued recourse to the chantwell narrator affirms that the calypsonian continues to have cultural, political, and literary resonance and relevance in contemporary Trinidadian society. See also David Chariandy's *Soucouyant* (2007), a novel that uses a calypso aesthetic to explore the memory loss associated with Alzheimer's.

CHAPTER 2 — "RECORD YOUR MEMORIES"

1. As Hijuelos reveals in his first novel, *Our House in the Last World* (1983), and his memoir *Thoughts without Cigarettes* (2011), the trajectory of the brothers was inspired by his own uncle's stint as a mambo musician in the 1940s and 1950s.

2. Hijuelos has, in fact, inserted the Castillo brothers into an actual episode of the *I Love Lucy* show where two Cuban cousins of Ricky Ricardo come to visit.

3. Because Hijuelos was the first Hispanic writer to win the Pulitzer, and since the novel's popular acclaim coincided with the second wave of the Latin boom, much of the scholarship on the novel situates it in ongoing debates about negotiating assimilation and hybridity. Early critics consider the novel too Anglocentric, written for a presumably unhyphenated American audience (Flores, *From Bomba* 167–169), but more recent readings use the notions of the *frontera*, or borderlands, to interrogate the novel's negotiation of an identity that is simultaneously Cuban and American (Elias, "Oscar Hijuelos' *The Mambo Kings*"; Meuleman, "Narrar (desde) los Borderlands"). Gustavo Pérez Firmat and William Luis go even further to attend equally to the novel's Cubanía and to its musical tropes in order to illuminate the ways that it "dance[s] between two cultures" (Luis, *Dance*

between Two Cultures) or instantiates "life on the hyphen" (Pérez Firmat) between Cubanness and Americanness, Spanish and English.

4. The LP-like structure is undercut by explicitly novelistic features, which include Eugenio's frame prologue and epilogue and a third brief closing "side" labeled "Toward the end, while listening to the wistful 'Beautiful María of My Soul.'"

5. Building on the work of Liam Bannon, Jonathan Sterne argues that recording technologies function more as tools of forgetting than remembering, even while remembering is the desired purpose ("Preservation Paradox" 58–59).

6. In the seventeenth century, *nostalgia* was used to describe the medical condition of Swiss students and soldiers who experienced a profound longing for familiar surroundings; prolonged displacement from home caused the afflicted to go mad from melancholy. Nostalgia later "became a central trope for both individual and national self-expression and identity, but which fragmented along with the fragmentation of the self under modernity" (Walder 939).

7. Lyrics here are from Irving Lara's 2018 version.

8. After his überpopularity in the United States waned in the early 2000s, Martin's Spanish-language albums, still hugely popular in Latin America, would begin to feature heavily nostalgic lyrics alongside his traditional fare of tropical rhythms celebrating life and casual romance and sweltering boleros testifying to longing, intimacy, and emotional fidelity. *Almas del Silencio* (2003)—his follow-up to the relative flop of *Sound Loaded* (2000), his second English-language release—was not only his first Spanish-language album in five years; it also debuted boleros of national longing. Listen, for instance, to the title song and tracks like "Tal Vez" and "Asignatura Pendiente," which personify his native Puerto Rico as a lost lover and depict his childhood as a lost idyllic state to which he longs to return. Returning to the Puerto Rico of his childhood is thus heralded by a return to both the Spanish language and his loyal and still outsize Hispanic fan base.

9. For this overview of Cuban American exile, I am indebted to the work of González-Pando, Gann and Duignan, and Domínguez. More recently, Alberto Laguna has argued that nostalgia and sadness are not the only registers that define Cuban exile; humor, *diversión*, and play are central to the community's self-fashioning as well. *The Mambo Kings Play Songs of Love* affirms that reading in its very title.

10. Most accounts of Cuban exile ignore those Cubans who left the island prior to the revolution—like Hijuelos's parents, the fictional Cesar and Nestor, and real-life early wave musicians—who considered themselves émigrés, at least until the revolution made them de facto exiles.

11. Fidel Castro died on November 26, 2016, and the news was received with much celebration in the streets of Little Havana. In the decade before then, changes in Cuba and in U.S. policy sustained Cuban exiles' hope that an end to the regime was close. In 2009, Castro's brother Raúl assumed control of the regime and initiated a series of policies that has allowed some small business ownership, real estate transactions, and automobile sales. In 2011, U.S. president Barack Obama responded to the regime change by easing restrictions on travel to the island by American-based exiles, and in 2015, he began the first overtures to reestablishing diplomatic relations between the two nations.

12. In "The Human Factors of Cubanidad," Fernando Ortiz distinguishes *cubanidad*, legal status as Cuban, from *cubanía*, conscious and deliberate spiritual status of Cuban belonging and identity (458).

13. The clave are the two percussion sticks that form the base (foundational) rhythm in Latin music; from Spanish for *key*, the clave is the key to all Latin music (Morales xviii).

14. Consider the mortification of lawyers during the defamation case brought by a dancer who claims Hijuelos plagiarized her life story for his novel. The court was tasked overnight with reading hundreds of pages of the novel, and then during the deposition, scandalized lawyers read aloud the most salacious passages detailing Cesar's lurid exploits. See Oscar Hijuelos, Oscar Hijuelos Papers, box 1, folder 2.

15. In original drafts for the musical version of the novel ("First draft, 2/18/96"), Hijuelos meant for the same actress to play both Maria and Delores. See Hijuelos, Hijuelos Papers, box 13, folder 1, p. 34.

16. Hijuelos, *The Mambo Kings Play Songs of Love: Drafts*.

17. For a historical account of machismo and Latin American fixation on male sexuality, see Ilan Stavans's "The Latin Phallus," in which he argues that Latina mothers are complicit in Latino men's hyperphallic performance of manhood, as they often fetishize the penis from the boy's infancy. This fetishization further creates an idealization of and dependency on the mother.

18. In an early draft of the musical version of the novel, the framing device is Cesar's appearance on a Hispanic radio show where, realizing that no one remembers the mambo king, he mournfully recalls and recounts the story of his and Nestor's brief dalliance with fame. See Hijuelos, Hijuelos Papers, box 12, folder 1, p. 118.

19. Because of their notational illiteracy, the brothers arranged their songs by writing lyrics and basic chords, then translating the memorized melodies for a musician with the dual literacies required to extrapolate sound to written music (*TMK* 29).

20. I want to make clear that in my use of the terms *forward* and *backward*, I am not making a moral judgment associating forwardness with Americans and backwardness with Cubans. I am using the terms solely for their valence in describing the relative cultural orientations of peoples plagued by trauma and memory in contrast to the dominant cultural narrative in the United States and the West regarding progress and modernity.

21. In his first novel, his memoir, and numerous unfinished teleplays, Hijuelos performs an intertextual narrative rememory of his quest for his "lost" Cubanness following a traumatic event as a young boy. Already too blond and "too Anglo," his ludic Cuban vacation is shattered when he falls prey to a mysterious illness. During his year-long convalescence in a sanitarium that already isolates him from his Spanish-speaking parents, an American nurse locks the young Hector—or Oscar, or Albert—in a closet as a punishment for speaking Spanish. Traumatized by the darkness, starvation, isolation, and repeated physical punishment, the boy finally represses his mother's tongue and becomes an American, effectively shattering his relationship with his mother, who can no longer speak to him, and breaking his last connection to his Cuban identity. See Hijuelos, Hijuelos Papers, box 2, folder 1, pp. 11a–12a.

22. Carolyn Birdsall traces the various articulations of the term *earwitness* and describes how it contrasts and complements the traditionally visual conception of history, memory, and traumatic witnessing.

23. Research in cognitive neuroscience strongly suggests that the confidence in the fidelity of vivid memories—and for my purposes here, the ability of recording media to accurately replay memories—might not be matched to the accuracy of the memories themselves (Loftus and Laney 825; Slotnick 100–101).

24. Luis, however, in a feat of bilingual textual analysis, discovers discrepancies in the Spanish-English translation of the lyrics and concludes that the song was written in English, like the novel, then translated (poorly) into Spanish by Hijuelos (*Dance between Two Cultures* 203).

25. I am thinking here of Tsitsi Jaji's figuration of stereomodernism in Pan-African musicality, particularly "the ways that stereo might be thought of as an effect, that which creates the impression of being surrounded by the contours of a voluminous, extensive three-dimensional body" (11).

26. As a synecdoche of the two positions sketched here in very broad terms, compare Rick Altman ("Material Heterogeneity") and James Lastra ("Reading, Writing").

27. In other words, although *LP* stands for "long-playing" record, one side of a 33 rpm record only holds about twenty-two minutes of music. *The Mambo Kings*, on the other hand, records *years* of memories. What is the memory media or format that can hold all these memories, if not the novel itself?

CHAPTER 3 — RE-MEMBERING "BODY AND SOUL"

1. For instance, the charred bodies of the victims of 9/11 remind him of violated black bodies throughout history, whether the lynched boys who became "strange etching fruit" or the innocent girls killed during the bombing of the Sixteenth Street Baptist Church in Birmingham, Alabama, in 1963 (Brathwaite, *Born to Slow Horses* 108).

2. Readings by Nick Nesbitt, Martin Munro, and Jason Herbeck consider the novel within a jazz and blues frame and attend to novelistic analogs to jazz improvisation or the blues mode. Such overly formalist readings tend to subsume other improvisational music and literary narration under a jazz aesthetic in the vein of Brathwaite's initial proposition. Some of this attention to jazz in this novel is warranted: Maximin himself cites "music" broadly as an influence to his consciousness (*Lone Sun* xxi). But while jazz musicians and records show up often throughout his work, so do a number of other Caribbean and black Atlantic music forms.

3. Maximin's French text and its English translation pun on the term *exile* to foreground the experience of being away from the island or *île*. Compare *exilé* (exiled) and *ex-îlé* (ex-isled; *Lone Sun* 102; *L'isolé* 115). I use the term *ex-isled* throughout this book to underscore the sense of loss that Caribbean peoples experience for the island homeland when they are "off-shored" to various degrees and for various reasons.

4. As Carol Bailey has argued, authors like Earl Lovelace, Marlon James, and Colin Channer often eschew masculinist narrative perspectives and modes to deploy a female narrator and "female-centred discourse" with an attention to issues of gender and power. Bailey suggests that such "womanist-feminist poetics" by regional male authors is inextricable from the performance culture of the Caribbean, where forms of carnivalesque masking are central to disruptive and generative politics and self-fashioning (9).

5. With Maximin's admission of the book's initial inspiration from Hélène Cixous, numerous scholars have discussed the novel's instantiation of "*l'écriture féminine*," a form of writing the body championed by early French feminists such as Cixous, Luce Irigaray, and Julia Kristeva (see, for instance, Zimra, "Négritude"; and Scharfman). But Curdella Forbes has interrogated the binary essentialisms of the categories of "masculine" or "feminine" text to argue that, although the region's literature seems to adhere to the nonlinear, hybrid, and collaborative modes of narrative that have been gendered as feminine,

a "feminine" text is more accurately defined as an ideological and discursive positioning and can be and has been performed by male writers (*From Nation* 27).

6. Yarimar Bonilla explains that Césaire's quest was for equality but that the French state was not ready or willing to concede it; "Césaire was not oblivious to the pitfalls of assimilation. In an interview with filmmaker Patrice Louis, he explained . . . 'Assimilation means to become similar . . . but I felt that for us, Martinicans, the descendants of Africans, that type of assimilation is a form of alienation. And I could not be in favor of alienation'" (22).

7. Siméa's pregnancy is perhaps an intertextual allusion to Jacqueline Manicom's 1972 novel *Mon examen de blanc*, which describes how Madévie comes to reject *lactification*. As in the later novel, Madévie's thorough assimilation is troped through her romance with a white French student in Paris, and her subsequent racial awakening is marked by her decision to abort her pregnancy, her return to Guadeloupe, and her subsequent romance with a Black trade unionist. See Zimra's discussion of Manicom's novel in "Négritude" (65).

8. In 1930s France, as Marie-France Morel outlines in "Histoire de l'avortement," abortion was a misdemeanor punishable by a fine and hard labor under several penal codes that dated from 1810 (Article 317) and were modified in 1920 and 1923. It was upgraded to a crime punishable by death under the February 15, 1942, Vichy Code (Allison, "The Right to Choose" 224). Between 1870 and 1939, when "Siméa's Journal" is set, methods for the necessarily clandestine abortions in France included ingesting herbal teas and medicinal concoctions like quinine sulfate, inserting household items such as sewing needles and hat feathers into the cervix, or introducing boiling or soapy water into the uterus with a syringe (Morel). For discussions of the clinical procedures involved at different stages of pregnancy, see "Fetal Development and Abortion"; and Rousset et al.

9. For detailed discussions of the erasure of the Nardal sisters and Suzanne Césaire from the canonical story of negritude, see T. Denean Sharpley-Whiting; Jennifer Wilks; and Brent Hayes Edwards. See also Maryse Condé's interrogation of the male-centeredness of negritude in "Pourquoi la Négritude?"

10. See Anne Donadey's discussion of how Maximin reconceptualizes the island's status as "*outre-mer*" (overseas), connecting it by its "*mer*" to closer geographies (50).

11. Laura Putnam has shown how Havana and other Caribbean ports "were part of the culturally contiguous space within which the Jazz Age and its deeply cosmopolitan music and dance were created" (157). Ned Sublette's biblical *Cuba and Its Music* chronicles how Cuba's Oriente province received and germinated Afro-Haitian music forms that then spread to New Orleans and elsewhere in the early 1800s, with a significant population hailing originally from then Saint-Domingue (123).

12. In Brathwaite's terms, such a form aligns with negritude to express and inspire the awakening of black consciousness and black protest and also the tension between individual alienation and group solidarity (*Roots* 55).

13. See also Brathwaite's description of a limbo/lembe space as a threshold or transitional space that archives submerged memory that can be remembered in or as habit memory ("Caribbean Cosmology" 15).

14. Here I disagree with Scharfman's reading that Siméa's textual performance enables her to "recuperate her baby" in an act of writing as engendering (242–243).

15. I am using *signification* here in the structuralist sense. In comparison, see Nesbitt's riff on Henry Louis Gates Jr.'s term to read Hawkins's performance as an example of structural signifyin' par excellence (Nesbitt 160).

16. See my discussion of reverb in dub music in chapter 5.

17. This is likely modeled on the real-life Césaires, Gerty Archimède, and René Ménil, Martinican founders of negritude and the literary magazine *Tropiques*, which ran during the Vichy regime.

18. In contrast to Nesbitt, who focuses on the "master" texts like Césaire, Damas, and Breton that Siméa, Marie-Gabriel, and Maximin rewrite and revision, Scharfman traces the lineage between Maximin's novel and Suzanne Césaire's writings to show *Lone Sun*'s indebtedness to a feminist literary practice rooted in reading and writing "mother texts" (233–245). Maximin's fascination with Césaire as an intellectual and creative muse is also evident in his 2009 edition of a collection of her essays from the *Tropiques* era, *Le grand camouflage / The Great Camouflage*.

19. In "Can the Empire Really Write Back," Clarisse Zimra considers the "unbounded" contours of the three novels *L'Isolé soleil*, *Soufrières*, and *L'île et une nuit* as a single amorphous "text" of Marie-Gabriel's life (81).

20. For ethnomusicological studies on gwoka, see Jerome Camal, "DestiNation" and "Creolizing Jazz"; Dominique Cyrille, "Sa Ki Ta Nou" and "Creole Quadrilles"; Brenda Berrian; Kathe Managan; and the documentary *Gwoka: L'âme de Guadeloupe?*

21. Bonilla explores the ways that "as the 'national liberation' model lost its plausibility and promise, Guadeloupean militants found themselves reconceptualizing their anticolonial movement as a workers' movement. . . . The result is a social movement that infuses labor struggles with battles over historical memory, Creole-language use, racial and ethnic politics, and the search for alternative forms of political and historical repertoire of this movement" (4).

22. For Jean Bernabé, Patrick Chamoiseau, and Raphaël Confiant, crafters of the Créoliste manifesto *Éloge de la Créolité*, by revaluing Creole language and culture, Antilleans would battle "the crisis of exteriority" that plagued them in the wake of departmentalization (75–78). They advocated a return to orality, Creole language, and Creole ways of knowing in opposition to Frenchness or even Africanness, since both "mother Africa" (as espoused by Césairian negritude) and France (as privileged by colonization and departmentalization) are external to Antillean reality and contribute to their false consciousness. Their call for a collective and inward turn or "interior vision" is inspired by Glissant's writings on natural poetics. While the French Caribbean concept of Creoleness (a state of being Creole or Caribbean) is distinct from Brathwaite's conception of Creolization (the process of becoming Creole or Caribbean), there are many synergies in the call for an oppositional revaluing of Afro-Caribbean folkways that cut across linguistic boundaries, as Brathwaite himself noticed when he encountered Glissant's writings on natural versus forced poetics (*Roots* 270). For example, for both Brathwaite and Glissant, the true potential for Caribbean becoming and futurity lies in recuperating the communal "we," with orality as its privileged mode, and to infuse writing and literature with that communal consciousness.

23. Throughout his scholarship, Camal has traced manifestations of musical creolization and the way that Guadeloupean gwoka interfaces with elements outside the island even as it is positioned as nationalist music par excellence, whether Lockel's Parisian experience with jazz, which influences his project of modernizing gwoka and working with the AGEG to make gwoka the sound of independent Guadeloupe ("DestiNation"), or David Murray's work with Guadeloupean gwoka musicians to fuse jazz and gwoka into jazz-ka ("Creolizing Jazz").

24. See bell hooks, *Salvation*; Audre Lorde, "Uses of the Erotic," and Patricia Hill Collins, *Black Sexual Politics*. Chapter 4 takes up the issue of the romantic and erotic in black female restoration and cultural memory more fully.

25. See also Caroline Rody's theorization of mother-daughter texts such as the pair of Charlotte Brontë's *Jane Eyre* and Jean Rhys's *Wide Sargasso Sea*.

26. The end of the novel is also its beginning in a reverse-chronological timescale; it also collapses the chronotope of sending and receiving letters, as we read the reply before the original, the name of the signatory is delayed to the end of the letter, and only seconds pass between reading the letters and their replies—very much like a contemporary social media feed.

27. See also Herbeck's discussion of how the ongoing dialogue with fragments of previous texts stages a "continual process of re-production" (172).

CHAPTER 4 — ROOTS, ROMANCE, REGGAE

1. See, for instance, Abram Gabriel, "A Biologist's Perspective."

2. Channer uses the novelistic version of Marley's "Waiting in Vain" to index male devotion in the face of female inconstancy, but to do so, he subverts the song's historical context—written for Marley's white Jamaican paramour—to index a turning from the white Jamaican Blanche, as "wrong love," to the Afro-Syrian Sylvia, as the true love.

3. Both Hall and Glissant dispense with notions of identities as fixed and rooted. In *Poetics of Relation*, Glissant draws on Deleuze and Guattari's postmodernist rhizome theory to argue for a conceptualization of Caribbean identities as creolized and relational—less a singular tree-root system and more the entangled web of the Creole garden (11).

4. The term *yardie* referred originally not to Jamaicans at home but to Jamaican gangs in Britain. In circulation at least since the 1990s, when it was popularized by Jamaican-British writer Victor Headley's gangland novel of the same name, the term has often been deployed by Britons of Jamaican descent to identify with their country of origin rather than their host country (see Bhopal and Myers 70–71; and Geoff Small 363–369). It has also become one of the many ways the British establishment collapses all black British bodies into the categories of outsiders, usurpers, criminal, and Jamaican, as notoriously illustrated by British historian David Starkey in a BBC interview about the source of the London Riots of 2011.

5. The sound system "deejay" (he who toasts/talks/ raps over a "riddim" track) is distinct from both the DJ (radio disc jockey) and the "selector" (he who selects and spins records in the Jamaican dancehall).

6. Marley himself was temporarily exiled in Delaware and then London at two separate periods of his life, the latter following an attempt on his life in December 1976. Others like Sugar Minott traveled and maintained homes between Kingston and London, cross-pollinating musical ideas between the two spaces. In addition, migrating Jamaicans like the parents of DJ Kool Herc carried with them the LPs and the techniques that would enable them to innovate on the turntable and pioneer American hip-hop.

7. This is according to an interview with Rita Marley in the 2012 documentary *Marley*.

8. The exception seems to be "Is This Love." See, for example, the set list for the November 30, 1979, show in Oakland, California.

9. For a discussion of how the early-twentieth-century mobility of Claude McKay, Marcus Garvey, and C. L. R. James trouble conceptions of the nation-state as a bounded entity,

see Michelle A. Stephens's *Black Empire*. By establishing McKay as a literary father for Fire, who writes his Somerset Maugham short-listed novels on an "Underwood manual, a 1930 No. 5 that had once belonged to Claude McKay" (*WIV* 238), Channer invites us to read *Waiting* in the tradition of *Home to Harlem*: consider McKay's use of black music as a literary form, his celebration of black bodies and sensual pleasure, and his positioning against respectable middle-class black culture à la W. E. B. Du Bois, who in his review of *Home to Harlem* famously declared wanting to take a bath after reading it (*Crisis* 202).

10. Whereas Edmondson interrogates Channer's framing of the reggae aesthetic as a marker of "literary authenticity" (*Caribbean Middlebrow* 4), Faith Smith situates the novel in turn-of-the-millennium anxieties about authenticity and globalized identities and critiques the novel's attachment to "codes of authenticity" or external markings of Jamaicanness that the diasporic citizen must master in order to qualify for repatriation. She argues that Channer's romance novel reinforces an ideology that "traveling nationalists and diasporic subjects must come home, but [that] they must master complex codes to do so" (59).

11. In his contribution to Alain Locke's *The New Negro*, W. A. Domingo noted that in the 1920s, West Indian denizens of Harlem often felt distinct from African Americans and indeed stood apart by their assertive, unorthodox, defiant blackness that "irritated American Negroes" (346). Terry-Ann Jones's more recent study finds that, even in the twenty-first century, "depending on the circumstances, [Afro-]Jamaicans have demonstrated a tendency to distance themselves from other blacks in [the United States], in some instances, even from other West Indians" (120).

12. Sources that depict lovers rock as a diasporic British idiom include *The Story of Lovers Rock*; de Koningh and Griffith (186–189); and Hebdige (129–130). Lisa Palmer, however, traces a genealogy that includes reggae love songs by Jamaican-based artistes.

13. Marley began his career singing doo-wop covers that grew increasingly Jamaicanized in style and accent, and he would continue to sing love songs as a central part of his oeuvre. The revolutionary *Exodus* and "soft" romantic *Kaya* albums were recorded in the same sessions in London in 1977; "Waiting in Vain" was in fact issued as a B-side to the "Exodus" single in January/February 1977 (Steffens and Pierson 94).

14. For discussions of the duality in Marley's lyrics between the sexual and spiritual, see Carolyn Cooper, *Sound Clash* (73–98); and Kwame Dawes, *Natural Mysticism* (143–164).

15. Haile Selassie's claim to the earthly throne is as a purported descendant of the biblical king Solomon and the Abyssinian queen of Sheba. For Rastafarians, Song of Songs describes the desire between Solomon and this dark-skinned lover later chronicled in the *Kebra Negast*. In both Jewish and New Testament exegesis of Song of Songs, the romantic and erotic exchange between the beloved and the lover is read as an allegory for the love between God as bridegroom king and the congregation as betrothed bride.

16. In her series of books on love, bell hooks proposes a "love ethic," a restorative loving among black folk to heal broader social and psychological damage (*Salvation*), while Audre Lorde has theorized the erotic as a liberatory practice, a "source of power" that releases creative and spiritual energies and connects us to both self and others (54–56). Lisa Amanda Palmer rejects the notion that lovers rock's turn to female romance is a retreat from politics; indeed, she argues, the idiom allows female singers and listeners to narrate their otherwise disallowed interiorities and to articulate black female romantic and sexual desire within the public sphere of the music industry (183). However, the songs are often written by men, including Dennis Bovell.

17. Although the novel focuses on Sylvia's and Fire's shared Jamaican blackness, the responsive "wining" cited above is accomplished by Blanche, whose name and multiply hyphenated ancestry contribute to her inappropriateness as Fire's ultimate mate. In fact, the novel is least convincing in its explication of why Blanche is Fire's wrong love, leaving the repeated focus on Sylvia's ethnicity as the locus of her "rightness." In the Marley mythos as well, heavy focus remains on his official wife, the dark-complexioned Rita, despite his high-profile relationship with the phenotypically white Miss Jamaica, Cindy Breakspeare. In fact, major Marley hits like "Wait in Vain" and "Turn Your Lights" were rumored to be written for Breakspeare (Steffens 200).

18. For a Caribbean feminist critique of the heteronormativity of the male-authored romance and women writers' response to the form, see Donette Francis, *Fictions of Feminine Citizenship*.

19. Channer has placed in Sylvia's mouth Geoffrey Philp's poem "Exile."

20. For a Caribbeanist critique of the North Atlantic orientation of Gilroy's theorization of diaspora, see Nadi Edwards, "Roots, and Some Routes Not Taken."

21. For a discussion of the history of black-Indian tensions in Jamaica and the wider Caribbean, see Mervyn Alleyne, "The Role of Africa." The latest available census identifies a 91 percent black population, with Indo-Jamaicans at 3.4 percent ("National Census Report 2001" 35). I also explore Indo-Caribbean marginalization within music cultures more fully in chapter 5.

22. Ian's behaviors map almost too perfectly onto the categories of dancehall masculinity outlined throughout Hope's *Man Vibes*. Like Cooper, who has reread "slackness" as lyrical play (*Sound Clash* 145), Bucknor reads *Waiting*'s obsession with sex talk as evidence of staged masculinity, an insistence on male prowess through linguistic performance.

23. Of course, more musically savvy auditors could bypass the conservative strictures of radio airplay with either live sound clashes or recordings thereof.

24. Listen, for instance, to Simpleton's 1992 hit "Coca Cola Bottle Shape," a sonic "big up" to women ("girls") with the anatomical perfection enshrined by the shape of the popular soft drink.

25. The OED defines a meme as "a cultural element or behavioural trait whose transmission and consequent persistence in a population, although occurring by non-genetic means (esp. imitation), is considered as analogous to the inheritance of a gene."

26. The same is true for Marley's music, which, until the fall 1980 Madison Square Garden show and ultimately his second to last performance, his brand of reggae drew a largely white audience (Steffens 375).

27. For a fuller discussion of the deportee figure, see Kezia Page, *Transnational Negotiations* (103–125).

28. In fact, "roots" is a retroactive label applied to early reggae to designate sonic authenticity despite its hybridity. Even as roots reggae artists continue to use the form to interrogate social injustice, purists often take a protectionist stance against innovation in a bid to protect the music and culture so designated from the depredations of newer trends. Ironically, even contemporary artists like Chronixx and Protoje, whose music operates along the reggae-dancehall continuum, take up the label "reggae revival" to describe their music. In contrast to the tendency toward conservatism in roots reggae, dancehall is constantly mutating, ephemeral, and fast-paced, as much in touch with traditional folk idioms as in constant dialogue with other Caribbean and black Atlantic music.

CHAPTER 5 — MEMORY AS MIXTAPE

1. See also Rosanne Kanhai, "The Masala Stone Sings."

2. See her essays "The Absent Voice" and "The Invisible Woman in West Indian Fiction," her short stories "Barred: Trinidad 1987" and "Indian Cuisine," and her poetry collection *Nuclear Seasons*. For a similar critique of the representation of Indo-Caribbean women in fiction, see also Brinda Mehta's *Diasporic Dislocations* (2).

3. Readings of music in the novel center on hybridity, or music as gendered and sexual resistance. See Brinda Mehta ("Engendering History"); Shalini Puri ("Canonized Hybridities"); and Paula Morgan.

4. The question of voice has implications for other subaltern constituencies beyond the scope of this project, in particular for Chinese Caribbeans, who have also been unseen and unheard in national discourse and popular culture despite their important contributions. See Staceyann Chin's memoir, *The Other Side of Paradise*, that describes her finding a voice and a form in which to be heard as a mixed-race Chinese Jamaican lesbian; and Tessanne Chin's turn on the American singing competition *The Voice* discussed in Tzarina Prater's "Look Pon Likkle Chiney Gal."

5. Cesar, Hijuelos's mambo musician (chapter 2), attempts something similar when he takes his record player and mambo and bolero records into the Hotel Splendour. With this early, unwieldy version of a Walkman, Cesar brings his reminiscing away from the attention and interruption of his family. But without bidirectional headphones to direct the sounds only to his ears, he risks disturbing fellow guests and his trip down memory lane is also constantly interrupted by the sounds of the loudly copulating couple that filter through the adjoining wall.

6. Consumer mixtapes are distinct from the professional mixtapes popular in hip-hop, where an artist compiles a short-playing collection of her music to test the market or apprise audiences and industry insiders of what she has been working on.

7. In her study of the soundscapes of post–oil boom Trinidadians, for example, Robin Balliger discovered that Trinidadians "consume an incredible variety of music which often has less to do with identity than functionality" (58), while both Helen Myers and Tina Ramnarine have documented not only music genres that can be labeled "Indian" but a variety of local (Afro-Creole and hybrid) and foreign music as well.

8. In his famous "Massa Day Done" address at the so-called University of Woodford Square, the rebaptized public square in Port of Spain, Trinidad, Eric Williams declared, "Massa believed in the inequality of races. Today, as never before, the PNM has held out to the population of Trinidad and Tobago and the West Indies and the world the vision and the practice of interracial solidarity" (730).

9. As chutney moved from the female, private, Indian space to the public sphere, it intermingled with calypso and soca and came to public consciousness in the 1990s during the same historical moment that saw the election of the republic's first Indian prime minister, Basdeo Panday. Chutney soca is in many ways the culmination of the incorporation of the Indo-Trinidadian musical presence within calypso; it brings to the faster soca music the *tassa* drums, suggestive lyrics, and fast-paced pelvic gyrations associated with the private, female-centered *matikor* chutney and often features Hindi words. As many commentators note, chutney soca is considered a *dougla* form and was largely fronted by dougla artists like Brother Marvin (see, for instance, Reddock 193, 199).

10. In *Making Men*, Belinda Edmondson traces how Caribbean writers of both sexes created writing selves in the guise of British men, envisioning authority and authorship as gendered male and writing as linked to the phallic pen.

11. For instance, an engineer or mixer might reintroduce reverb into the mix if the sound was too clean or flat (Morton 142–143).

12. Hebdige notes that "nowadays, Jamaican studios contain equipment which can handle up to twenty-four tracks instead of just two, and the potential for experimentation in dub is vast" (84).

13. See also Rodolphe Solbiac's exploration of how the novel's treatment of diasporic memory unsettles standard conceptions of diaspora (230).

14. For a discussion of the differences between exilic and diasporic consciousness, see Curdella Forbes, *From Nation to Diaspora* (229–230).

15. In her chapter "Race, Rape, and Representation," Puri reads Espinet's novel and her story "Barred" as evidence of *dougla* or hybrid Afro-Indian negotiation, in "an attempt to renegotiate constructions of Indianness by articulating that which is 'barred' from dominant representations of race and sexuality" (261). See also Kamala Kempadoo's elaboration of what she calls a "dogla perspective" from which she makes diasporic art.

16. See, for instance, "Crusoe's Island" in Walcott's *Collected Poems* (68–72).

CODA

1. For instance, 1985's "Sleng Teng" has the distinction of being the first dancehall riddim created on a computer (Paul 634).

2. For a discussion of the distinctions between meme and memory, see Jacob Dorman's *Chosen People* (6–7).

3. Brathwaite defines *tidalectic* as "the movement of the water backwards and forwards as a kind of cyclic, I suppose, motion, rather than linear" (Mackey, "Interview" 14), while Glissant takes the Caribbean's archipelagic form to conceptualize his theory of relationality, regional identity, and memory (see Thomas 28).

4. For a more detailed discussion of the act of reading electronic books and the connection between print books and embodiment, see Bolter (68, 80).

5. For discussions of Brathwaite's SVS, see Kelly Baker Joseph, "Versions of X/Self"; de Matas, "Ctrl+Alt"; and Annie Paul, "Log On."

Works Cited

Aching, Gerard. *Masking and Power: Carnival and Popular Culture in the Caribbean.* U of Minnesota P, 2002.

Adorno, Theodor W. "The Form of the Phonograph Record." *October*, vol. 55, 1990, pp. 56–61.

Aiyejina, Funso. "Novelypso, Earl Lovelace and Bacchanal Tradition." *A Place in the World: Essays and Tributes in Honour of Earl Lovelace at 70*, edited by Funso Aiyejina, Lexicon, 2008, pp. 163–200.

———. *Self-Portraits: Interviews with Ten West Indian Writers and Two Critics.* UWI School of Continuing Studies, 2003.

Alexander, M. Jacqui. "Not Just (Any) Body Can Be a Citizen." *Feminist Review*, vol. 48, 1994, pp. 5–23.

Alleyne, Mervyn C. "The Role of Africa in the Construction of Identities in the Caribbean." *A Pepper-Pot of Cultures: Aspects of Creolization in the Caribbean*, edited by Gordon Collier and Ulrich Fleischmann, *Matatu*, vols. 27–28; Rodopi, 2003, pp. 29–42.

Allison, Maggie. "The Right to Choose: Abortion in France." *Parliamentary Affairs: A Journal of Comparative Politics*, vol. 47, no. 2, 1994, pp. 222–231.

Altman, Rick. "The Material Heterogeneity of Recorded Sound." *Sound Theory, Sound Practice*, edited by Rick Altman, Routledge, 1992, pp. 15–31.

Anderson, Ben. "Recorded Music and Practices of Remembering." *Social and Cultural Geography*, vol. 5, no. 1, 2004, pp. 3–20.

Anderson, Benedict. *Imagined Communities: Reflections on the Origins and Spread of Nationalism.* Verso, 1983.

Anim-Addo, Joan, editor. *Centre of Remembrance: Memory and Caribbean Women's Literature*, Mango, 2002.

Anthony, Marc. "Como Duele." *Contra la Corriente*, Universal Music, 1997.

Anyidoho, Kofi. "Atumpan: Kamau Brathwaite and the Gift of Ancestral Memory." *Caribbean Culture: Soundings on Kamau Brathwaite*, edited by Annie Paul, U of the West Indies P, 2007, pp. 39–53.

Appadurai, Arjun. *Modernity at Large: Cultural Dimensions of Globalization.* University of Minnesota P, 1996.

Assmann, Aleida, and Jan Assmann. "*Membra Disiecta*: Embalmment and Anatomy in Egypt and Europe." *ReMembering the Body*, edited by Gabriele Brandstetter and Hortensia Völckers, Hatje Cantz, 2000, pp. 44–101.

The Astronauts. "Born Jamaican." *Born Jamaican.* Thunder Bolt, 1982. TB-LP-02.

Bailey, Carol. *A Poetics of Performance: The Oral-Scribal Aesthetic in Anglophone Caribbean Fiction*. U of the West Indies P, 2014.

Bakhtin, Mikhail M. *The Dialogic Imagination: Four Essays*. Translated by Caryl Emerson and Michael Holquist, U of Texas P, 1981.

———. *Rabelais and His World*. MIT P, 1968.

Balliger, Robin. "Popular Music and the Cultural Politics of Globalization among the Post–Oil Boom Generation in Trinidad." *Identity, Ethnicity and Culture in the Caribbean*, edited by Ralph Premdas, UWI School of Continuing Studies, 1998, pp. 54–79.

Baucom, Ian. "Frantz Fanon's Radio: Solidarity, Diaspora, and the Tactics of Listening." *Contemporary Literature*, vol. 42, no. 1, 2001, pp. 15–49.

Beliso-De Jesús, Aisha M. *Electric Santería: Racial and Sexual Assemblages of Transnational Religion*. Columbia UP, 2015.

Benítez-Rojo, Antonio. *The Repeating Island: The Caribbean and the Postmodern Perspective*. Duke UP, 1992.

Benjamin, Walter. *Illuminations*. Edited by Hannah Arendt. Translated by Harry Zohn, Harcourt, 1968.

Bennett, Louise. *Jamaica Labrish*. Sangsters, 1966.

Berliner, Paul. *Thinking in Jazz: The Infinite Art of Improvisation*. U of Chicago P, 1994.

Bernabé, Jean, et al. *Éloge de la Créolité / In Praise of Creoleness*. Translated by M. B. Taleb-Khyar, Johns Hopkins UP, 1990.

Berrian, Brenda F. *Awakening Spaces: French Caribbean Popular Songs, Music, and Culture*. U of Chicago P, 2000.

Best, Curwen. *Culture @ the Cutting Edge: Tracking Caribbean Popular Music*. U of the West Indies P, 2010.

Bhopal, Kalwant, and Martin Myers. *Insiders, Outsiders and Others: Gypsies and Identity*. U of Hertfordshire P, 2008.

Bilby, Kenneth. *The Caribbean as a Musical Region*. Woodrow Wilson International Center for Scholars, 1985.

Birdsall, Carolyn. "Earwitnessing: Sound Memories of the Nazi Period." *Sound Souvenirs*, edited by José van Dijck and Karin Bijsterveld, Amsterdam UP, 2009, pp. 169–181.

Bob Marley and the Wailers. "Bad Card." *Uprising*, Island, 1980.

———. "Bob Marley & the Wailers—Upgraded Amandla Festival Full Concert 1979-7-21 Harvard Stadium, Boston." *YouTube*, uploaded by BobMarleyConcerts, 23 Aug. 2012, https://www.youtube.com/watch?v=SrgOztpbDGc.

———. *Exodus*, Island, 1977.

———. "Is This Love?" *Kaya*, Island, 1978.

———. "No Woman No Cry." *Live!*, Island, 1975.

———. "Turn Your Lights Down Low." *Exodus*, Island, 1977.

———. "Waiting in Vain." *Exodus*, Island, 1977.

Bolter, Jay David, *Writing Space: Computers, Hypertext, and the Remediation of Print*. Lawrence Erlbaum, 2001.

Bonilla, Yarimar. *Non-sovereign Futures: French Caribbean Politics in the Wake of Disenchantment*. U of Chicago P, 2015.

Bradley, Lloyd. *This Is Reggae Music: The Story of Jamaica's Music*. Penguin, 2000.

Brandstetter, Gabriele. "Choreography as a Cenotaph: The Memory of Movement." *ReMembering the Body*, edited by Gabriele Brandstetter and Hortensia Völckers, Hatje Cantz, 2000, pp. 102–135.

Brant, Daniel. "Disaster Cosmopolitanism: Catastrophe and Global Community in the Fiction of Daniel Maximin and Maryse Condé." *International Journal of Francophone Studies*, vol. 17, no. 2, 2014, pp. 215–237.

Brathwaite, Kamau. *The Arrivants: A New World Trilogy*. Oxford UP, 1994.

———. "Caribbean Literature: The Black Rock of Africa." *African Forum*, vol. 1, no. 4, 1966, pp. 32–52.
———. *Contradictory Omens*. Savacou, 1974.
———. *Born to Slow Horses*, Wesleyan UP, 2005.
———. "Notes on Caribbean Cosmology." *River City: A Journal of Contemporary Culture*, vol. 16, no. 3, 1996, 1–17.
———. *Roots*. U of Michigan P, 1993.
Brereton, Bridget. *A History of Modern Trinidad: 1783–1962*. Heinemann, 1981.
Brodber, Erna. *Louisiana: A Novel*. U of Mississippi P, 1994.
———. "Reggae as Black Space." *Global Reggae*, edited by Carolyn Cooper, Canoe, 2012, pp. 21–36.
———. *A Study of Yards in the City of Kingston*. Institute of Social and Economic Research, 1981.
Bucknor, Michael A. "Staging Seduction: Masculine Performance or the Art of Sex in Colin Channer's *Waiting in Vain*." *Interventions*, vol. 6, no. 1, 2004, pp. 67–81.
Buju Banton (Mark Myrie). "Boom Bye Bye." Single, VP, 1992.
———. "Deportee (Things Change)." Single, Penthouse, 1993.
———. "Hills and Valleys." *Inna Heights*, Penthouse, 1997.
———. "Untold Stories." *'Til Siloh*, Penthouse, 1995.
Bull, Michael. "The Auditory Nostalgia of iPod Culture." *Sound Souvenirs*, edited by José van Dijck and Karin Bijsterveld, Amsterdam UP, 2009, pp. 83–93.
Burning Spear. "Slavery Days." *Marcus Garvey*, Island, 1975.
Camal, Jerome. "Creolizing Jazz, Jazzing the Tout-monde: Jazz, Gwoka and the Poetics of Relation." *American Creoles: The Francophone Caribbean and the American South*, edited by Martin Munro and Celia Britton, Liverpool UP, 2012, pp. 165–179.
———. "DestiNation: The Festival Gwoka, Tourism, and Anticolonialism." *Sun, Sea, and Sound: Music and Tourism in the Circum-Caribbean*, edited by Timothy Rommen and Daniel T. Neely, Oxford UP, 2014, pp. 213–237.
Campbell, Tevin. *T.E.V.I.N.* Qwest/Warner Brothers, 1991.
Carey, Mariah. *Charmbracelet*. MonarC/Island, 2002.
Cartey, Wilfred. "Introduction." *Negritude: Black Poetry from Africa and the Caribbean*, edited and translated by Norman R. Shapiro, October House, 1970, pp. 17–37.
Caruth, Cathy. *Unclaimed Experience: Trauma, Narrative, and History*. Johns Hopkins UP, 1996.
Césaire, Aimé. *Cahier d'un retour au pays natal*. Présence Africaine, 1939.
Césaire, Suzanne. *The Great Camouflage: Writings of Dissent (1941–1945)*. Edited by Daniel Maximin. Translated by Keith L. Walker, Wesleyan UP, 2009.
Chancy, Myriam J. A. *Framing Silence: Revolutionary Novels by Haitian Women*. Rutgers UP, 1997.
———. *Searching for Safe Spaces: Afro-Caribbean Women Writers in Exile*. Temple UP, 1997.
Chang, Kevin O'Brien, and Wayne Chen. *Reggae Routes: The Story of Jamaican Music*. Temple UP, 1998.
Channer, Colin. "Introduction." *Iron Balloons: Hit Fiction from Calabash Writer's Workshop*, Akashic, 2006, pp. 1–28.
———. "Preface." *Wheel and Come Again: An Anthology of Reggae Poetry*, edited by Kwame Dawes, Peepal Tree, 1998, pp. 13–15.
———. "The Problem with Women? Men." *Essence*, May 2002, p. 114.
———. *Waiting in Vain*. One World, 1998.
Chariandy, David. *Soucouyant*. Arsenal Pump, 2007.
Chevannes, Barry. "Jamaican Diasporic Identity: The Metaphor of *Yaad*." *Nation Dance: Religion, Identity, and Cultural Difference in the Caribbean*, edited by Patrick Taylor, Indiana UP, 2001, pp. 129–137.

Chin, Staceyann. *The Other Side of Paradise: A Memoir*. Scribner, 2009.
Chude-Sokei, Louis. "When Echoes Return." *Transition*, vol. 104, 2011, pp. 76–92.
Chronixx (Jamar McNaughton). *Chronology*. Virgin/ EMI, 2017.
———. *Dread and Terrible*. Chronixx Music, 2014.
Cixous, Hélène. "The Laugh of the Medusa." Translated by Keith and Paula Cohen. *Signs: Journal of Women in Culture and Society*, vol. 1, no. 4, 1976, pp. 875–893.
Collins, Merle. "Shame Bush." *Lady in a Boat*, Peepal Tree, 2003, pp. 50–22.
Collins, Patricia Hill. *Black Sexual Politics: African Americans, Gender, and the New Racism*. Routledge, 2005.
Condé, Maryse. "Pourquoi la Négritude? Négritude ou Révolution." *Négritude africaine, négritude caraïbe*, edited by Jeanne-Lydie Goré, Éditions de la Francité, 1973, pp. 150–154.
Connerton, Paul. "Seven Types of Forgetting." *Memory Studies*, vol. 1, no. 1, 2008, pp. 59–71.
Cooper, Carolyn. *Noises in the Blood: Orality, Gender, and the "Vulgar" Body of Jamaican Popular Culture*. Duke UP, 1995.
———. *Sound Clash: Jamaican Dancehall Culture at Large*. Palgrave, 2004.
Count Ossie and the Folkes Brothers. "Oh Carolina." Single, Bluebeat, 1959.
Cowley, John H. "Calypso and the Trinidad Carnival Tradition." *West Indian Rhythm: Trinidad Calypsos on World and Local Events; Featuring the Censored Recordings—1938–1940*, edited by the Classic Calypso Collective, Bear Family Records, 2007, pp. 14–37.
Culbertson, Roberta. "Embodied Memory, Transcendence, and Telling: Recounting Trauma, Re-establishing the Self." *New Literary History*, vol. 26, no. 1, 1995, pp. 169–195.
Cyrille, Dominique O. "Creole Quadrilles of Guadeloupe, Dominica, Martinique, and St. Lucia." *Creolizing Contradance in the Caribbean*, edited by Peter Manuel, Temple UP, 2009, pp. 188–208.
———. "Sa Ki Ta Nou (This Belongs to Us): Creole Dances of the French Caribbean." *Caribbean Dance from Abakua to Zouk: How Movement Shapes Identity*, edited by Susanna Sloat, U of Florida P, 2002, pp. 221–246.
Damas, Léon-Gontran. *Pigments-Névralgies*. Présence Africaine, 2003.
D'Amico, Angela, and Richard Pittenger. "A Brief History of Active Sonar." *Aquatic Mammals*, vol. 35, no. 4, 2009, pp. 426–434.
Daniel, Yvonne. *Caribbean and Atlantic Diaspora Dance: Igniting Citizenship*. U of Illinois P, 2011.
David Murray and the Gwo-Ka Masters. *Gwotet*, Feat. Pharaoh Sanders, Justin Time Records, 2004.
Davis, Fred. *Yearning for Yesterday: A Sociology of Nostalgia*. Free Press, 1979.
Dawes, Kwame. *Natural Mysticism: Towards a New Reggae Aesthetic*. Peepal Tree, 1999.
———. "Ramabai Espinet." *Talk Yuh Talk: Interviews with Anglophone Caribbean Poets*, U of Virginia P, 2001, pp. 108–123.
Domingo, W. A. "Gift of the Black Tropics." *The New Negro: Voices of the Harlem Renaissance*, edited by Alain Locke, Touchstone, 1992, pp. 341–349.
Domínguez, J. I. "US-Cuban Relations: From the Cold War to the Colder War." *Journal of Interamerican Studies and World Affairs*, vol. 39, no. 3, 1997, pp. 49–75.
Donadey, Anne. "Beyond Departmentalization: Feminist Black Atlantic Reformulations of Outre-Mer in Daniel Maximin's *L'Isolé Soleil*." *International Journal of Francophone Studies*, vol. 11, no. 1–2, 2008, pp. 49–65.
Dorman, Jacob S. *Chosen People: The Rise of American Black Israelite Religions*. Oxford UP, 2013.
Douglas, Marcia. *The Marvellous Equations of the Dread*. Peepal Tree, 2016.
Du Bois, W. E. B. "Review of *Home to Harlem*." *Crisis*, September 1928, p. 202.
Edmondson, Belinda. *Caribbean Middlebrow: Leisure Culture and the Middle Class*. Cornell UP, 2009.

———. *Making Men: Gender, Literary Authority, and Women's Writing in Caribbean Narrative*. Duke UP, 1999.

Edwards, Brent Hayes. *The Practice of Diaspora: Literature, Translation, and the Rise of Black Internationalism*. Harvard UP, 2003.

Edwards, (Norval) Nadi. "Roots, and Some Routes Not Taken: A Caribcentric Reading of the Black Atlantic." *Found Object*, vol. 4, 1994, pp. 27–35.

———. "Talking about Culture: Rethinking the Popular." *Small Axe: A Caribbean Journal of Criticism*, vol. 9, 2001, pp. v–viii.

Elias, Amy. "Oscar Hijuelos' *The Mambo Kings Play Songs of Love*, Ishmael Reed's *Mumbo Jumbo*, and Robert Coover's *The Public Burning*." *Critique: Studies in Contemporary Fiction*, vol. 41, no. 2, 2000, pp. 115–128.

Ellison, Ralph. *Invisible Man*. Vintage Books, 1995.

Espinet, Ramabai. "The Absent Voice: Unearthing the Female Epistemology of Cane." Colloquium on Sugar Cane and Society, 16–18 June 1989, Toronto, Canada. Presentation.

———. "Barred: Trinidad 1987." *Green Cane and Juicy Flotsam: Short Stories by Caribbean Women*, edited by Carmen Esteves and Lizabeth Paravisini-Gebert. Rutgers UP, 1991, pp. 80–85.

———. "Indian Cuisine." *The Massachusetts Review*, vol. 35, no. 3/4, 1994, pp. 563–573.

———. "The Invisible Woman in West Indian Fiction." *World Literature Written in English*, vol. 29, no. 2, 1989, pp. 116–126.

———. *Nuclear Seasons: Poems*. SisterVision, 1991.

———. *The Swinging Bridge*. Harper Flamingo, 2003.

Felman, Shoshana, and Dori Laub. *Testimony: Crises of Witnessing in Literature, Psychoanalysis, and History*. Routledge, 1992.

"Fetal Development and Abortion." First Coast Women's Services, 2018, http://fcws.org/issues/fetal-development-and-abortion.

Fitzgerald, Ella. "Body and Soul." *Frank Sinatra: A Man and His Music + Ella + Jobim*, NBC, 13 Nov. 1967, Warner/Elektra/Atlantic.

Flores, Juan. *From Bomba to Hip-Hop: Puerto Rican Culture and Latino Identity*. Columbia UP, 2000.

———. "In Cortijo's Wake: *Crónica* and Popular Music." *Music, Writing, and Cultural Unity in the Caribbean*, edited by Timothy J. Reiss, Africa World, 2005, pp. 257–270.

Forbes, Curdella. "Fracturing Subjectivities: International Space and Discourse in *Waiting in Vain* and *Mr. Potter*." *Small Axe: A Caribbean Journal of Criticism*, vol. 12, no. 1, 2008, pp. 16–37.

———. *From Nation to Diaspora: Samuel Selvon, George Lamming and the Cultural Performance of Gender*. U of the West Indies P, 2005.

Francis, Donette A. *Fictions of Feminine Citizenship: Sexuality and the Nation in Contemporary Caribbean Literature*. Palgrave Macmillan, 2010.

———. "'Travelling Miles': Jazz in the Making of a West Indian Intellectual." *Caribbean Culture: Soundings on Kamau Brathwaite*, edited by Annie Paul, U of the West Indies P, 2007, pp. 142–151.

Frank, Arthur W. *The Wounded Storyteller: Body, Illness, and Ethics*. U of Chicago P, 1995.

Frederick, Rhonda D. "Making Jamaican Love: Colin Channer's *Waiting in Vain* and Romance-ified Diaspora Identities." *Small Axe: A Caribbean Journal of Criticism*, vol. 42, 2013, pp. 63–84.

Freud, Sigmund. "Beyond the Pleasure Principle." *On Freud's "Beyond the Pleasure Principle,"* edited by Salman Akhtar and Mary Kay O'Neil, Karnac, 2011, pp. 13–72.

———. "Remembering, Repeating, Working-Through." *The Complete Psychological Works of Sigmund Freud*, edited by James Strachey and Anna Freud, Hogarth, 1966, pp. 145–156.

Frydman, Jason. *Sounding the Break: African American and Caribbean Routes of World Literature*. U of Virginia P, 2014.

Fulani, Ifeona, editor. *Archipelagos of Sound: Transnational Caribbeanities, Women and Music*. U of the West Indies P, 2012.

Gabriel, Abram. "A Biologist's Perspective on DNA and Race." *Genetics and the Unsettled Past: The Collision of DNA, Race, and History*, edited by Keith Wailoo, Alondra Nelson, and Catherine Lee, Rutgers UP, 2017, pp. 43–66.

Gann, Lewis H., and Peter Duignan. *The Hispanics in the United States: A History*. Westview, 1986.

Garvey, Marcus. *Selected Writings and Speeches of Marcus Garvey*. Edited by Bob Blaisdell, Dover, 2004.

Gill, Margaret D. "Calypso Aesthetic in George Lamming's *In the Castle of My Skin*." *Music, Writing, and Cultural Unity in the Caribbean*, edited by Timothy J. Reiss, Africa World, 2005, pp. 181–200.

Gilroy, Paul. *The Black Atlantic: Modernity and Double Consciousness*. Harvard UP, 1993.

Gitelman, Lisa. *Scripts, Grooves, and Writing Machines: Representing Technology in the Edison Era*. Stanford UP, 1999.

Glissant, Édouard. *Caribbean Discourse: Selected Essays*. Translated by J. Michael Dash, U of Virginia P, 1989.

———. *Poetics of Relation*. Translated by Betsy Wing, U of Michigan P, 1990.

Golding, Bruce. Interview by Stephen Sackur. Hardtalk. BBC. 20 May 2008, http://news.bbc.co.uk/2/hi/programmes/hardtalk/7410382.stm.

González-Pando, Miguel. *The Cuban Americans*. Greenwood, 1998.

Grant, Heather. "Mek Wi Put Things Right." Vinyl Single. Nura, 1992.

Guevara, Gema R. "Narratives of Racial Authority in Cuban Popular Music." *Journal of Popular Music Studies*, vol. 17, no. 3, 2005, pp. 255–274.

Guilbault, Jocelyne. *Zouk: World Music in the West Indies*. U of Chicago P, 1993.

Gwoka: L'âme de la Guadeloupe? Directed by Caroline Bourgine and Olivier Lichen, Les Films du Village/TLT, 1995.

Halbwachs, Maurice. *On Collective Memory*. Edited by Lewis A. Coser, U of Chicago P, 1992.

Hale, Thomas A. *Griots and Griottes: Masters of Words and Music*. Indiana UP, 1998.

Hall, Stuart. "Caribbean Culture: Future Trends." *Caribbean Quarterly*, vol. 43, 1997, pp. 25–33.

———. "Cultural Identity and Cinematic Representation." *Ex-Iles: Essays on Caribbean Cinema*, edited by Mbye B. Cham, African World, 1992, pp. 220–236.

Hamilton, Njelle. "'From Silent Wounds to Narrated Words': Calypso Storytelling in Lawrence Scott's *Night Calypso*." *Anthurium: A Caribbean Studies Journal*, vol. 10, no. 1, 2013, article 3, https://scholarlyrepository.miami.edu/anthurium/vol10/iss1/3.

———. "Mourning Mixtape: A Memoir." Unpublished manuscript.

———. "'Music and a Story': Sound Writing in Ramabai Espinet's *The Swinging Bridge*." *Critical Perspectives on Indo-Caribbean Women's Literature*, edited by Joy Mahabir and Mariam Pirbhai, Routledge, 2013, pp. 70–92.

———. "On Memory and the Archives of History: A Conversation with Trinidadian Novelist Lawrence Scott." *Wasafiri*, March 2017, http://www.wasafiri.org/article/conversation-lawrence-scott.

———. "'Rastaman Vibrations': Sound, String Theory, and 'Anti-Clock' Temporalities in Marcia Douglas's *The Marvellous Equations of the Dread*." Unpublished manuscript.

Harewood, Susan. "Masquerade Performance and the Play of Sexual Identity in Calypso." *Cultural Studies, Critical Methodologies*, vol. 5, no. 2, 2005, pp. 189–205.

Harter, Deborah A. *Bodies in Pieces: Fantastic Narrative and the Poetics of the Fragment*. Stanford UP, 1996.

Hawkins, Coleman. "Body and Soul." *Body and Soul (Remastered)*, BMG Music, 1996.

Hebdige, Dick. *Cut 'n' Mix: Culture, Identity and Caribbean Music*. Comedia, 1987.

Henriques, Julian. *Sonic Bodies: Reggae Sound Systems, Performance Techniques, and Ways of Knowing*. Continuum, 2011.

Herbeck, Jason. "'Jusqu'aux limites de l'improvisation': Caribbean Identity and Jazz in Daniel Maximin's *L'Isolé soleil*." *Dalhousie French Studies*, vol. 71, 2005, pp. 161–175.
Hijuelos, Oscar. *Beautiful Maria of My Soul*. Hyperion, 2010.
———. *The Mambo Kings Play Songs of Love*. Farrar, 1989.
———. Oscar Hijuelos Papers 1974–2005, Rare Books and Manuscripts, Columbia University Library, MS1490.
———. *Our House in the Last World*. Washington Square, 1983.
———. *A Simple Habana Melody (From When the World Was Good)*. Harper, 2002.
———. *Thoughts without Cigarettes: A Memoir*. Gotham, 2011.
Hilar, A. P. *Sonar: Detector of Submerged Submarines*. Office of the Chief of Naval Operations, 1946.
Hill, Edwin C., Jr. *Black Soundscapes White Stages: The Meaning of Francophone Sound in the Black Atlantic*. Johns Hopkins UP, 2013.
hooks, bell. *Salvation: Black People and Love*. Harper Perennial, 2001.
Hope, Donna P. *Inna di Dancehall: Popular Culture and the Politics of Identity in Jamaica*. Ian Randle, 2006.
———. *Man Vibes: Masculinities in the Jamaican Dancehall*. Ian Randle, 2010.
Hopkinson, Nalo. *Midnight Robber*. Warner, 2000.
Hornby, Nick. *High Fidelity*. Riverhead, 1996.
Huntington, Julie Anne. *Sounding Off: Rhythm, Music, and Identity in West African and Caribbean Francophone Novels*. Temple UP, 2009.
"In a Nutshell: The Jamaica Constitution, 1962." *Jamaica Information Service*, 23 July 1962, http://jis.gov.jm/media/constit.pdf.
Infante, Guillermo Cabrera. *Three Trapped Tigers*. Dalkey Archive Press, 2004.
Irving Lara y Su Orquestra, "Tristezas," *Rumba Pá Ti*, Xqenda, 2018.
Jaji, Tsitsi Ella. *Africa in Stereo: Modernism, Music, and Pan-African Solidarity*. Oxford UP, 2014.
"Jamaica's Gully Queens." *Vice Magazine*, 28 July 2014, https://www.vice.com/en_us/article/kwpn4n/young-and-gay-jamaicas-gully-queens-288.
James, Marlon. *A Brief History of Seven Killings: A Novel*. Riverhead, 2014.
———. "From Jamaica to Minnesota to Myself." *New York Times Magazine*, 10 Mar. 2015, https://www.nytimes.com/2015/03/15/magazine/from-jamaica-to-minnesota-to-myself.html.
Jansen, Bas. "Tape Cassettes and Former Selves: How Mix Tapes Mediate Memories." *Sound Souvenirs*, edited by José van Dijck and Karin Bijsterveld, Amsterdam UP, 2009, pp. 43–54.
Jones, Ann Rosalind. "Writing the Body: Towards an Understanding of *L'Écriture Féminine*." *Feminisms: An Anthology of Literary Theory and Criticism*, edited by Robyn R. Warhol and Diane Price Herndl, Rutgers UP, 1997, pp. 370–383.
Jones, Terry-Ann. *Jamaican Immigrants in the United States and Canada: Race, Transnationalism, and Social Capital*. LFB, 2008.
Joseph, Anthony. *The African Origins of UFOs*. Salt, 2006.
Joseph, Kelly Baker. "Versions of X/Self: Kamau Brathwaite's Caribbean Discourse." *Anthurium: A Caribbean Studies Journal*, vol. 1, no. 1, 2003, article 4, http://scholarlyrepository.miami.edu/anthurium/vol1/iss1/4.
Juliá, Edgardo Rodríguez. *Cortijo's Wake: El Entierro De Cortijo*. Duke UP, 2004.
Kanhai, Rosanne. "The Masala Stone Sings: Poetry, Performance and Film by Indo-Caribbean Women." *Matikor: The Politics of Identity for Indo-Caribbean Women*, edited by Rosanne Kanhai, UWI School of Continuing Studies, 1999, pp. 209–237.
Kearney, Richard. "Narrating Pain: The Power of Catharsis." *Paragraph*, vol. 30, no. 1, 2007, pp. 51–66.
Kempadoo, Kamala. "Negotiating Cultures: A 'Dogla' Perspective." *Matikor: The Politics of Identity for Indo-Caribbean Women*, edited by Rosanne Kanhai, UWI School of Continuing Studies, 1999, pp. 103–113.

King, Nicola. *Memory, Narrative, Identity: Remembering the Self.* Edinburgh UP, 2000.
de Koningh, Michael, and Marc Griffith. *Tighten: The History of Reggae in the UK*. Sanctuary, 2003.
Krus, Patricia. "The Ethic of Postcolonial Healing in Astrid Roemer's *Trilogy of Suriname*." *Perspectives on the 'Other America': Comparative Approaches to Caribbean and Latin American Culture*, edited by Michael Niblett and Kerstin Oloff, Rodopi, 2009, pp. 75–96.
LaCapra, Dominick. *Writing History, Writing Trauma*. Routledge, 2001.
Laguna, Alberto Sergio. *Diversión: Play and Popular Culture in Cuban America*. NYU, 2017.
Lamming, George. *The Pleasures of Exile*. U of Michigan P, 1992.
Landsberg, Alison. *Prosthetic Memory: The Transformation of American Remembrance in the Age of Mass Culture*. Columbia UP, 2004.
Lanser, Susan Sniader. *Fictions of Authority: Women Writers and Narrative Voice*. Cornell UP, 1992.
Lastra, James. "Reading, Writing, and Representing Sound." *Sound Theory, Sound Practice*, edited by Rick Altman, Routledge, 1992, pp. 65–86.
Latin Music USA. Public Broadcasting Company, 2009.
Levitin, Daniel J. *This Is Your Brain on Music: The Science of a Human Obsession*. Plume, 2007.
Liu, Tessie. "Teaching the Differences among Women from a Historical Perspective: Rethinking Race and Gender as Social Categories." *Women's Studies International Forum*, vol. 14, no. 4, 1991, pp. 265–276.
Loftus, Elizabeth F., and Cara Laney. "Traumatic Memories Are Not Necessarily Accurate Memories." *Canadian Journal of Psychiatry*, vol. 50, no. 13, 2005, pp. 823–828.
Lorde, Audre. *Sister Outsider: Essays and Speeches*, Crossing, 2007.
Lovelace, Earl. *The Dragon Can't Dance*. Longman, 1979.
———. *Is Just a Movie*. Haymarket, 2011.
Luis, William. *Dance between Two Cultures: Latino Caribbean Literature Written in the United States*. Vanderbilt UP, 1997.
Mack, Douglas R. A. *From Babylon to Rastafari: Origin and History of the Rastafarian Movement*. Frontline, 1999.
Mackey, Nathaniel. "An Interview with Kamau Brathwaite." *The Art of Kamau Brathwaite*, edited by Stewart Brown. Mid Glamorgan, 1995, pp. 13–32.
Mahabir, Joy, and Mariam Pirbhai. "Introduction: Tracing an Emerging Tradition." *Critical Perspectives on Indo-Caribbean Women's Literature*, edited by Joy Mahabir and Mariam Pirbhai, Routledge, 2013, pp. 1–21.
Mais, Roger. *Brother Man*. Heinemann, 1974.
Managan, Kathe. "Guadeloupean Women Performing Gwo Ka: Island Presences and Transnational Connections." *Archipelagos of Sound: Transnational Caribbeanities, Women and Music*, edited by Ifeona Fulani, U of the West Indies P, 2012, pp. 93–118.
Manovich, Lev. *The Language of New Media*. MIT Press, 2001.
Manuel, Peter, et al. *Caribbean Currents: Caribbean Music from Rumba to Reggae*. Temple UP, 1995.
Marley. Directed by Kevin MacDonald, Magnolia, 2012.
Martin, Ricky. *Almas del Silencio*, Sony Music Entertainment, 2003.
———. "Asignatura Pendiente." *Almas del Silencio*, Sony Music Entertainment, 2003.
———. "Casí Un Bolero." *Vuelve*, Sony Music Entertainment, 1998.
———. "Isla Bella." *A Quien Quiera Escuchar*, Sony Music Entertainment, 2015.
———. *Sound Loaded*, Sony Music Entertainment, 2000.
De Matas, Jarrel. "Ctrl + Alt / HyperText: Toward a Remediated Caribbean Literary Aesthetic." *Journal of West Indian Literature*, vol. 25, no. 2, 2017, pp. 9–27.
Mathes, Carter. *Imagine the Sound: Experimental African American Literature after Civil Rights*. U of Minnesota P, 2015.
Maximin, Daniel. *L'île et une nuit: Roman*. Éditions de Seuil, 1995.

———. *Lone Sun*. Caraf/ U of Virginia P, 1989.

______. *L'Isolé soleil*. Éditions du Seuil, 1981.

———. *Soufrières*. Éditions de Seuil, 1987.

McKay, Claude. *Banana Bottom*. Harper, 1933.

———. *Harlem Shadows*. Harcourt, 1922.

———. *Home to Harlem*. Northeastern UP, 1987.

Mehta, Brinda. *Diasporic (Dis)Locations: Indo-Caribbean Women Writers Negotiate the Kala Pani*. U of the West Indies P, 2004.

———. "Engendering History: A Poetics of the *Kala Pani* in Espinet's *Swinging Bridge*." *Small Axe: A Caribbean Journal of Criticism*, vol. 21, 2006, pp. 19–36.

The Melodians. "Rivers of Babylon." The Harder They Come Original Soundtrack, Island/ Universal Music, 1972.

"Meme." *Oxford English Dictionary*, 2018, https://en.oxforddictionaries.com/definition/ meme.

Meuleman, Sarah. "Narrar (desde) los Borderlands: *The Mambo Kings Play Songs of Love* de Oscar Hijuelos." *Confluencia*, vol. 24, no. 1, 2008, pp. 29–40.

Miller, Kei. *There Is an Anger That Moves*. Carcanet, 2007.

Mintz, Sidney W. *Caribbean Transformations*. Columbia UP, 1989.

Mistral, Gabriela. *Selected Poems of Gabriela Mistral*, edited by Ursula Le Guin, U of New Mexico P, 2003.

Mohammed, Patricia. "From Myth to Symbolism: The Construction of Indian Femininity and Masculinity in Post-indentured Trinidad." *Matikor: The Politics of Identity for Indo-Caribbean Women*, edited by Rosanne Kanhai, UWI School of Continuing Studies, 1999, pp. 62–99.

Morales, Ed. *The Latin Beat: The Rhythms and Roots of Latin Music from Bossa Nova to Salsa and Beyond*. Da Capo, 2003.

Morel, Marie-France. "Histoire de l'avortement: Incertitudes sur les débuts de grossesse jusqu'au XVIII siècle." *Réalités en gynécologie obstétrique*, vol. 76, December 2002, pp. 51–53. http://www.societe-histoire-naissance.fr. Accessed June 16, 2016.

Morgan, Paula. "With a Tassa Blending: Calypso and Cultural Identity in Indo-Caribbean Fiction." *Anthurium: A Caribbean Studies Journal*, vol. 3, no. 2, 2005, article 10, https:// scholarlyrepository.miami.edu/anthurium/vol3/iss2/10.

Morton, David L., Jr. *Sound Recording: The Life Story of a Technology*. Johns Hopkins UP, 2006.

Motherland: A Genetic Journey. Directed by A. Baron and T. Jackson, Takeaway Media, 2003.

Munro, Martin. *Different Drummers: Rhythm and Race in the Americas*. U of California P, 2010.

Murray-Román, Jeannine. *Performance and Personhood in Caribbean Literature: From Alexis to the Digital Age*. U of Virginia P, 2016.

Myers, Helen. *Music of Hindu Trinidad: Songs from the India Diaspora*. U of Chicago P, 1998.

Naipaul, V. S. *The Middle Passage: The Caribbean Revisted*. Vintage, 2002.

"National Census Report 2001," Caricom Secretariat, https://www.caricomstats.org/Files/ Publications/NCR%20Reports/Jamaica.pdf.

Negus, Keith. "Narrative Time and the Popular Song." *Popular Music and Society*, vol. 35, no. 4, 2012, pp. 483–500.

Nelson, Alondra. *The Social Life of DNA: Race, Reparations, and Reconciliation after the Genome*. Beacon, 2016.

Neptune, Harvey R. *Caliban and the Yankees: Trinidad and the United States Occupation*. U of North Carolina P, 2007.

Nesbitt, Nick. *Voicing Memory: History and Subjectivity in French Caribbean Literature*. U of Virginia P, 2003.

Niranjana, Tejaswini. *Mobilizing India: Women, Music, and Migration between India and Trinidad*. Duke UP, 2006.

Njoroge, Njoroge M. *Chocolate Surrealism: Music, Movement, Memory, and History*. UP of Mississippi, 2016.

Nkwabong, Elie, and Joseph Nelson Fomulu. "Dilatation and Curettage versus Manual Vacuum Aspiration for First Trimester Clandestine Abortions." *International Journal of Reproduction, Contraception, Obstetrics and Gynecology*, vol. 4, no. 3, 2015, pp. 716–720.

Nora, Pierre. "Between Memory and History: *Les Lieux de Mémoire*." *History and Memory in African-American Culture*, edited by Geneviève Fabre and Robert O'Meally, Oxford UP, 1994, pp. 284–300.

Nyre, Lars. *Sound Media: From Live Journalism to Music Recording*. Routledge, 2008.

Obejas, Achy. *Memory Mambo*. Cleis, 1996.

O'Brien Chang, Kevin, and Wayne Chen. *Reggae Routes: The Story of Jamaican Music*. Temple UP, 1998.

O'Callaghan, Evelyn. *Woman Version: Theoretical Approaches to West Indian Fiction by Women*. Macmillan, 1993.

Ong, Walter J. *Orality and Literacy: The Technologizing of the Words*. Routledge, 1982.

Ortiz, Fernando. *Cuban Counterpoint: Tobacco and Sugar*. Translated by Harriet de Onís, Duke UP, 1995.

———. "The Human Factors of Cubanidad." Translated by João Felipe Gonçalves and Gregory Duff Morton. *HAU: Journal of Ethnographic Theory*, vol. 4, no. 3, 2014, pp. 445–480.

Page, Kezia. "From Diasporic Sensibility to Close Transnationalism: *The Aguëro Sisters*, *The Dew Breakers* and *The Brief Wondrous Life of Oscar Wao*." *The Routledge Companion to Anglophone Caribbean Literature*, edited by Michael Bucknor and Allison Donnell, Routledge, 2014, pp. 226–235.

———. *Transnational Negotiations in Caribbean Diasporic Literature: Remitting the Text*. Routledge, 2014.

Palmer, Lisa Amanda. "'Ladies a Your Time Now!': Erotic Politics, Lovers' Rock and Resistance in the UK." *African and Black Diaspora: An International Journal*, vol. 4, no. 2, 2011, pp. 177–192.

Paquet, Sandra Pouchet, et al., editors. *Music, Memory, Resistance: Calypso and the Caribbean Literary Imagination*. Ian Randle, 2007.

Paul, Annie. "Log On: Toward Social and Digital Islands." *The Routledge Companion to Anglophone Caribbean Literature*, edited by Michael Bucknor and Allison Donnell, Routledge, 2014, pp. 626–635.

Pérez Firmat, Gustavo. *Life on the Hyphen: The Cuban-American Way*. U of Texas P, 1994.

Philip, Marlene NourbeSe. "Fugues, Fragments and Fissures: A Work in Progress." *Music, Memory, Resistance: Calypso and the Caribbean Literary Imagination*, edited by Sandra Pouchet Paquet, Patricia J. Saunders, and Stephen Stuempfle, Ian Randle, 2007, pp. 75–93.

———. "In the Matter of Memory: A Work in Progress." *Centre of Remembrance: Memory and Caribbean Women's Literature*, edited by Joan Anim-Addo, Mango, 2002, pp. 3–13.

———. *Zong!* Wesleyan UP, 2008.

Philp, Geoffrey. "Exile." *In This Breadfruit Kingdom: An Anthology of Jamaican Poetry*, edited by Mervyn Morris, Blouse and Skirt, 2017, p. 27.

Pollard, Velma. *Dread Talk: The Language of Rastafari*. McGill-Queen's UP, 2000.

Prado, Pérez. "Mambo No. 5." *Lo Mejor de Pérez Prado*, BMG Music, 1999.

———. "Que Rico el Mambo." *Lo Mejor de Pérez Prado*, BMG Music, 1999.

Prater, Tzarina T. "'Look Pon Likkle Chiney Gal': Tessanne Chin, *The Voice*, and Digital Caribbean Subjects." *Anthurium: A Caribbean Studies Journal*, vol. 12, no. 1, 2015, article 11, http://scholarlyrepository.miami.edu/anthurium/vol12/iss1/11.

Puri, Shalini. "Canonized Hybridities, Resistant Hybridities: Chutney Soca, Carnival, and the Politics of Nationalism." *Caribbean Romances: The Politics of Regional Representation*, edited by Belinda Edmondson and A. James Arnold, U of Virginia P, 1999, pp. 12–38.

———. "Memory-Work: Reading Merle Collins and the Poetics of Place." *The Routledge Companion to Anglophone Caribbean Literature*, edited by Michael Bucknor and Allison Donnell, Routledge, 2014, pp. 490–497.

———. "Race, Rape, and Representation: Indo-Caribbean Women and Cultural Nationalism." *Matikor: The Politics of Identity for Indo-Caribbean Women*, edited by Rosanne Kanhai, UWI School of Continuing Studies, 1999, pp. 238–282.

Putnam, Laura. *Radical Moves: Caribbean Migrants and the Politics of Race in the Jazz Age*. U of North Carolina P, 2013.

Radway, Janice A. *Reading the Romance: Women, Patriarchy and Popular Literature*. U of North Carolina P, 1991.

Ramazani, Jahan. "The Wound of History: Walcott's *Omeros* and the Postcolonial Poetics of Affliction." *PMLA*, vol. 112, no. 3, 1997, pp. 405–417.

Ramcharitar, Raymond. *Breaking the News: Media and Culture in Trinidad*. Lexicon, 2005.

Ramnarine, Tina K. *Creating Their Own Space: The Development of an Indian-Caribbean Musical Tradition*. U of the West Indies P, 2001.

Reddock, Rhoda. "Jahaji Bhai: The Emergence of a Dougla Poetics in Contemporary Trinidad and Tobago." *Identity, Ethnicity and Culture in the Caribbean*, edited by Ralph R. Premdas, UWI School of Continuing Studies, 1998, pp. 185–210.

Regis, Louis. *The Political Calypso: True Opposition in Trinidad and Tobago, 1962–1987*. U of the West Indies P, 1999.

Regis, Pamela. *A Natural History of the Romance Novel*. U of Pennsylvania P, 2003.

Reiss, Timothy J. "Introduction." *Music, Writing, and Cultural Unity in the Caribbean*, edited by Timothy J. Reiss, Africa World, 2005, pp. 1–34.

Rice, Tom. "Sounding Bodies: Medical Students and the Acquisition of Stethoscopic Perspectives." *The Oxford Handbook of Sound Studies*, edited by Trevor Pinch and Karin Bijsterveld, Oxford UP, 2012, pp. 298–319.

Ricoeur, Paul. *Memory, History, Forgetting*. Translated by Kathleen Blamey and David Pellauer, U of Chicago P, 2004.

Roach, Joseph R. *Cities of the Dead: Circum-Atlantic Performance*. Columbia UP, 1996.

Rody, Caroline. *The Daughter's Return: African-American and Caribbean Women's Fictions of History*. Oxford UP, 2001.

Rohlehr, Gordon. *Calypso and Society in Pre-independence Trinidad*. Peepal Tree, 1990.

Roots: The Next Generations, written by Alex Haley and Ernest Kinoy, directed by John Erman, Warner Brothers, 1979.

Rothberg, Michael. *Multidirectional Memory: Remembering the Holocaust in the Age of Decolonization*. Stanford UP, 2009.

Rousset, C., et al. "Posttraumatic Stress Disorder and Psychological Distress following Medical and Surgical Abortion." *Journal of Reproductive and Infant Psychology*, vol. 29, no. 5, Nov. 2011, pp. 506–517.

Rudnicki, Robert W. *Percyscapes: The Fugue State in Twentieth-Century Southern Fiction*. Louisiana State UP, 1999.

Sacks, Oliver. *Musicophilia: Tales of Music and the Brain*. Vintage Books, 2007.

Saunders, Patricia J. "Introduction: Mapping the Roots/Routes of Calypso in Caribbean Literary and Cultural Traditions." *Music, Memory, Resistance: Calypso and the Caribbean Literary Imagination*, edited by Sandra Pouchet Paquet, Patricia J. Saunders, and Stephen Stuempfle, Ian Randle, 2007, pp. xv–xxviii.

Schafer, R. Murray. *The Soundscape: Our Sonic Environment and the Tuning of the World*. Destiny Books, 1994.

Scharfman, Ronnie. "Rewriting the Césaires: Daniel Maximin's Caribbean Discourse." *L'Héritage de Caliban*, edited by Maryse Condé, Editions Jasor, 1992, pp. 233–245.

Schwarz-Bart, Jacques. *Soné-Ka-Là*, Universal Music Jazz France, 2007.

Scott, Dennis. "An Echo in the Bone." *Plays for Today*, edited by Errol Hill, Longman, 1985, pp. 73–138.

Scott, Lawrence. "King Sailor One J'Ouvert Morning." *Ballad for the New World and Other Stories*, Heinemann, 1994, pp. 9–16.

———. "Matura Days: A Memoir (for Earl)." *A Place in the World: Essays and Tributes in Honour of Earl Lovelace at 70*, edited by Funso Aiyejina, Lexicon, 2008, pp. 153–160.

———. *Night Calypso*. Allison and Busby, 2004.

———. *Witchbroom*. Papillotte, 2016.

Selvon, Samuel. *The Lonely Londoners*. Longman, 2007.

Semaj-Hall, Isis. "Constructing a Dub Identity: What It Means to Be 'Back Home' in Jamaica." *Cultural Dynamics*, vol. 30, no. 1–2, 2018, pp. 96–109.

Shakespeare, William. *The Tempest: Sources and Contexts, Criticism, Rewritings and Appropriations*. Norton, 2004.

Shapiro, Norman R. *Negritude: Black Poetry from Africa and the Caribbean*. October House, 1970.

Sharpley-Whiting, T. Denean. *Negritude Women*, U of Minnesota P, 2002, pp. 80–104.

Sheffield, Rob. *Love Is a Mix Tape: Life and Loss, One Song at a Time*. Three Rivers P, 2007.

Shiga, John. "Sonar: Empire, Media, and the Politics of Underwater Sound." *Canadian Journal of Communication*, vol. 38, 2013, pp. 357–377.

Simpleton (Christopher Harrison). "Coca Cola Bottle Shape." Feat. Louie Culture, Single, VP, 1992.

Slotnick, Scott D. *Cognitive Neuroscience of Memory*. Cambridge UP, 2017.

Small, Geoff. *Ruthless: The Global Rise of the Yardies*. Warner, 1995.

Smith, Faith L. "'You Know You're West Indian If . . .': Codes of Authenticity in Colin Channer's *Waiting in Vain*." *Small Axe: A Caribbean Journal of Criticism*, vol. 10, 2001, pp. 41–59.

Snyder, Bob. *Music and Memory: An Introduction*. MIT P, 2000.

Solbiac, Rodolphe. "Revising Female Indian Memory: Ramabai Espinet's Reconstruction of an Indo-Trinidadian Diaspora in *The Swinging Bridge*." *Critical Perspectives on Indo-Caribbean Women's Literature*, edited by Joy Mahabir and Mariam Pirbhai, Routledge, 2013, pp. 229–252.

Sommer, Doris. *Foundational Fictions: The National Romances of Latin America*. U of California P, 1991.

Spottswood, Dick. "Recording for the Decca: Calypsos in Trinidad 1938–1940." *West Indian Rhythm: Trinidad Calypsos on World and Local Events; Featuring the Censored Recordings—1938–1940*, edited by the Classic Calypso Collective, Bear Family Records, 2007, pp. 111–121.

Stanley Niaah, Sonjah. *Dancehall: From Slave Ship to Ghetto*. U of Ottawa P, 2001.

Stavans, Ilan. "The Latin Phallus." *Transition*, vol. 65, 1995, pp. 48–68.

Steffens, Roger. *So Much Things to Say: The Oral History of Bob Marley*. Norton, 2017.

Steffens, Roger, and Leroy Jodie Pierson. *Bob Marley and the Wailers: The Definitive Discography*. LMH Publishers, 2005.

Stephens, Michelle A. *Black Empire: The Masculine Global Imaginary of Caribbean Intellectuals in the United States, 1914–1962*. Duke UP, 2005.

Sterne, Jonathan. *The Audible Past: Cultural Origins of Sound Reproduction*. Duke UP, 2003.

———. *MP3: The Meaning of a Format*. Duke UP, 2012.

———. "The Preservation Paradox in Digital Audio." *Sound Souvenirs*, edited by José van Dijck and Karin Bijsterveld, Amsterdam UP, 2009, pp. 55–68.

Stewart, Tinga. "Nuh Wey Nuh Betta Dan Yard." *Vinyl Single, 56 Hope Road/Tuff Gong, 1981*.

Stines, L'Antoinette Osunide. "Claiming Naming: Redefining Naming in Caribbean Dance through the Paradigm of L'Antech." *Caribbean in Transit Arts Journal*, vol. 1, no. 2, 2012, pp. 38–51.

Stoever, Jennifer L. *The Sonic Color Line: Race and the Cultural Politics of Listening*. New York UP, 2016.

The Story of Lovers Rock. Directed by Menelik Shabazz, ArtMattan Productions, 2011.

Sublette, Ned. *Cuba and Its Music: From the First Drums to the Mambo*. Chicago Review, 2004.

Thelwell, Michael. *The Harder They Come: A Novel*. Grove, 1988.

Thomas, Bonnie. "Edouard Glissant and the Art of Memory," *Small Axe: A Journal of Caribbean Criticism*, vol. 30, 2009, 25–36.

Thomas, Deborah A. *Modern Blackness: Nationalism, Globalization, and the Politics of Culture in Jamaica*. Duke UP, 2004.

T. O. K. "Chi Chi Man." Single, VP, 2001.

Trouillot, Michel-Rolph. *Silencing the Past: Power and the Production of History*. Beacon Press, 2015.

Turino, Thomas. *Nationalists, Cosmopolitans, and Popular Music in Zimbabwe*. U of Chicago P, 2000.

The Upsetter: The Life and Music of Lee "Scratch" Perry. Directed by Ethan Higbee and Adam Bhala Lough, Upsetter/Permanent Marks Films, 2011.

Van Dijck, José. "Remembering Songs through Telling Stories: Pop Music as a Resource for Memory." *Sound Souvenirs*, edited by José van Dijck and Karin Bijsterveld, Amsterdam UP, 2009, pp. 107–122.

Van Dijck, José, and Karin Bijsterveld, editors. *Sound Souvenirs*. Amsterdam UP, 2009.

Vazquez, Alexandra T. *Listening in Detail: Performances of Cuban Music*. Duke UP, 2013.

Veal, Michael E. *Dub: Soundscapes and Shattered Songs in Jamaican Reggae*. Wesleyan UP, 2007.

Vété-Congolo, Hanétha. *The Caribbean Oral Tradition: Literature, Performance, and Practice*. Palgrave Macmillan, 2016.

Walcott, Derek. *What the Twilight Says: Essays*, Farrar, 1998.

———. *Collected Poems, 1948–1984*. Farrar, 1986.

Walder, Dennis. "Writing, Representation, and Postcolonial Nostalgia." *Textual Practice*, vol. 23, no. 6, 2009, pp. 935–946.

Warner, Keith Q. *Kaiso! The Trinidad Calypso: A Study of the Calypso as Oral Literature*. Three Continents, 1982.

Warner-Lewis, Maureen. *Central Africa in the Caribbean: Transcending Time, Transforming Cultures*. U of the West Indies P, 2003.

———. *Guinea's Other Suns: The African Dynamic in Trinidad Culture*, Majority, 1991.

Weber, Heike. "Taking Your Favorite Sound Along: Portable Audio Technologies for Mobile Music Listening." *Sound Souvenirs*, edited by José van Dijck and Karin Bijsterveld, Amsterdam UP, 2009, pp. 69–82.

Weheliye, Alexander G. *Phonographies: Grooves in Sonic Afro-Modernity*. Duke UP, 2005.

West Indian Rhythm: Trinidad Calypsos on World and Local Events; Featuring the Censored Recordings—1938–1940. Edited by the Classic Calypso Collective. Bear Family Records, 2007.

Wilks, Jennifer. *Race, Gender, and Comparative Black Modernism: Suzanne Lacascade, Marita Bonner, Suzanne Césaire, Dorothy West*. Louisiana State UP, 2008.

Williams, Eric. "Massa Day Done: Public Lecture at Woodford Square, 22 March 1961." *Callaloo*, vol. 20, no. 4, 1997, pp. 725–730.

Wilson, Kathleen. *The Island Race: Englishness, Empire, and Gender in the Eighteenth Century*. Routledge, 2003.

Winks, Christopher. "Cuba, the Night, and the Music: Guillermo Cabrera Infante's Havana *Son et lumière*." *Music, Writing, and Cultural Unity in the Caribbean*, edited by Timothy J. Reiss, Africa World, 2005, pp. 271–286.

Wuest, Ruth. "The Robber in the Trinidad Carnival." *Caribbean Quarterly*, vol. 36, 2017, pp. 42–53.
Wynter, Sylvia. *The Hills of Hebron: A Jamaican Novel.* Simon and Schuster, 1962.
Yates, Frances A. *The Art of Memory*. U of Chicago P, 1966.
Zimra, Clarisse. "Can the Empire Really Write Back: Maximin's Unbounded Narrative." *American Journal of Semiotics*, vol. 18, no. 1–4, 2002, pp. 67–86.
———. "Négritude in the Femininc Mode: The Case of Martinique and Guadeloupe." *Journal of Ethnic Studies*, vol. 12, no. 1, 1984, pp. 53–77.

Index